TRACK TECHNIQUE
ANNUAL '83

Edited by Vern Gambetta

Tafnews Press
Los Altos, California

1982 tafnews

Books from Track & Field News

New Books

THE HURDLES: Contemporary Theory, Technique and Training. Jess Jarver, ed. Latest entrant in our "Contemporary" series. A modern guide to present-day hurdling concepts and training. $8.50

THE HIGH JUMP BOOK. Superb discourses on flop jumping by Dwight Stones, Greg Joy, Jacek Wszola and Dr. David Martin. $8.50

TRACK MANAGEMENT, Andy Bakjian. Top TAC official offers valuable check lists for track officials and meet directors, etc. $5.00

HOW HIGH SCHOOL RUNNERS TRAIN. All-new 2nd edition, edited by Frank P. Calore. Profiles of Ketchum, Richardson, Butler, Zishka, Hopp, 39 others. $6.00

Other Popular Titles

A SCIENTIFIC APPROACH TO DISTANCE RUNNING, David Costill. Our best-selling book. "Definitely the best book of its kind," Alex Ayers, *Running Times.* 1979. $5.00

TRACK AND FIELD OMNIBOOK, 3rd ed. 1980. Ken Doherty's colossal work . . . America's No. 1 track text. 550pp. $16.95

RUNNING AND YOUR BODY, Bernie Dare. Applying physiological principles to track training. 1980. 160pp. $6.50

TRACK AND FIELD: TECHNIQUE THROUGH DYNAMICS, Tom Ecker. Applying the principles of body mechanics to each track & field event. $4.95

THE "CONTEMPORARY THEORY, TECHNIQUE AND TRAINING" SERIES, Jess Jarver, ed. Superb collections of original articles, reprints and new translations of articles, providing contemporary guides to the event groups covered for coach and athlete.

The Jumps, 2nd ed. 1981. 128pp. $8.50
The Throws, 2nd ed. 1980. 160pp. $8.50
Long Distances. 1980. 160pp. $8.50
Middle Distances. 1979. 128pp. $8.50
Sprints and Relays. 1978. 128pp. $8.50

ALL ABOUT ROAD RACING, Tom & Janet Heinonen. ABCs of racing for the beginner and others. 96pp. 1979. $4.50

COMPUTERIZED RUNNING TRAINING PROGRAMS, Gardner & Purdy. Still an immensely valuable and popular book for coach and runner. $6.95

HOW WOMEN RUNNERS TRAIN, ed. by Vern Gambetta. Profiles of Benoit, Warren, Waitz, etc. Good training suggestions. 1980. $5.50

HOW ROAD RACERS TRAIN, ed. by Greg Brock. 40 training profiles, incl. Virgin, Lindsay, Rodgers, Shorter, etc. 1980. $5.00

GUIDE TO TRACK AND FIELD INJURIES, Kruger & Oberdieck. 1978. $4.50
GETTING STARTED IN TRACK AND FIELD, R.S. Parker. 2nd printing 1981. $5.00
HOW THEY TRAIN: HIGH SCHOOL FIELD EVENTS, ed. by Frank P. Calore. 64 training programs, incl. Mike Carter, Joe Dial, etc. 1980. $6.00

Add $1.00 per book for postage and handling. Calif. residents add 6% sales tax.

Tafnews Press

BOOK DIVISION OF TRACK & FIELD NEWS
BOX 296, LOS ALTOS, CA. 94022

TRACK TECHNIQUE ANNUAL '83

VERN GAMBETTA
Editor

JANET VITU
GRACE LIGHT
ESTHER REEVES
SCOTT DEACON
Production Editors

SCOTT DEACON
Cover Design

Track Technique Annual 1983 is published by Tafnews Press (Book Division of Track & Field News, Inc.).

Copyright © 1982 by Track & Field News.

Track Technique Annual is published in November of each year. For rate information, write to Track & Field News, Box 296, Los Altos, CA 94022.

From the Editor
vern gambetta

Longevity—Dave Moorcroft's recent success has prompted me to question why the good European athlete tends to compete longer and continues to improve—often achieving world record levels—long after American athletes of similar skills have retired. The answers are varied but simple. First of all, in the U.S. we are always in a hurry. We do not allow our athletes to gradually progress. Once talent is recognized, the athletes are pushed at younger ages to work harder and compete often, many times before their bodies are ready to assume a heavy workload. This can lead to a premature end to their career due to injuries, burnout, or general discouragement in not being able to maintain the instant success they achieved.

Another major reason is that the opportunities for competition and coaching beyond college are limited unless the athlete is a superstar. For every Dave McKenzie who perseveres and rises to the top, there are many more who become discouraged and quit. The late developer and those who have not had the opportunity of a top collegiate program must be given the opportunity to continue to compete and develop.

U.S. Summer Track Circuit—It never ceases to amaze me that for over 90% of our athletes, their season ends just when they are rounding into peak form and ready to compete. The cream, the seasoned competitors, are off to Europe after the NCAA or TAC meets to compete for another three months. The next level of athletes—the future stars—are finished. For them, there may be a few all comer meets but nothing at a level to provide significant competitive experience.

It is hard to believe that a country with the resources and available facilities that we have cannot put together a competitive summer track circuit that would extend the season at least through July. Corporate sponsorship could be tapped. With proper financing and organization, we could attract the top Europeans to compete in the U.S. during the summer. Besides the resources and facilities, we also have more consistent good weather conditions than Europe to attract these top people. This circuit would do much to build interest in track and field in this country, something we sorely need in light of the upcoming Olympics.

Coaching Certification—Last December at the TAC Convention, I was appointed to chair a committee to explore the possibilities of developing a certification program. Hopefully, our recommendations and plan will be adopted at the TAC Convention this December in Philadelphia.

I personally perceive a great need for a certification and coaches education program. We are at a turning point in our sport. High schools have been forced to cut back and fewer coaches are trained in physical education or have had a good background in track and field. There is a void in the coaching ranks that must be filled.

A comprehensive scheme of coaching certification will ensure that our young developing athletes will get proper training from certified, qualified coaches. The program will take time to implement and, most likely, will not have an immediate impact. When the program is fully operational, a coach will not be eligible for employment unless he or she has achieved TAC certification.

I see this program as a step toward developing a true national system. A hierarchy of coaching expertise will exist, beginning with the novice coach and continuing on up to the level of national coach. The programs will ensure that every coach has a common body of knowledge. This in turn will result in a standardization in teaching the various event skills.

Obviously, much work needs to be done, but it is a beginning. It will take time, but I believe that the time and effort will pay off in improved future performances on the track.

*****In closing, I quote a portion of a letter that I received from Kevin McGill, Asst. Coach at Columbia and Editor of *TAC Hammer Notes*—a real aficionado of the throws and a keen observer of the track scene in the U.S. He comments on the unwillingness of top coaches to share any information of substance concerning the hammer:

> ....What I think has been exposed is that a few of the top coaches... still feel that if they had any clue to the event, they ... would not reveal it to other coaches. At least with the hammer, I felt the need to do that to get the event off the ground all over the U.S. But, again it goes back to the ego of the coaches, and that is an obstacle which is baffling. What this event needs is a John Wooden, or Bobby Knight, an American coach who can command attention. What that coach needs is to produce a 275'7'' hammer thrower and who will do that on his own? The Russians have a hammer school where the coaches get together and hash out battle plans. Until that unity occurs, I don't see any progress. For every foot McKenzie improved, McArdle, Bessette, Djerassi, Galle dropped down two feet. I told one coach, that one thrower doesn't make a revolution.

This is a problem that we have in all events. Let's all share information and help the sport rather than concentrating on our own egos.

CONTENTS

3

Helping the Preps

PLANNING A TRAINING PROGRAM

by Robert Thayer, Canada

The principles behind the planning and organization of a well-conceived year-round training program are presented. A very important article for anyone who seeks to maximize their potential, whatever the level of development. Coaching Review, *Vol.3, No. 17, September/October 1980.*

Stimulus. Stimulus may be simply defined as the physical task which the coach has the athlete perform. It may be a conditioning exercise or the practicing of a specific skill. In a well planned program the training stimulus will be either decreased or increased depending on the time of year. To maximize the athlete's potential, the proper timing, in terms of application of stimulus, is critical.

Overload, Adaptation and Training Effect. As an athlete is exposed to a training stimulus, his coach hopes his performance will improve. Continued exposure to the same stimulus over a prolonged period, however, may result in a plateau or even a decrease in performance.

Therefore the volume or intensity of training must be progressively increased, resulting in an overload. The athlete adapts to each new training load. This adaptive process, where the athlete adjusts physiologically to the work load, is termed the training effect. The above relationship may be represented by the following scheme (**Figure 1**).

Super Compensation Cycle. The entire process, of Stimulus, Overload, Adaptation and Training Effect, has been referred to as the super compensation, or super adaption, cycle. In order to take full advantage of this cycle the coach must plan for the correct alternation between effort and rest. The overall cycle may be represented by **Figure 2**.

Figure 2 is based on the rationale that training results in fatigue, which may cause a decrease in an athlete's performance over a weekly practice schedule. If the coach fails to plan for recovery, during the week and between weeks, eventually he may have a group of fatigued athletes on his hands, who cannot respond favorably to a training stimulus.

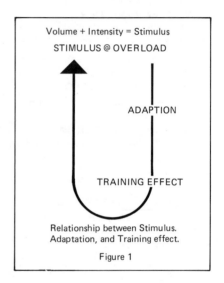

Volume + Intensity = Stimulus

STIMULUS @ OVERLOAD

ADAPTION

TRAINING EFFECT

Relationship between Stimulus. Adaptation, and Training effect.

Figure 1

An adequate degree of rest, or compensation, following an exhaustive 2 to 3 weeks of practice may allow the athlete to recover to the point where he or she is ready for a greater training stimulus, or super compensation. One method of determining the proper timing of rest and overload is to use the morning pulse rate and practice session pulse rates.

A RESTED ATHLETE IS A TRAINABLE ATHLETE

In figure 2 we have athletes participating in three different programs. It is obvious in the one case that the coach is pushing the athletes too hard and is not providing for adequate rest intervals in the training program.

So the coach provides a training stimulus, but the fatigued athlete fails to respond (see

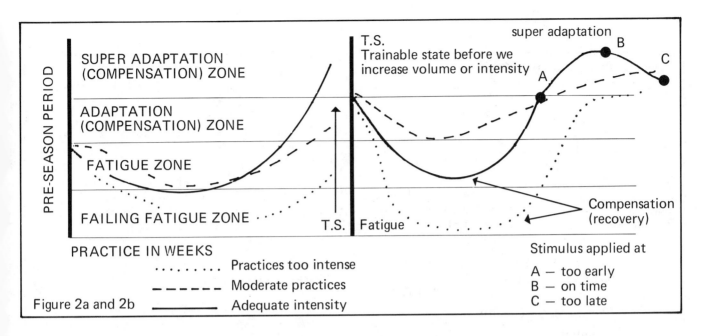

figure 1). In fact, the athlete's performance may decrease.

In contrast, the coach who provides adequate recovery intervals, supplies the proper stimulus and the athlete responds with improved performance. Weight training is a prime example. An athlete works hard in the weight room, attempts a maximum lift, fails and then takes a week off. After the rest period walks into the weight room and makes the lift. The possible explanation, the super adaptation zone.

THE READINESS FACTOR

The Readiness Factor determines the appropriate time to overload the athlete. Increasing the intensity of practice at a time when the athlete has not fully recovered from previous sessions, when he is still in the failing adaptation zone, may be frustrating for both coach and athlete since no improvement in performance will occur.

However the stimulus appropriately applied will result in a maximum training effect (see Figure 2b).

COACHING TIPS—REST

Too Little Rest

1. Excessively high heart rates between work intervals in spite of the appropriate rest periods.

2. Performance times in quality work are very poor or skill level appears to drop.

3. Competitive results are below expectations. Athlete displays signs of physical fatigue.

4. The morning pulse rate (normal resting heart rate) experiences a dramatic rise which persists for several days.

5. A marked change in attitude, i.e., complains in practice
    reluctant to work
    constant focus on injuries
    begins to miss practice

6. The sudden appearance of small nagging injuries which appear to be legitimate.

7. Repeated failure to complete required number of sets or reps if interval training.

8. Failure to respond when challenged in practice.

Too Much Rest

1. Athlete will complete interval work out without too much effort. Check heart rate immediately following a specific drill to see if the drill is demanding enough. May have to shorten rest interval.

2. If there is too much rest between work intervals or practices are not intense enough (suspected by the coach) the morning pulse rate will plateau or perhaps increase slightly over a period of time. This is especially important during the pre-season where the coach is attempting to build an endurance base. If the practices are not intense enough the planned for bradycardia (decrease in resting heart rate) may not occur.

3. If a coach suspects that the relief intervals between periods of work are too long to substantiate the suspicion he or she must check pulse rate. For example a work-relief ratio of 4:1 may have to be reduced to 2:1 to stress the

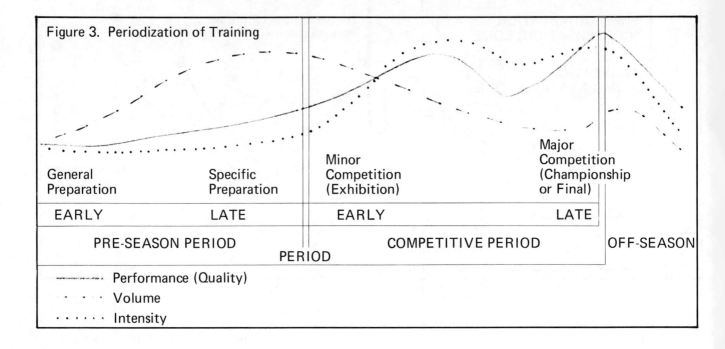

Figure 3. Periodization of Training

General Preparation	Specific Preparation	Minor Competition (Exhibition)	Major Competition (Championship or Final)
EARLY	LATE	EARLY	LATE
PRE-SEASON PERIOD		COMPETITIVE PERIOD	OFF-SEASON
	PERIOD		

— · — · — Performance (Quality)

· · · · Volume

· · · · · · Intensity

athlete sufficiently.

4. Communication with the athletes may support the coach's feelings that the practices are not intense enough.

5. Poor competitive result may also be an indication of insufficient work.

PLANNING THE TRAINING PROGRAM

With the above concepts in mind the coach must not only plan the weekly practice schedule but also the annual training plan. The various stages of training are represented by **Figure 3.**

The overall training program must take into consideration the maximal development of the following areas:

1. physical preparation
2. technical preparation
3. tactical preparation
4. psychological preparation.

Furthermore in order for the coach to attack the four above areas in a logical fashion he or she must divide the season into the following:

1. pre-season
2. competitive season

3. off season

THE PRE—SEASON

General guidelines

Physical preparation emphasis in the early portion of the pre-season should be on the improvement of general motor fitness.
—maximum aerobic capacity
—muscular endurance and strength flexibility.

The volume of exercises for their development is high but intensity is low. However, as we get into the late stages of the pre-season, exercises become more specific to the sport and volume decreases as intensity increases.

Proper physical preparation in the pre-season is essential in order to insure the maximum learning of technical skills. For example, a coach who allows his athletes to neglect aerobic fitness in the pre-season, may retard the athlete's skill learning because of their premature fatigue.

Technical Preparation

To introduce new and fundamental

techniques of the sport. In the latter portion of the pre-season drilling the techniques are more intense with a greater emphasis on refinement of skill.

Psychological Preparation

In this early phase the coach should primarily concentrate on the motivational area. However, towards the end of this phase the coach should work on the psychological preparation for competition. This may be done by the simulation of competitive situations during practice.

Tactical Preparation

Introduction of tactical elements necessary to competition.

THE COMPETITIVE SEASON

General guidelines

Physical Preparation

The coach should concentrate on maximum development of motor fitness components specific to the sport. Intensity is high and volume low. Late in the competitive season where major competitions are planned the coach must insure adequate recovery as practices are specific and intense in nature. Training is highly specific.

Technical Preparation

The emphasis here is a stabilization of technique and quality performance of technique. The technique drills should be related to the competitive situation. In the latter stages of the competitive season technical preparation should be performed under competition conditions. High intensity drills, scrimmages and competitions are the major component of this period.

Psychological and Tactical Preparation

Work in this area is confined to preparation for specific competitions.

THE OFF-SEASON

General guidelines

The major emphasis in this period is threefold:

1. the athlete's psychological and physiological recovery

2. to evaluate the past year's performance and plan for the new season

3. to provide a period of active rest in order to prevent a significant decrease in motor fitness. Athlete may be involved in other sporting activites to maintain fairly high fitness level. Volume may be quite high but intensity is low.

THE WEEKLY PRACTICE PLAN

Planning the weekly practice schedule is a complex process demanding a high degree of organization on the part of the coach. The weekly plan should be based on scientific principles, a few of which are outlined at the beginning of the article.

As well the weekly practice schedule must reflect a specific phase of the overall seasonal plan. For example the weekly plan in the competitive season will have to be geared to the competitive schedule. The weekly practice plan must also reflect the delicate balance of the following:

a) the volume—intensity relationship
b) the stimulus—adaptation—training effect relationship
c) the overload principle of training
d) the specificity of training principle.

The coach should employ the above principles when planning for one super adaptation cycle. What does this mean? Perhaps the best way to illustrate is to use a specific example. In the pre-season the coach is concerned with the enhancement of cardio-vascular fitness.

There is evidence to show that the super adaptation cycle for endurance fitness is three to four weeks. In other words the coach provides a stimulus over a three to four week period with a variety of drills and exercises designed to improve endurance fitness.

However, prolonged exposure to these exercises without planned rest may lead to a fatigued athlete. Therefore the coach plans for a rest interval after three to four weeks which allows the athlete to recover. Hopefully this will coincide with the super adaptation zone.

The coach will then introduce a stronger stimulus (overload) to induce a training effect. Other physical parameters such as flexibility and strength should be considered on a similar basis.

As mentioned previously the time of the year in the overall training plan will dictate the intensity of the weekly plan. For example, volume is high but intensity low in the pre-season.

CONCLUSION

Planning the yearly training program is a complex and demanding task for both the coach and athlete. With the development of the yearly training plan both coach and athlete leave nothing to chance. Therefore the competitive results attained by the athlete should reflect this diligent preparation by the coach.□

THE APPROACH IN THE LONG AND TRIPLE JUMPS

by Tom Tellez, University of Houston

Tellez discusses methods and mechanics of developing consistent acceleration patterns in the jump approaches.

THE APPROACH

Sprinters attain maximum acceleration at approximately 60 yards (180 feet). The approach should be as long as possible, depending on the jumper's: a) Experience b) Speed c) Strength d) Acceleration ability e) Running mechanics, etc.

Sprint speed is dependent on: a) Stride length (best opportunity for improvement) b) Stride frequency (governed by individual differences). Stride length is improved by: a) Muscular strength b) Elasticity and range of motion in the joints c) Stride length is increased primarily by force exerted against the ground, acting behind the body's center of gravity d) Greater stride length *cannot* be achieved by placing the forward foot ahead of the body's center of gravity.

When the runner is moving slower over the ground, he/she applies force backwards to set the body in motion. Hence the short strides in the beginning, followed by longer strides as acceleration is increased (force applied downward) to gain more ground per stride. The transitional strides of getting the body in motion until reaching full running stride should be gradual. In a good approach, you must have a compromise between stride length and frequency (cadence). The last few strides of the approach should be of a cadence to allow for an active take-off.

The success of the entire approach, and for that matter, the entire jump, will depend on the length and consistency of the first two or three strides of the approach run. The approach run should be one of gradual acceleration, beginning with the first stride and ending with maximum controlled acceleration at take-off (relaxed). The approach is of great importance and a large percentage of training time should be spent by coach and athlete on developing good sprinting mechanics and the approach run.

DEVELOPING THE RUN

The run should be developed on the track, not on the runway. The run should be developed where there is *no* take-off board, vaulting box, high jump bar or pit. They tend to give the athlete visual cues when developing the acceleration pattern. The athlete must feel (physical sensation) the acceleration pattern.

Decide on the length of the run and the number of strides that you want the athlete to take.

a) The athlete will take an even number of strides if he begins his run with the foot he takes-off with as the forward foot.
b) The athlete will take an odd number of strides if he begins his run with the foot opposite his take-off foot as the forward foot.
c) High jump—9 to 12 strides
d) Pole vault—17 to 21 strides
e) Long jump—17 to 21 strides
f) Triple jump—17 to 21 strides

Check marks should be used during early development of the run. They are used when he/she is moving slower over the ground, in the first two or three strides. Check marks for the coach to see are placed four to six strides from the take-off point.

Check marks for the athlete should be eliminated as soon as possible. There is a tendency for the athlete to cue on them for the acceleration pattern. A check mark for the coach to see should always be used. Encourage the athlete to start the run with his take-off foot forward. Work on consistency. The first strides are the key to the whole approach.

Don't let the take-off board, vaulting box or cross bar influence the acceleration pattern. □

THE NECESSITY OF A FINISHING SPRINT

by Tony Benson, Australia

Former Australian Olympian and record holder, Tony Benson, gives his thoughts on the need and development of a finishing kick. Reprinted courtesy of Asian Runner *magazine.*

One obvious feature to emerge over the last decade of middle and long distance running has been the necessity of developing a finishing sprint. Yet many athletes feel that it is an innate ability which one either possesses or does not. Many feel that working on a kick is a waste of time.

If the record of the frontrunner is examined it will show that even the most notable frontrunners, Steve Prefontaine and David Bedford, were unable to win the races most important to them. Despite their ability to run fast times and break away from the kickers in some more minor competitions, medals of any sort eluded them in major races. The only frontrunners who have been able to win—Filbert Bayi (1974 Commonwealth Games 1500 meters), Brendan Foster (1974 European 5000 meters) and Alberto Juantorena (1976 Olympic 800 meters)—have possessed finishing bursts as strong as any of their rivals.

Another notable fact about the frontrunner/kicker comparison is that more kickers have set world records since 1970. It should be noted that the kickers are more likely to set their records in high quality races, whereas the frontrunners tend to set theirs in races where the opposition is weaker.

This should not be interpreted as a denigration of the frontrunners efforts because they usually break records by bigger margins. Rather it is just that the best kickers are more likely to be present, and far harder to shake off in races run for high stakes.

A "kick" is basically a mental thing born of a very strong desire to win or perhaps a very great fear of losing. It is not the desire to win as expressed before the race or during the early stages. It is the will to win as expressed by action in the late stages when at various points, each athlete is forced to face his moment of truth.

The moment of truth will come only in the late stages of the race for the following reasons: First, no frontrunner can expect to crush a top class field before the last twenty five percent of the race. Second, the strategic frontrunner cannot afford to initiate his mid-race breakaway until at least the halfway point and cannot expect to be clear of the field until the final stages. Third, the strategic kicker will only move within the last twenty five or thirty percent of the race and must expect company from the pure kickers until almost on the finishing line. Finally, the pure kickers must throw everything into a dynamic burst at some spot during the final lap that allows them to outwit the other kickers and pass everyone else.

A finishing sprint involves a significant mental compliment and is not based purely on natural ability. For instance, runners like Kip Keino, Ben Jipcho, John Walker, Dave Wottle, Lasse Viren, Mohammad Gammoudi, Bronislaw Malinowski, Steve Scott, Suleiman Nyambui, Steve Ovett and Sebastian Coe have often finished faster than others who are actually superior at the shorter distances of 400, 800 or 1500 meters.

It is important to recognize the fact that not only is overall last lap speed vital but that the movement must be sudden and dynamic. This is the real strength of Yifter's kick.

If at the moment of the kick one athlete can cover nine meters in one second while another can cover only eight, the second athlete cannot win unless he is actually faster and he has sufficient time to make up the distance before the first reaches the finishing line. There are numerous incidents of second and third place finishers covering the last 100, 200 or 300 meters faster than the winner, but losing because of poor timing and lack of initiative or aggression.

To win a race involving others with equal or perhaps greater speed requires greater mental strength, a greater need to win and a greater degree of mental control. To pace and move too early for one's capacity or to be passive and wait too long hoping to be able to respond to someone else's initiative is equally disasterous.

Last lap speed revolves around sudden dynamic changes of pace which can just as effectively be employed at other times of the race. Although extra speed in the last lap is always desirable, most athletes will never be true kickers. For example, I remember seeing Dave Bedford lead the first lap of a 5000 meter race in 69 seconds before blasting the next three laps in 61 seconds. While 4.13 for the first 1600 meters could be considered reasonable it shook the opposition when done this way. After a couple of 63's he had the race to himself. This was a pure frontrunners way to "kick" since the 61's at this point were as devastating as a 53 second last lap later on.

The strategic frontrunners and the strategic kickers variations have been best exemplified by Brendan Foster's mid-race 58 and 59 second laps and Lasse Viren's final laps of 56 seconds which were built on finishing 1600 meter times as fast as 4:01.

Noticeably the later the move the faster the critical lap(s) had to be, but all methods have negated the 53's or 54's of the pure kickers. Equally vital however, was the fact that *the success of the move depended exclusively on the athlete committing himself completely at the point he believed was his best chance of victory*—exactly as Yifter or Ovett do in the last 400 meters. Once the move is made the athlete must be determined to lead to the finish.

Most runners of all types either do not understand this or lack the courage of their pre-race convictions when their moment of truth arrives. In the actual mental and physical battle for dominance it is easier to drop off the pace or delay the move that represents their best chance of winning.

The same runners can later be found out on a training run—which true exhaustion would preclude—commenting on how they felt good at the finish and wished they had hung on for longer or made a move earlier. In truth they simply lost the mental battle.

When it comes to the physical battle any athlete who wishes to improve his finishing speed must devote time to basic sprint work. Ideally, to save time this can be done during minor workouts or as a form of easy day training.

Anything involving from one to six sets of two to six repetitions over distances from thirty to three hundred meters is sufficient and will not affect, or be affected by an easy ten to fifteen mile run.

The best final lap kick is the one where the athlete covers his last 200, 300 or 400 meters in a time as close as possible to his personal best for the same distance. Pure speed is quite useless if a 49 second 400 meter best time drops to 54 seconds while another runner, capable of only 50 seconds, has the strength to run 52 seconds in the last lap.

Specific kicking sessions must duplicate the athlete's state of fatigue when he enters the final lap. Repetitions, intervals, long runs or sprints are not the answer. Rather the athlete's workouts should include sessions like 3000 meters of 50 meters sprinting and 50 meters striding; 5000 meters of 100 meters sprint/stride; twenty minutes of sprint finishes—one per lap—over distances from 50 meters to 350 meters with only the minimum recovery between each burst; or two to four sets of three to five times 200 meters. Another good method is to alternate sprints where pairs of athletes run together with one having to wait until the other kicks before trying to make up the lost ground. Twenty minutes of running with two bursts per 400 meters is an exhausting workout.

The essential ingredient of any 'kicking' workout must be the sudden dynamic burst followed by a top speed carry for as long as possible. The athlete need not be concerned about the distance of this carry as other aerobic and anaerobic training sessions will develop the strength for this.

It is vital that top speed be reached in as few meters as possible. Supplementary background workouts like hill springing, hill sprinting and sand running will be needed to develop strength in the legs and arms and shoulders. Without the powerful drive of the sprinter, the move will be little more than an accelerated surge which will cause the real kickers little problem.

Very few athletes can afford to rely exclusively on a last lap kick but extra speed can only be an asset to any runner and when combined with some other race strategy may be the difference between winning and losing, between a world record and a fast time. □

CHAMPIONSHIP SHOT PUTTING

by   George Dunn, Jr., Oak Lawn High School, Oak Lawn, Illinois

A year-round training program for the development of strength and power in shot putters. Dunn's discussion includes specific schedules for weight training, plyometric routines, and variable weight shot and running programs. From U.S. Strength Coaches Journal, *Vol. 3, No. 6, Dec. '81/Jan. '82.*

I have found that the athletes who follow this program make substantial gains in their strength and power and *never* plateau. Power is the most important aspect of a successful shot putter. If an athlete has great strength, but lacks explosive, ballistic power, his success in the shot put will be limited. The theories of my weight program were gathered from experience and from correspondence with Peter Tschiene of West Germany, and Jimmy Pedemonte of Italy. These men have had contact with the East Germans and Russians, who because of their state systems are able to do substantial research. The only problem has been that when we get this information, it is often outdated or incomplete. Thus we must stumble around experimenting to find the right combinations, systems, sets, weights, repetitions, etc.

Our program is geared so that the athletes will "peak" for the conference, district, and state meets at the end of May. I strive to have these top level throwers in a state of condition where they will be their strongest, most explosive, fastest, technique sound and *fresh.* They must be mentally alert and hungry, not tired, bored and burnt out. During the outdoor season, we have three track meets a week, but to reach the level we want to obtain, we must train "through" these meets, actually training before or after the dual meets on week days.

The program extends over eleven months. August is vacation month from the weight room. Training for each season starts on the first day of school in September. The following is our strength training program for each month. You will note an undulating progression in intensity as the program nears the state meet, and you will note that there is an alternation of the extensive and intensive levels to give variety.

The Vladimir Mihailovic Zaciorskiy table (Table #1) shows the percentages given to the number of repetitions used in each exercise. Research by Zaciorskiy indicates that if one were to do only three reps at 75%, there is no physiological change in the muscle to enhance neuro-muscular stimulation. In other words, one would be wasting one's time.

Table 1.

1	—	100%	Maximal
2-3	—	95%	Sub-maximal
4	—	90%	
5	—	85%	High
6	—	80%	
7	—	75%	
8	—	70%	
9	—	65%	Medium
10	—	60%	

September (60%)

Back Squats	3 x 10
Front Squats	3 x 10
Supine Single Leg Press	3 x 10
Bench Press	3 x 10
Shoulder Press	3 x 10
Power Cleans	3 x 10
Shot Put Sit-Ups	3 x 10

October (75+80+85+90+95%)

Back Squats	5 x 7+6+5+4+3
Lunges	4 x 6-8 (80-70%)
Incline Bench	5 x 7+6+5+4+3
Bench Press	5 x 7+6+5+4+3
Power Cleans	5 x 7+6+5+4+3
Shot Put Sit-Ups	4 x 10

November (70%)

Back Squats	3 x 8
Front Squats	3 x 8
Supine Single Leg Press	3 x 8
Bench Press	3 x 8
Push Press	3 x 8
Power Cleans/Snatch	3 x 8
Shot Put Sit-Ups	5 x 10

December (85%)

Back Squats	4 x 5
Front Squats	4 x 5
Supine Single Leg Press	4 x 5
Bench Press	4 x 5
Incline Bench	4 x 5
Power Cleans/Snatch	4 x 5
Shot Put Sit-Ups	5 x 10

January (75%)

Back Squats	5 x 7
Front Squats	5 x 7
Supine Single Leg Press	5 x 7
Bench Press	5 x 7
Push Press	5 x 7
Power Cleans/Snatch	5 x 7
Shot Put Sit-Ups	5 x 10

February (95%)

Back Squats	5 x 3
Power Cleans	5 x 3
Push Press/Incline Bench	5 x 3
Shot Put Sit-Ups	5 x 10

March (60+75+85+85+75%)

Back Squats	5 x 10+7+5+5+7
Supine Single Leg Press	5 x 10+7+5+5+7
Push Press	5 x 10+7+5+5+7
Incline Bench	5 x 10+7+5+5+7
Power Cleans/Snatch	5 x 10+7+5+5+7
Shot Put Sit-Ups	5 x 10

April (85+90+92+95+100)
(Twice a week only)

Back Squats	5 x 5+4+3+2+1
Supine Single Leg Press	5 x 4 (90%)
Push Press	5 x 5+4+3+2+1
Incline Press	5 x 5+4+3+2+1
Shot Put Sit-Ups	5 x 10

May (85+92+95+100+92%)
(First Week)

Back Squats	5 x 5+3+2+1+3
Incline Bench	5 x 5+3+2+1+3
Power Cleans	5 x 5+3+2+1+3

May (85+92+95+100%)
(Second Week)

Back Squats	4 x 5+3+2+1
Incline Bench	4 x 5+3+2+1
Power Cleans	4 x 5+3+2+1

May (85+92+95%) (Third Week)

Back Squats	3 x 5+3+2
Incline Bench	3 x 5+3+2
Power Cleans	3 x 5+3+2

May (Fourth Week)

Tuesday:	Back Squats	1 x 3 (95%)
	Incline Bench	1 x 3 (95%)
Thursday:	Back Squats	1 x 2 (95%)
	Incline Bench	1 x 2 (95%)

June and July

"Body building time!" When the athletes begin to mature, there are some great gains in muscle definition and bulk. They have a good base to start with, so there is no harm in them going directly into such programs. They use a Pause Rest Routine, Pre-Fatigue, Training to Failure, Forced Reps, Negative Reps, Super Sets, etc. This is not easy, but it fires their imaginations and motivation.

During the month of August, I want them to get away from it all, to get out of the weight room and relax. But, there are always those who are highly motivated and continue lifting even through the month of August.

The "new" trend in Europe and Russia for alternating extensive and intensive workouts is now to use shorter micro-cycles. Peter Tschiene considers my system too "static." He states Kreyer of Russia says the changes must be every one to three weeks. You can change the program I have outlined into shorter micro-cycles. Remember, you want to "shock" the neuromuscular system out of plateauing.

As you look at the program I have outlined, you will note that there is an undulating type of progress that gradually gets more intense. The "old" one or two peak systems do not exist anymore in top level training; it is okay for the youngsters, however.

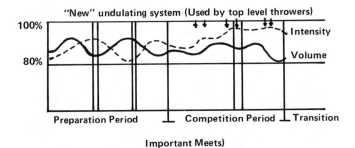

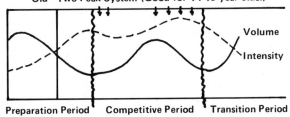

There are several other programs or modifications I insert for two-to-four week blocks. The first of these is the "Auxtonic Training Routine." 50% of maximum, 3 to 5 sets with 10 reps; the barbell is moved 5 seconds up and 5 seconds down. You can use this method for bench press, half squats, press behind the neck, etc. The psychological stress with this method is very high and requires high motivation.

The other method for weight training comes from Bulgaria. The basis of this method is that the throwers carry out sets of special jump exercises along with their great quantity of weight exercises. The training consists of so-called "weight units." One unit equals 2 reps=95%, 4=90%, 6=80%, 8=75%, 10=70%, and 12=60%. After every 5th set of each exercise, the thrower carries out 3 sets of jumps with varying quantities according to the period. After this first week, the following schedule is used:

2nd Week: 3 sets of jumps after the 3rd and 5th set.
3rd Week: 1 set of jumps after each set.
4th Week: Active recovery with tests.
(The basic exercises are the bench press, half or full squat, power cleans and snatch.)

A favorite modification is what Peter Tschiene calls "load leaping." Bondarchuk, the Russian hammer coach, devised the method and calls it the "three week cycle training program." He used it when he, Syedikh, and Tamm swept the hammer in the 1976 Olympics.

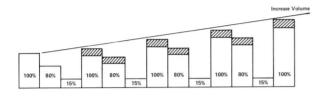

The first week is 100%, which means the volume of work, in tons lifted, number of throws, number of jumps, etc. is at a high intensity. There should be fatigue at the end of the week. An athlete will not be able to go at the same pace the following week, so we lower it to 80%. Again, this means the volume. The intensity is the same as the 100%. Physiologically, the organism is fatigued due to the intensity of the work and so we give him an opportunity to rest during the third week. This 15% volume is in the form of jogging, basketball, volleyball, even some swimming. There are no special exercises. In our case, because the throwing starts late January, we do throw during the rest week.

The fourth week or new cycle is a little bit more in volume than the last cycles 100%. This is an example of a one-to-three week change in the program. What is important after the week of rest is that there is this sudden jolt of hard work that sends a new stimulus to the neuro-muscular system.

Remember, athletes should have a solid background of hard work. I might mention that it does not matter if there is a meet during a 100% week. There can or cannot be meets scheduled during this time. An example of what the weight program might look like:

1st Week (100%)   5 x 3 (95%)   6 x 3 (95%)   7 x 3 (95%)
2nd Week (80%)   4 x 3 (95%)   5 x 3 (95%)   6 x 3 (95%)
3rd Week (15%)   Active Rest...jogging...volleyball...
                  basketball...swimming...

Even a pyramid routine can be used, as long as it is in the upper levels: 5 x 5(85) + 4(90) + 3(92) + 2(95) +1 (100).

Another program I will sometimes insert is called the "Mixed or Combined Routine." The examples below are from Peter Tschiene and Jimmy Pedemonte. The program from Peter was used by Bondarchuk to train a couple of 70m hammer throwers at a hammer clinic in Germany. Peter observed them doing this two days in a row. It is a high intensity training program.

Monday
High Pulls 7 x 30 (30kg).
Heavy hammer 1 x 10 (12kg).

Power Cleans 7 x 20.
Dead Lifts 6 x 16.
Throw weight 1 x 10 (20kg).
Squats 4 x 16 (for active recovery).

Tuesday
Weight throws 1 x 15 (20kg).
Dumbbell exercises, like body builders: 4 x 10 (circles in front of body) 3 x 120 (extended side curls).
Heavy hammer 1 x 15.
Dumbbells 5 x 15 (back circles).
Flat Bench 6 x 30.

Examples of Jimmy Pedemonte's Mixed Routines:
(I)
15 throws with light shot (10 lbs).
3 x 3 Push Press (95%).
10 Standing throws with 16lb shot.
3 x 3 Power Cleans (95%).
10 Throws backward with 35lb barbell plate.

(II)
Snatch (6 x 10 + 7 + 5 + 5 + 7 + 10).
20 throws with variable method (2 + 1 + 1).
Power Cleans (4 x 5 + 3 + 2 + 1 + 2 + 3).
20 Throws with variable method (2 + 1 + 1).

JUMP PROGRAM

Peter Tschiene said, "The engine for the long throw apparatus...are the legs." We feel so strongly about this, that besides the squats in the strength program, we include a high volume of various kinds of jumps. There has been much positive research by the Russians and East Germans in this regard that all their top level training includes an extensive jump program.

Jumps are necessary for the development of maximum neuro-muscular reflex. There is a high correlation betweel leg *power* and success in the shot put.

There are many different kinds of jumps, from depth jumping to triple jumping drills. What we are trying to do is develop the "stretch reflex" of the legs. Jumps should be performed only two times a week. A few of the jumps we use every Tuesday and Thursday are as follows:
1. Double leg hops over hurdles.
2. Hopping over low, then high hurdles.
3. Double and single leg hops up and down stadium stairs.
4. Progressive squat jumps.
5. Squat jumps over mini-hurdles.
6. Hopping back and forth the length of benches placed end to end.
7. Rapid leg splits or frog kicks.
8. Rapid jump tucks (knees to the chest).
9. Hopping backwards on one leg for 30 to 50m.
10. Bounding.

11. Jump combinations:

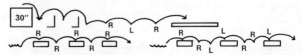

12. Triple jump boxes:

13. Depth jumping: We have 40", 30" and 18" boxes. These are the heights that are recommended by the Russian researchers. The most important aspect which must be stressed by the coach is that when the athlete makes contact with the mat after jumping from the box, he *cannot, must not* allow his legs to "give" before rebounding to the next box. The rebound or "explosive reflex" must be immediate from legs that are in a flexed position.

1. 30" to 18"
2. 18" to 30"
3. 40" to 18"

Brian and Andrew Miller in *Circle* magazine (1) have come up with a new "twist" in box jumping. Shot putting is a rotational or twisting event. Why not put rotation or twists into the box jump drills? Examples:

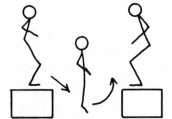

(1)

½-twist jump after the jump down-land facing opposite direction.

(2)

½-twist off box so athlete faces box he just jumped from. Immediately bound backward onto box.

(3)

Jump backwards off box. Upon landing, ½-twist and jump onto box.

(1) *Bounding and Depth-Jumping: A Review* by Brian and Andrew Miller, CIRCLE, March 1981.

PENDULUM SHOT AND SHOT BOX

The pendulum shot and shot box are plyometric drills developed by Sergio Zanon of Italy. These are used to develop the "ballistic reflex" of the throwing arm and power leg of the shot putter.

For the arm, we use the pendulum shot. It is a 10kg weight, hanging on a suspended *rigid* pole 5 to 6m in length. The weight is pushed out by the left hand (a), the pendulum is stopped by the right hand, placed in the throwing position (b), and followed by a normal shot put action (c) after the amortization phase.

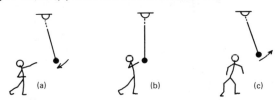

The Shot Box is an exercise to develop the supporting and driving leg in the shot. This is performed by executing the start of a glide from an elevated position about 30 to 40m high. The athlete lands on level surface to perform a normal delivery.

Zanon recommends that 5 to 8 repetitions and 6 to 10 sets of the exercises be performed in a training unit with 10 to 15 minutes rest between sets. Each repetition is performed flat out to develop maximum neuro-muscular effort. When the pendulum is used, it is advisable to progress by increasing the pendulum (drop) instead of increasing the weight of resistance. The breaking or amortization phase should be as short as possible and performed without changing the basic pattern of the movement. This allows for maximum strength to be developed in the second part of the acceleration phase.

All plyometric exercises should be discontinued ten days before important competitions. The intensity must follow an undulatory course, with a frequency of about 20 days.

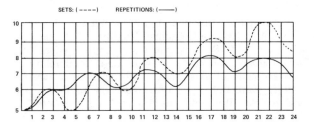

RUNNING PROGRAM

The running program is very simple. I do not believe in endurance running. The bulk of our running consists of sprints from the blocks of no more than 8 to 10m. Each sprint must be all out and as explosive as possible.

Starting in October, during our Tuesday-Thursday workouts, we do a form of agility sprints of 8 to 10m. We start at four sprints and gradually work up to 20 sprints. These, along with all the jumping drills which are increasing in number, result in a very exhausting workout. Example of agility sprints:

1. Squat jump sprints
2. Forward roll sprints
3.
4.
5.
6.
7.
8.
9.
10.

(→→→) Direction of sprint. On whistle, they get up as fast as they can and sprint.

We do other agility/mobility drills such as: forward and backward rolls, cartwheels, flip-flops, round-offs, etc. We will also do 360 degree turn-jumps over a hurdle, 360 degree turn runs, 360 degree-stretch leap followed by a forward roll (do a series of these), etc. Shot putters are usually big men and those who possess good body control have the most success in developing good technique through body awareness.

VARIABLE WEIGHT SHOT PROGRAM

The use of different or variable weight shots is as necessary as changing the weight program. The neuro-muscular system must be shocked if there is to be any progress. The purpose is to develop maximum ballistic power of the arm.

There are three different phases to the variable program. One phase is called "Analytical." Within this phase, there is the power component, where a heavy or overweight shot is used at maximum speed at 80% of maximum during all periods. The other component is speed, using a light weight shot at maximum speed. In the early part of the season, a large volume of this phase is called for. Do not use the analytical speed component during the competitive season.

The second phase of the variable training is called the "Variable Phase." This uses a combination of light, regular and overweight shots. What combination you will use depends upon the athlete's need:

Light	Regular	Overweight	Need
2	1	1	Speed
1	2	1	Regular
1	1	2	Power

The third or "Synthetic Phase" is used in conjunction with the analytical block during the competitive season. Only the twelve pound shot is used during this phase.

One final note concerning preparation for the big meet. There are many misconceptions about what to do during the last few days. What you do as a coach can have some beneficial or disastrous results for that potential champion. One rule to keep in mind is that there is no rest for the champions. Research has shown that a weight lifting session the day before the big meet is essential if the "tonus" of the neuro-muscular system is to "stay up." The Russians have shown that nerve excitation actually rises despite an intense workout the day before competition. It must be a short work program of specialized training for that specific event. □

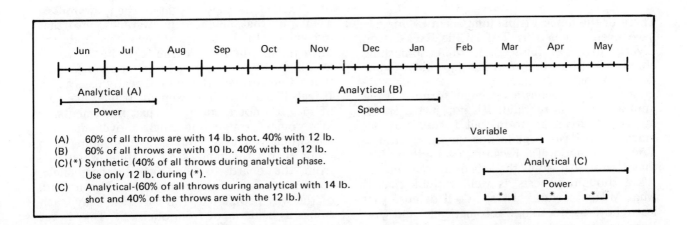

(A) 60% of all throws are with 14 lb. shot. 40% with 12 lb.
(B) 60% of all throws are with 10 lb. 40% with the 12 lb.
(C)(*) Synthetic (40% of all throws during analytical phase. Use only 12 lb. during (*).
(C) Analytical-(60% of all throws during analytical with 14 lb. shot and 40% of the throws are with the 12 lb.)

WILLIE BANKS ON TRIPLE JUMP TECHNIQUE

by Scott Brady-Smith, Antioch High School, Antioch, California

Banks gives his views on technique, training, attitude, rest and diet for the triple jump.

Willie Banks is the American record holder at 57-7½(17.56) and the indoor world record holder at 57-1½(17.41). During the 1981 season Banks compiled the greatest series of performances in the history of the event. Banks' top five marks averaged better than 57 feet. He had 10 meets with legal jumps over 17 meters (55-9¼). Banks' unprecedented consistency at such a high level is due to years of development and an insightful understanding of himself and the event. Here Banks discusses his holistic approach to the triple jump which includes philosophy, technique, training, attitude, rest, and diet.

Who were your coaches?

In high school I had Ken Barnes, Eugene Lentz, and Bill Christopher, who wasn't a coach but he essentially taught me how to do the triple jump correctly. I guess when the coaching began to show a significant effect was with Tom Tellez, then Jim Kiefer, Japanese coach Koqaki, Bob Larsen, and Milan Tiff.

Three of the longest triple jumpers in US history have been coached by Tiff (Willie Banks, Ron Livers, and Tiff himself). Is there something about his philosophy which has aided your development?

Yes. He teaches a different form of triple jumping. It's more fluid. It's not just a sport. Milan calls it an art form, but I would say it's more of an Eastern philosophy in doing things. You see in Judo, Tai Kwando, or anything like that it's not just doing the acts of movements. . . it's a thought process as well. I think that is what Milan teaches. Just as in self defense you learn how to do things automatically and you learn to put your body through movements in such a way as to do them fluidly and precisely. That's the way he teaches the triple jump. Not as a sport in Western philosophy but as a way of doing things in Eastern philosophy.

You have called the triple jump "power ballet." Can you expand on that?

I once went to the American Ballet Theater and I watched the dancers do their leaps and their bounds. It was very similar to the way we jump, only theirs were more graceful in the sense that they didn't seem to jump as powerfully as we do. In the triple jump we are using power through the event. It's not like we jump on our toes; we jump on our flat foot. We jump in a way that we use the strong parts of our body and they use the weaker muscles.

Tiff's triple jump philosophy seems to be a combination of technique and mental work.

Martial arts athletes have to get themselves prepared to do an act or a movement. When they do that, they put themselves in somewhat of a trance or they heighten their awareness. They put that heightened awareness into that movement. In the triple jump we have to do the same thing. When we do the triple jump, we are at a high state of awareness. It's a good feeling. When I go through the jump it really feels good. It feels like a natural movement. It feels like part of me. It's not a sport, it's just movements. . . just going through one single movement. Just like when you take your arm from point A to point B, it's the same kind of thing when I go from the board to the pit. It's one single, continuous movement of my body. If you think of the way people teach in the West, they teach things as being apart from one's self. They never teach things as being a part of the person. So if someone is teaching the triple jump they teach it in terms outside of one's self rather than explaining it as the movements being a part of your body. A coach should say, "you have to put this movement within you. This is how you create these movements from within."

Tiff told me, "You could jump far but you just won't let yourself jump far." I thought about that and there are a lot of things that were holding me back from jumping far. The fear of jumping far. . . that is scary enough in itself. There are all kinds of physical things, like gravity, that can hold you back but those physical things can be overcome in certain ways. People say you should lift weights to improve your strength so you can push your body further away from the ground. Tiff says you don't have to lift weights. . . you don't need that external aid. You can increase your strength by simply doing the triple jump. . . you just jump further.

How do you work on your strength?

I think the hardest thing I ever did was to bound 220 yards across a polo field with Milan. The first 50 yards was no problem, because I'd done that before. At the end of the first 50 yards I started to feel a little tired and a little weak. After 100 yards I was dying. . . and I still had 120 yards to go! Pretty soon my bounds were only about three feet long. My arms weren't getting up very high and pretty soon I couldn't even lift my arms and shoulders. My knees started dropping. The last 20 yards I couldn't even make it. Whereas Tiff, who was more than 30 years old, did it with no problem. He's smaller than me but he was stronger than me as related to triple jumping. After a while I could do that with no problem. Now, I saw that as being strength. It wasn't strength from lifting weights; it was strength created from triple jumping. When I took that strength to the triple jump runway, it was already there within me. Now if I go into the weight room and lift, lift, lift, I don't go out on the triple jump runway and lift weights! I go out and triple jump. So why should I go into the weight room and risk becoming muscle-bound and injury prone. I would as soon just triple jump.

How could a young jumper benefit from this philosophy you have developed?

If an athlete is serious about the triple jump he's going to have to study the event and become knowledgable about the event. It's not the type of thing where the athlete can say, "Oh, I read this and I can go out and become a great triple jumper." You have to live it. What are you going to get out of reading an article is not the success, but you can gain the will to do it or the encouragement to participate. Then you have to find it within yourself to do the things that will help you go farther. So you analyze what people say and you try to put it into movements. When the movements become fluid, then you try to increase on that through doing technical exercises (triple jump drills, stretching). Then you should get together with other jumpers and get the adrenalin going by having a "jump party."

You make the triple jump look so easy and so natural, but you have said there is much sacrifice involved in the triple jump. What do you mean?

Little do people know that I have had two fractured ankles, a wrenched back, pulled hamstrings in both legs, and numerous sprained ankles. There is a lot that a jumper has to go through. I have seen a lot of great jumpers not make it through the wars because they could not handle the pain of jumping. It's quite a difficult thing to jump through the years. But you find that the older jumpers are those that go the farthest. So if you make it through the first few injuries and come back strong, you'll be all right. Just as in any other thing that you do, you are going to have your ups and your downs. You have to hang in there because the triple jump can be a very painful event.

You can't sacrifice practice. It is very important. When I was preparing for the 1980 Olympic season, I would go out every day including Saturday and Sunday. I did jogging, sprinting, bounding, stretching, and other general conditioning exercises to prepare myself to do my best. This is important for all competitors in the triple jump.

What do you do in practice?

Everyday I come out, I jog 3-4 laps. I spend 30 minutes stretching and doing other warm up exercises. That will be followed by 4 warm up strides over 150 meters. *My entire warm up takes about 45 minutes. Many people are done with their training in that time!* The actual practice begins with short bounding—nothing strenuous—just a few bounds into the pit to get used to it. Then, depending on the day, I do different drills. One day I might concentrate on runways. I'll take some run throughs, then some hops off the board just to make sure my run is on. After that I would do sprint drills such as flying 50s, flying 75s and 150s for speed and strength. I also run up short hills for strength.

On other days I might do bounding and/or

box drills. I do various box drills for 30-60 minutes. I try to improve my strength and resiliency through depth jumping, so when I use a high hop I'll be able to handle it. A lot of athletes use a flat arc on their hop because they can't handle anything above that flat arch. I can come down from a high arch then, BOOM, come off it because I'm used to doing this off boxes.

Was that years of development?

Yes, it took some time to do it . . . it took some pain, too! I threw my hip out doing box drills, but once you get to a high level of development, the box drills are invaluable. It took three or four years before I mastered box drills. I think one can become more proficient in the box drills sooner . . . I only did them once a week until recent years.

How many days a week would you use boxes or bounding drills during a hard training cycle?

Twice a week is pretty good with box drills. You have to be careful with box drills . . . you have to spread them out. Those boxes are very, very difficult. It's like triple jumping with a heavy barbell on your shoulders, but it's not just pushing up a weight. You're coming down, landing and taking off with a quick reaction time. When you do something like that you're risking injury, so you have to be very careful about spreading the box jumping days apart. You can't be tired. Your body has to be ready to do it.

Should a novice triple jumper come out and do box drills right away?

It's necessary to develop good bounding technique prior to using the boxes. It could be months, or even a year, before the jumper is ready to use box drills and then they should only be used once a week. When first using the boxes, they shouldn't be very high or far apart. Every time you start something new in triple jumping you should start from very low without too much speed. Just learn the technique of it. The novice should do the box drills very slow with the boxes very close. As your proficiency grows you should spread the boxes farther apart and use a little bit more speed and a little bit more stretch . . . and *move* through the boxes. Use the boxes to increase your speed and strength through the jump. The boxes also force you to concentrate on good technique because if you don't concentrate you will get hurt.

If there is an ultimate in the triple jump, will the hop phase be done with a flat arc or a high arc?

You have to get up—isn't the event called the triple *jump?* You have to take a long jump. You have to jump as if it is the long jump on your hop. I do the box drills to help me with the strength and timing required to come off of a high hop.

Basically, anyone can take a long high hop.

But the athlete won't be able to do anything with it after he comes down. Either the athlete will not be able to continue the jump or he will have a short step phase. You have to take three long jumps. It's one movement.

You have talked about the 60-foot triple jump. How far will your phases have to be?

My phases will be 19 feet-19-22 or 19-18-23. I want to have a long hop but I can't let the hop be so far as to impair my movement. My movement is geared for shorter hop and step phases than my jump phase, which is on my strong leg. From take-off to finish, the triple jump is one movement, but the one movement I go through is only geared for a hop, a step, and a *long* jump.

You are currently able to go over 20 feet on your jump phase. Apparently, you are able to maintain your speed through the entire triple jump.

There was a biomechanical study done by a graduate student at USC on various groups of triple jumpers in which I was a subject. The study found that speed from the hop to the step was directly related to distance of the TJ. Of all the jumpers, I was the only one who not only maintained my speed but increased my speed from the hop to the step. It sounds impossible to me that one could jump into the air, come down and increase his speed. When I come down and I go into my step, I am moving quicker because my knee is coming through like a sprinter. That one movement of riding over my take-off leg, WHOOSH, brings my body through very quickly. This enables me to increase my speed into the step then I slow down a little into the jump. But I still have plenty of speed left for a *long* jump. When I land from a good jump I fall forward. A lot of people think that is because of my landing technique which may be right, but I'd have to land on my back to not fall forward with the speed I am carrying.

Speed can be viewed many different ways—speed on the runway, speed through the jump, speed improvement. What are your views on speed?

As we were just saying, speed from the hop

to the step is very important in triple jumping. I believe that "speed bounding" and box drills develop this type of triple jump speed. Bounding will also increase your running speed, however sprinting in practice is even more effective. My runup does not appear too fast... it is a controlled sprint getting plenty of stretch out of my legs. I want to control the speed and come off the board in such a way that I can use the speed during the movements of the jump.

Some of your improvement is due to a new attitude about rest, isn't it?

I believe rest is an essential element in top flight triple jumping. You shouldn't rest all of the time. When I am not competing I will practice every day and it's fun. When I am competing I need rest to build up the inner strength to maintain my competitive edge.

I like to train on a two-week cycle during the competitive season. During the first week I train 6 days with rest on Sunday. During the second week I will have a medium workout on Monday, a light workout on Tuesday, a warm up on Wednesday, and rest on Thursday and Friday and I compete on Saturday.

What's the difference on Saturday? What do you feel like compared to your collegiate days when you were training through the entire week?

I feel lighter as if I have more spring in my legs. I can jump better because I am not tired.

Does visualization help you at all?

In the two days before a competition, I do mental work. I'll lie down in bed and go through a series of jumps. I concentrate on my movements. At times I actually start sweating during this visualization process. The movements aren't always perfect. Sometimes I have to keep the movements running back in my mind until I get to the place I want to be.

Is the visualization as important as the other facets of your training?

Yes, it is very important because you want everything to be automatic. If you can't visualize it then you know it won't be automatic.

Has your diet played a role in your improvement?

Yes, it is very important. Three years ago, I went to a doctor who believes that through nutrition you can increase your physical capabilities. Using hair follicle tests to determine what I was lacking nutritionally he was able to suggest vitamin & food supplements. I haven't eaten red meat in three years. I do eat chicken and fish. I eat a lot of vegetable, steamed only. I feel more stable emotionally because I don't eat a lot of sugar. I have more endurance and I feel lighter. I don't get sick as often, either.

What is your attitude toward competition?

I enjoy competition. It's fun. I don't go out to beat one single individual so much as I go out to compete with myself. If you don't have fun competing, why compete?

What is different about your triple jumping?

The event is a part of my life. It has become natural to me. When I was young, I didn't participate the way I do now. Triple jumping was simply a way to gain opportunities. At one point after I graduated from college I quit jumping. I eventually found that I missed it so much I had to go back to it. I accepted it as a part of me and my regular routine. I enjoy jumping and appreciate it a lot more now. It has taken on a new dimension since my temporary retirement. □

For the Coach

PRINCIPLES OF STRENGTH TRAINING IN ATHLETICS

by Bob Myers, Assistant Track Coach, University of Arizona

Myers gives a brief overview of basic strength training principles and suggests a daily weight program.

Strength is becoming a larger part of athletics; therefore, strength training time and education of proper lifting must be an integral part of an athlete's training program.

Strength training as a part of power training should follow the pyramid of power training:

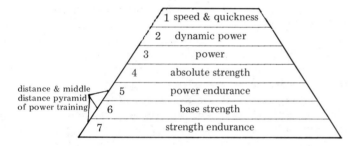

1 e.g., reaction time, movement drills, block start

2 e.g., short-quick explosive hops, bounds, vertical jumps

3 e.g., olympic lifts, explosive lifting

4 e.g. 4 x 1 @ 100%

5 e.g., multiple hops, bounds, skips, jumps

6 e.g., 4 x 4 @ 80%

7 e.g., 3 x 10 @ 50%

In developing a year round program:
1. Be systematic and progressive.
2. Develop training phases and cycles so the athletes have adequate rest physically and mentally. This will help prevent injuries and maintain motivation.
3. Adapt to the physical needs of the individual. An athlete is only as strong as his/her weakest link.
4. Adapt to the physical requirements of the event.
5. Adapt to the equipment and facilities available.
6. Be flexible in changing workouts due to injury, soreness or other outside stresses.

WARM UP

1. Jog or cycle 5-10 minutes (minimum) to increase the heart rate, body temperature and increase the circulation to the peripheral areas.
2. Static flexibility for 15-20 minutes (minimum) from the toes to the neck and shoulders (especially the upper body). This serves to thoroughly warm each muscle and prepare them for activity.
3. In some cases, special mobility or dynamic flexibility.
4. The warm up is decreased if the athlete is coming from another activity.

PRIMARY LIFTS

These are lifts which will primarily aid in developing strength/power in the dominant muscles used in that event. They are usually the legs, trunk and chest muscles, in that order.

1. Primary lifts are always performed first.
2. A minimum of 1-2 warm up sets are undertaken before starting the listed sets. During an orientation period 3-4 sets of a progression are used.
3. Always perform power or explosive lifts before strength or slow lifts (i.e., cleans or snatches will always be before squats or bench).
4. Always take the correct amount of rest between sets.
5. Always strive to use better technique while lifting.
6. Push yourself to make the sets/reps listed. "You only get out of it what goes into it."

SPECIFIC, SUPPLEMENTAL OR CIRCUIT LIFTS

These are lifts to develop muscles specifically for your event, specifically for your individual weaknesses or lifts to help your primary lifts.

1. Always done in order.
2. Always done with a minimum rest between sets/reps
3. Never performed during a max week. □

POWER DRILLS FOR DISTANCE RUNNING

by Joli Sandoz, Track Coach, Brandeis University

Power training isn't just for jumpers and throwers; distance runners can benefit from it too. The author synthesizes some of the best literature on the subject and applies it to distance running.

Most people do think of power as an explosive, short-duration quality. In track, it's usually something only sprinters and field eventers train for. So why worry about it in distance running?

Strength development is specific to movement patterns. This means in part that a muscle group must be trained at a particular speed or faster if it is to retain strength at that speed. Development of strength alone won't get the job done if it can't be maintained at speed; speed alone isn't enough because the force exerted by a muscle decreases as speed of movement increases. The specificity principle also means that competitive form must be duplicated exactly if the proper muscle fibers are to be strengthened and nerves educated to fire motor units in the right sequence. This is obviously impossible on weight machines . . . or in fact by any activity but running. So the strength developed in the weight room remains unusable without some supplemental training which will prepare muscles to deliver strength at speed *(power = strength x speed)*. Power drills bridge the gap.

Each particular drill is designed to imitate aspects of good running form, or to train a specific set of muscles to deliver strength at speed in a way that will ultimately mesh into efficient form. All of the drills require good upright body posture and coordinated movement of arms and legs. The following is part of one drill "set" which can be used several times a week as preparation for and companion to hill training.

1 x high knees, jog to make 100 yards
1 x 100-yard fast stride
1 x hop left leg, jog to make 100 yards
1 x 100-yard fast stride

The exercise segments (high knees, hopping, bounding, skipping, and so on) should be lengthened as you get stronger and more proficient at each drill. Since power drills can be hard on your legs, start very slowly and gradually increase the load.

The basic drill set (which we will go through once a day 2-4 times a week) is based on one used by Maricica Puica, the 1977 World Cross Country Champion who has run under 4:00 for 1500 meters. Over the years, she has worked her way up to four complete repetitions of a twenty segment drill set . . . up a 45 degree hill!.

One further aspect of power drills should be mentioned here. Exercise physiologist Kris Berg notes that it may be the timing of hip, knee, ankle and arm movements which separates excellent runners from good. The reasoning is: muscle has an elastic quality in that when stretched, it rebounds to its original length. This elastic capacity results in "free" work; it may be that this type of energy makes up as much as half the total energy used in activity. When stretched under tension, a muscle "snaps back" more or less according to the speed of the original stretch. This reaction can be increased by training which evokes the elastic quality; hence the power drills which involve jumping, hopping, bounding, downhill running. Optimal stride length and rate are important in allowing muscles to rebound—Berg's timing of movements.

The goal throughout all strength training is improvement of speed over the length of the run. The key is efficiency, made possible in part by training for:

1. Power
   a. Muscle strength
   b. Speed of muscle contraction

21

2. Neuromuscular skill
   a. Sequence of motor unit firings
      a. (1) Direction of forces
         (2) Timing
3. Anaerobic efficiency

STRENGTH FOR FLUID EFFICIENT FORM: POWER DRILLS (Drill Sets)

Directions
1. Warm up with 15-30 minutes of jogging.
2. Stretch.
3. Do drills on grass (not track).
4. No stopping during a drill set!
5. Think FORM. We'll begin slowly, and over time speed the movements up.
6. Warm down with 15+ minutes of jogging. Stretch!

Definitions

High Knees: Bring knees up as high as possible. Goal is thighs parallel to ground or higher. Check that buttocks are tucked under!

Fast stride: Smooth fast run. Tuck buttocks under to balanced position. Good knee lift and strong drive off ground.

Hop: Bring both arms forward and drive upward with left thigh as you extend right leg explosively (a). Bring right heel up to buttocks before landing on right leg and swinging arms and left leg back from hip (b and c). Spring up and forward again off right leg. Get as much height as possible.

Bounding: Exaggerated running action with tremendous drive from leg on ground. Hold position in air as long as possible. Keep body erect, land on flat foot spending only a fraction of a second on the ground. Goal is to bring thighs up parallel to ground.

Carioca: Turn right side to direction you wish to go. Now step in front of your right leg with your left. Swing your right leg toward goal X. Put left leg *behind* right. Swing right leg toward goal. Practice this before you try it at speed!! Purpose is to work rarely-used hip muscles. The second time this appears in the drill set, face the other direction.

Skipping: Very similar to hopping except you alternate legs, bouncing twice on each leg. Use single or double arm action. Try to skip as high as possible by driving opposite knee high.

Spring Jumps: Two-legged hops. Use double arm action. *Continuous movement!*

The Set

1 x high knees, jog to make 100 yards.
1 x 100 yards fast striding.
1 x hop left leg, jog to make 100 yards.
1 x 100 yards fast striding.
1 x hop right leg, jog to make 100 yards.
1 x 100 yards fast striding.
1 x bounding, jog to make 100 yards.
1 x 100 yards fast striding.
1 x carioca, jog to make 100 yards.
1 x 100 yards fast striding.
1 x skipping, jog to make 100 yards.
1 x 100 yards fast striding.
1 x spring jumps, jog to make 100 yards.
1 x 100 yards fast striding.
1 x carioca, jog to make 100 yards.
1 x 100 yards fast striding.
1 x high knee, jog to make 100 yards.
1 x 100 yards fast striding.

Progress
Test leg power periodically by measuring vertical jump, standing long jump, standing triple jump, distance covered by three spring jumps, and timing a 40-yard sprint. □

REFERENCES

1. Berg, Kris. "How to Maximize Running Efficiency." *Runner's World,* Vol. 14, No. 4, April, 1979. pp. 50-53.
2. Bonney, Alan. "Jump Training as a Key to All-Sports Performance." Unpublished clinic presentation.
3. Conniff, James, C.G. "James Nicholas: The Orthopedic Approach." *The Runner,* Vol. 3, No. 5, Feb., 1981. pp. 62-65, 77-78.
4. Costill, David. Presentation at Medalist Coaches Clinic in Newton, Massachusetts, January 31, 1981.
5. Daniels, Jack, Robert Fitts, and George Sheehan. *Conditioning for Distance Running.* New York: John Wiley and Sons, 1978.
6. Fox, Edward L. *Sports Physiology.* Philadelphia: W.B. Saunders Company, 1979.
7. Gambetta, Vern. "Plyometric Training." *California Track News,* Jan./Feb. 1977, p. 11.
8. Marks, Mike. "Weight Training for Track and Field." Presentation at the USOC Learn By Doing Clinic, Colorado Springs, CO, 1978.
9. Mathews, Donald K. and Edward L. Fox. *The Physiological Basis of Physical Education and Athletics.* Philadelphia: W.B. Saunders Company, 1976. 2nd ed.
10. Peterson, James A. "Weight Training: Health Insurance for Runners." *The Runner,* Vol. 3, No. 11, Aug. 1981. pp. 68-73.
11. Wilmore, J.H. "Alterations in Strength, Body Composition and Anthropometric Measurements Consequent to a 10-Week Weight Training Program" cited in Fox, Edward L. *Sports Physiology.* p. 158.
12. Wyrick, Waneen. "Biophysical Perspectives" in Gerber, Ellen W. *et. al. The American Woman in Sport.* Reading, MA: Addison-Wesley Publishing Company, 1974. pp. 403-529.

NEED AND USE OF PERFORMANCE ANALYSIS

by James G. Disch, Ph.D., Rice University

Disch stresses the usefulness of motor performance testing and profile data for selection, classification and diagnosis of track and field athletes.

"The proof is in the product" applies more directly to track and field than it does to numerous other sports. The fact that performance is directly measured gives track coaches a concrete criterion for selecting performers in the various events. The athlete that runs the fastest, or jumps the highest, or throws the longest is the one selected to compete.

Does this infer that motor performance testing of track athletes is not needed? Far from it. What this fact does point out is that performance testing in track is not well suited for selection, but for classification and diagnosis it is necessary and extremely useful. This is especially true with age group competitors.

The distinctions among the terms—selection, classification, and diagnosis—are important. *Selection* refers to choosing an athlete for a specific task or event. In team sports, selection processes involve choosing starters over non-starters or choosing varsity over junior varsity performers. In track actual performance is by far the best way to *select* a track squad.

Classification, on the other hand, involves choosing the specific event or events in which an individual would compete. A classification analogy in team sports would be determining playing positions in football, basketball, volleyball, etc. Classification processes in track allow coaches to channel performers into events for which they are best suited.

Diagnosis deals with analyzing an individual's ability level on a variety of tasks important to the performance of a given event. In track, for example, a long jumper's success will be based primarily in the motor abilities of sprinting speed and jumping ability. By concentrating on these tasks separately a coach can diagnose which ability needs to be developed more, in order to reflect the greatest change in event performance. This allows the coach to set up individualized workouts that optimally develop the performers.

Performance based data of this type is best associated with basic abilities such as speed, agility, jumping ability, strength, etc. The best way to present information of this nature is in performance profiles.

Performance profiles are charts that present a continuum of data based on a number of competitors and the data is displayed in such a way that individual and group performances can be plotted and examined.

USES OF PROFILE DATA

Classification is an extremely important use of profile data when dealing with age group athletes. Consider a study by Disch, Ward & Foreman in 1978 dealing with 41 female track athletes (age 11-21). The athletes were classified according to current event preference as either distance runners, throwers, or sprinters/jumpers. Using multiple discriminant analysis on a selected battery of tests it was possible to properly classify 38 of 41 athletes.

This may seem to be a foregone conclusion, because of the gross nature of the groups. However, this does confirm that a large percentage (90%) of the individuals tested fit the profile for their group. From a coaches point of view this means that they are performing the event(s) for which they are best suited.

Now consider the three athletes who were misclassified. It can be assumed that they were performing events for which they were not well suited. Inspection of the classification table indicated that one distance runner was classified as a sprinter and two sprinters/jumpers were classified as distance runners. This indicates that these athletes are better suited for other events.

By comparing individual profiles to group profiles specific variables can be isolated that indicate what caused the performer to be misclassified. For example, subject 7 was classified as a sprinter/jumper primarily because of her velocity at 5-10 yards in the 50 yard dash.

However, she had been performing distance events. Based on this information a coach could channel this runner into the shorter distance events or even the sprints and she would most probably be more successful.

Another utilization of performance data is for diagnosis. Consider the theoretical example of the female broad jumper who possessed a standing vertical jump of 25.5", but was not faring well in actual competition. Further examination of her profile data indicated that she was 25% body fat and ran 50y in 6.7.

Comparing her performance profile to the data for the athletes tested at Olympic Valley in August of 1980 it was found that she had more fat and a slower 50 than any of this group. However, her vertical jump was about 3.5" greater than any jumper tested.

By analyzing her results it was diagnosed that she should concentrate on reducing her body fat and increasing her speed. Therefore, an individualized training program and diet could be developed for her and this would hopefully hasten her development as a jumper.

The factors mentioned above would be picked up by most qualified coaches, but the virtue of performance data is that it provides a concrete means for making these assessments. Performance testing takes time and the development of performance profiles is somewhat tedious, but the values of this process far outweigh the problems associated with it! □

CONTINUOUS VS. INTERVAL TRAINING

by Duncan MacDougall and Digby Sale, McMaster University, Ontario, Canada

Both interval and continuous training are necessary in order to maximize the endurance athlete's potential for competition. The physiological basis for both forms of training is discussed and recommendations are made for year-round training and training to elevate the anaerobic threshold.

For years coaches and athletes have been debating the relative merits of interval vs. continuous training and asking scientists the question: "Which form of training is most effective for preparing the endurance athlete for competition?" The answer is both—but for different reasons.

OXYGEN AVAILABILITY

When the athlete is involved in a sport which requires a maximal energy expenditure over a time that exceeds approximately 2-½ minutes, the chief factor which limits his performance becomes his muscles' capacity for producing energy from the oxidation of glycogen and fat stores (Gollnick and Hermansen, 1973). This process can, in turn, only proceed at a rate which is set by that at which molecules of O_2 can be funneled into the mitochondria. As the duration of the event increases, this rate of oxygen delivery becomes even more important as a determining factor for success.

The delivery rate of O_2 into the mitochondria is directly dependent upon (1) the rate at which oxygen is delivered to the muscle and (2) the rate at which the muscle can extract or take up the oxygen. Thus, the successful endurance athlete is the one who can not only pump large quantities of blood to his exercising muscles but who can also extract a large quantity of O_2 from this blood.

Some authors have even gone so far as to suggest that approximately 50% of the increase in VO_2 max found in young healthy subjects after a training program can be attributed to enhanced O_2 extraction at the tissue level and 50% to enhanced O_2 transport (Rowell, 1974; Scheuer and Tipton, 1977). However, the phenomenon is probably too variable and complicated to make such generalizations.

INTERMITTENT EXERCISE

The theoretical basis for all interval training programs is the knowledge that when short rest periods are interspersed between periods of heavy exercise, the total accumulated exercise time can be greatly increased beyond that which could be achieved during a single continuous bout at the same intensity to exhaustion. For example, a highly motivated athlete could probably train continuously at an intensity corresponding to 100% of his VO_2 max for approximately 10 minutes before becoming too exhausted to continue. On the other hand, if he were to work at this same intensity for 2-3 minutes, interspersed by 2-3 minutes of recovery he would probably be able to maintain this pace for an hour or more before experiencing the same degree of fatigue (Astrand and Rodahl, 1979). Thus by using intermittent exercise he can increase his total training time at 100% VO_2 max to 30 minutes instead of 10.

Shorter work to rest intervals (e.g., 30 sec. on, 30 sec. off) at the same intensity would be even less fatiguing, however would not stress the oxidative capacity of the muscles to the same extent as would the longer (2-3 min.) intervals. The explanation for this phenomenon lies in the fact that during the brief work bouts a larger proportion of the total energy requirement is coming from the high energy phosphate pool and from O_2 bound to myoglobin, each of which have an opportunity to be partially restored during even the brief 30 sec. recovery period.

TRAINING TO INCREASE OXYGEN EXTRACTION OF MUSCLE

In theory, the muscles' capacity for extracting O_2 from the blood which it receives would be enhanced by any or all of: an increase in muscle capillary density (Brodal et al 1977), an increase in myoglobin (Pattengale and Holloszy 1967), an increase in mitochondrial enzyme activity (Holloszy 1975) or an increase in mitochondrial number and size (Hoppeler et al 1973). All of these adaptations have been documented as occurring as a result of physical training but the mechanisms which stimulate these changes are not yet known.

HYPOXIA THE KEY

Many physiologists feel that it is the reduced O_2 levels in the muscle during training which provides the stimulus for these changes. Such conclusions are based on studies which indicate that chronic exposure of humans to high altitude will result in increases in muscle myoglobin (Reynafarje, 1967), capillary density (Cassin, et al 1966; Rhan, 1966, but not Sillau et al 1980), mitochondrial enzyme activity (Reynafarje, 1962) and that even intermittent exposure to hypoxia will result in reduced lactic acid production at a constant workload (Bason, et al, 1973).

Physical training obviously simulates altitude exposure by reducing the O_2 tension in the active muscles to values which are considerably lower than they would be in resting man at sea level. For example, from differences in arterio-venous O_2 tensions one can estimate that when training at 70% of one's VO_2 max the O_2 tension in the working muscles would be approximately 51% of what it would be at rest. At 100% VO_2 max it would only be about 2% of what it is at rest. However, at supramaximal levels (e.g., "125% VO_2 max.") this value does not change—i.e. the muscle does not become any more hypoxic.

If it is the magnitude of this relative degree of hypoxia which provides the stimulus for structural and chemical changes in the muscle, it is apparent that training at workloads equivalent to 100% VO_2 max may be most effective. When the training intensity exceeds this level, apparently the stimulus is no greater and obviously the total exercise duration which can be tolerated becomes markedly reduced.

INTERVAL TRAINING

From the preceding it is apparent that the training method which would provide the muscle with the greatest degree of hypoxia for the longest total duration would be a work intensity which approaches 100% VO_2 max performed intermittently for 2-3 minutes and interspersed by 2-3 minutes of low intensity recovery. If such training is effective in stimulating structural and biochemical changes in the muscle which would increase its capacity for taking up and utilizing oxygen, it is obvious that such changes will only occur in those muscles (and indeed, only in those muscle fibers) which are used during training. Thus, for this form of training to be of any practical value to the athlete, it must be *specific to the event.*

As previously indicated, the optimal exercise intensity for this form of endurance interval training would appear to be that pace which is equivalent to 90-100% of the athlete's VO_2 max. When the pace exceeds this level, O_2 tension in the muscle is not significantly lower and the accompanying anaerobically generated acidosis will shorten the number of bouts which can be repeated. It should be noted that even at exercise intensities in the range of 90-100% VO_2 max, a significant proportion of muscle fibers will be contracting anaerobically and thus the athlete cannot avoid excess lactate accumulation at these intensities (Nagle et al 1970).

At intensities which are lower than this level (e.g., 70% VO_2 max) the O_2 tension in the muscle is probably not sufficiently reduced to provide a maximum training stimulus. Moreover, there is a possibility that the athlete may fail to train his fast twitch motor units which are apparently not recruited until the intensity exceeds approximately 90% VO_2 max (Gollnick, et al, 1975).

For practical purposes, an athlete may get a good indication of his training intensity by noting his pulse rate during the 15 seconds immediately following his work bout. It should be 3-5 beats per minute below his previously determined maximal heart rate for that exercise. If it is equal to his maximal heart rate, or if it does not drop to a value of 100-120 bpm at the end of the recovery interval, then the work intensity is too high.

TRAINING TO INCREASE OXYGEN TRANSPORT

Physiological factors which influence the athlete's maximal capacity for transporting oxygen include his pulmonary diffusing capacity, the concentration of hemoglobin in his blood, and his maximal cardiac output. Since athletes tend to differ very little from healthy non-athletic populations on these first two variables, it is generally accepted that an individual's maximal cardiac output is the most important factor affecting his ability to transport O_2.

Maximal cardiac output (the maximal amount of blood which the heart can pump in one minute) is the product of stroke volume (the volume of blood ejected by the heart in one contraction) and heart rate. Since it is well known that maximal heart rate does not increase with training, it is apparent that any change in maximal cardiac output with training must be entirely due to changes in maximal stroke volume. The mechanisms which lead to an increase in exercise stroke volume following a period of physical training are not fully understood and may be related to a larger ventricular volume, a slower heart rate during sub-maximal exercise (and thus a greater time for ventricular filling) or a greater contractility (more complete emptying) of the heart muscle. The fact that physical training can increase the contractility of the heart has been demonstrated in animal preparations where ventricular diastolic volumes and heart rates have been held constant (Bersohn and Scheuer, 1976).

Increasing Stroke Volume of the Heart

At the risk of oversimplification, we may think of the heart (cardiac muscle) as being analagous to skeletal muscle (e.g., the biceps). Just as the body builder is aware that overloading his biceps will result in an increase in size and strength, it is known that overloading of the heart will also lead to some degree of increased size and strength of the cardiac muscle of the endurance athlete (Morganroth et al 1975).

The contractile force of the heart is probably at its maximum at work intensities of approximately 75% VO_2 max and is not significantly increased at higher intensities. The number of repetitions would be synonymous with the total number of contractions during the training period, or heart rate times the duration of the exercise.

If one accepts that the most effective method for training the heart musculature is that which causes it to contract maximally for the greatest total number of contractions, then a program where intensity is approximately 75% VO$_2$ max and the exercise is continuous would appear to be optimal. At intensities above this level there is probably little to be gained in terms of additional contractile force of the heart and the total duration of the training session will be shortened because of fatigue, thus negating the total number of contractions, despite the elevated heart rate. If one substitutes near maximal interval training as previously outlined, it can be shown that the total number of contractions over the same training period (e.g., 45 min.) would still not be as great as that accumulated during continuous training, since heart rate declines very rapidly during the recovery intervals. Moreover the magnitude of the average force of contraction would also be reduced since it also rapidly declines during the rest interval.

CONTINUOUS TRAINING

Theoretically the most effective form of training for stressing the central oxygen transport system and for stimulating adaptive changes in the heart musculature would be continous exercise involving as large a muscle mass as possible at an intensity which approximates 75% of the athlete's VO$_2$ max. The exact intensity will depend upon the level of the athlete's anaerobic threshold (see MacDougall, 1977) which varies among individual athletes.

If an athlete's threshold occurs at 75% of his VO$_2$ max, his ideal training intensity would be 74 / VO$_2$ max; if his anaerobic threshold is 83% VO$_2$ max, his ideal training intensity would be 82% VO$_2$ max, and so on. When exercise intensity exceeds this threshold the accompanying lactacidosis will increase the subjective feelings of fatigue and eventually shorten the duration of the training session. On the other hand, at intensities just below the anaerobic threshold it is possible for an athlete to train up to 60 min. or more in a single bout, without feeling exhausted.

Although for the most part, it would be optimal for the exercise to be specific to the sport for which the athlete is training (e.g., the runner should train by running and the nordic skier by skiing), this principle is not quite as important for this form of training. For example, the skier or rower who finds it difficult to pursue his sport in the off-season because of climatic conditions would still be able to transfer much of the adaptation in O$_2$ transport gained by a running or cycling program, to their specific sports. This fact provides the athlete with an important advantage of this form of training, and that is that he can incorporate *variety* into his program and on a given day substitute an activity such as swimming, cross country skiing, cycling, etc., and still gain a training effect on the cardiac musculature which would be transferrable to his specific sport.

Again, for practical purposes, the training heart rate provides the athlete with an approximate indication of the correct training intensity. A somewhat crude, but generally effective, target heart rate for training can be calculated from the equation THR = RHR + 75% (MHR-RHR), where: THR = the target heart rate; RHR = the athlete's resting heart rate, and MHR = the athlete's maximal heart rate as measured during controlled laboratory tests. Anaerobic threshold can only be accurately measured in a laboratory setting, however the experienced athlete will subjectively learn to recognize the abrupt increase in his ventilation which occurs if his intensity exceeds the threshold. Thus, using his calculated target heart rate as an approximate guide and then by trial and error adjusting his pace either upward or downward according to his anaerobic threshold, the athlete should be able to select his most effective intensity for continuous training.

ESTABLISHING A BALANCE BETWEEN THE TWO TYPES OF TRAINING

In establishing a year-round training program for the endurance athlete several points must be kept in mind:

It takes much less effort to maintain a training effect than it does to reproduce it in the first place. Thus an athlete can reduce his weekly training load considerably and still maintain the changes in VO$_2$ max which he has previously achieved. This applies especially to continuous training (Bryntsson and Sinning, 1973) and to a lesser extent to interval training (Mathews and Fox, 1976, p. 307).

Proper endurance interval training is considerably more taxing—both physiologically, and psychologically, and therefore requires more motivation.

It would appear that adaptation in the O$_2$ extraction mechanisms at the local muscle level are lost more rapidly than those involved in the central O$_2$ transport mechanisms, when the athlete reduces his training. Evidence for this is furnished by reports of considerable seasonal fluctuations in VO$_2$ max of swimmers while swimming despite no changes in VO$_2$ max measurements during treadmill running over the same period (Holmer, 1974; Magel, et al, 1975).

The degree of glycogen depletion will be considerably greater following a session of interval training than following a session of continuous training. Consequently the athlete who is performing heavy interval training should allow a minimum of 48 hours between training sessions in order to ensure adequate glycogen repletion (Piehl, et al, 1974; and MacDougall, et al, 1977a). On the other hand, continuous training can generally be carried out on a daily basis since the degree of glycogen depletion following a normal training session would not normally be of sufficient magnitude that it could not be replenished by the athlete on a normal carbohydrate diet within 24 hours.

With these points in mind, one can hypothesize that the most effective program would be one which concentrates on continuous submaximal training for the majority of the off-season, and then progressively phases in interval training approximately 3 months prior to the competitive season. The transition is made possible by a progressive reduction of the time devoted to continuous training and it is assumed that any gain in central O$_2$ transport mechanisms will be maintained throughout this period by the combination of reduced continuous load and the augmented interval training. The interval training must be continued up to and (at varying levels) throughout the competitive season, probably most effectively by alternating a "heavy" interval day with a "light" continuous day. To attempt to introduce interval training early in the off-season, and to attempt to maintain the effect throughout the year would not only be inefficient and more stressful to the athlete but would require considerably more motivation.

TRAINING TO ELEVATE THE ANAEROBIC THRESHOLD

In addition to his state of training and his VO_2 max, an athlete's ability to perform long-term exercise is directly related to his anaerobic threshold. This is especially true in the longer distance events where VO_2 at anaerobic threshold is probably a better predictor of success than is VO_2 max (MacDougall, 1977). While anaerobic threshold may be partially pre-determined by % fiber type (Ivy, et al, 1980) it can also be affected by training, however it is not yet known which form of training yields the best results.

Many European coaches feel that long-duration continuous sub-anaerobic threshold training is the most effective means of elevating the threshold and this has to a certain extent been supported in recent investigations (Davis, et al, 1979). Additional support for this theory can also be found in laboratory test results of elite long distance athletes such as 10,000m runners and marathoners who tend to have higher thresholds than do elite middle distance athletes such as 1,500m runners and oarsmen (Mac Dougall, 1977). The longer-distance athletes traditionally devote more training time to long-duration submaximal training, while the middle distance athletes generally do more interval work.

On the other hand, many sports scientists feel that the most effective method of elevating the threshold would be to promote local changes at muscle level which would enhance its extraction and oxidative potential. Since it is known that skeletal muscles have the potential to adapt their oxidative capacity to a degree which is greater than that which is reflected by a change in VO_2 max (Saltin et al, 1977) it is conceivable that such changes may permit the athlete to tax a higher percentage of his VO_2 max without the accumulation of lactic acid. An increase in oxidative capacity of all fiber types could elevate the threshold by both forestalling the point of anaerobiosis (and thus lactic acid production) and by enhancing the uptake of lactic acid by slow twitch fibers, from those fibers which may be beginning to contract anaerobically. As previously outlined, these changes can probably best be accomplished through higher intensity endurance interval training, and indeed there is also evidence which indicates that this type of training will dramatically reduce lactic acid production at the same submaximal workload (Fox, 1975). Moreover, it would seem that this form of training would also be the most effective method of recruiting the fast twitch fibers and thus stimulating adaptation in these fibers as well. For these reasons the authors of this paper tend to support endurance interval training for elevating the anaerobic threshold; however, the topic needs more investigation.□

TESTING OF POTENTIAL TALENT

by Jess Jarver, Australia

Identifying potential talent has been too often a trial-and-error process. TT Annual *Foreign Editor Jess Jarver here outlines methods used by the Soviet and West German coaching staffs.*

Some problems with talent identification have been: 1) Lack of reliable test batteries. 2) Access to more sophisticated laboratory testing. 3) The absence of norms to compare the test results.

The following samples of simple field tests used in the Soviet Union and West Germany are not going to solve the problems of talent search and identification.

What we need is a standardized testing scheme that will provide best possible test batteries and reliable norms for each event. The following examples are meant to show that it is possible to base the selection of potential talent on unsophisticated methods, readily available to the coach.

The first set of sample tests is used in Soviet Youth Sports Schools for the 10 and 11 year old youngsters. The battery is divided into five categories—running, hurdling, jumping, throwing and multi-events. It includes some anthropometric measurements, according to the demands of a particular group of events.

A closer look at the test batteries reveals that no anthropometric measurements are recorded for runners. Height is considered important for hurdlers, jumpers, throwers and multi-events, while the throwers' battery includes also information on weight and arm span.

Looking at the tests of speed components shows that runners, hurdlers and jumpers are expected to produce similar times in the 30 meters sprint from a flying start and 60 meters from a standing start. Slightly less speed is expected from throwers, particularly in the 60 meters test.

It is also interesting to note the emphasis placed on leg power for throwers, expected to achieve better distances in the standing long jump than the jumpers (20cm in both age groups). Jumpers, in contrast, are looking for significantly better performances in the standing triple jump.

The West German talent identification tests, published in a series of articles in Die Lehre der Leichtathletik in 1977, are claimed to be practical but not ideal. The choice of the test batteries was based on:
* Tests that can be carried out without difficulties anywhere.
* Tests that are well known and need no special knowledge by the testers.
* Tests that are suitable to establish the level of basic motor ability.

In addition, the following information was collected for the final evaluation:
* Anthropometric measurements.
* Training age.
* Training frequency.
* Training load and intensity.

Below are selected examples of the West German tests. The tests include no norms for comparison. The final evaluation is made by the testing panel, based on the combined results of the collected information.

100 METERS HURDLE—FEMALE

1. Anthropometric measurements:
   Height, weight, height/weight index, leg length, thigh length.
2. Training information:
   Best 100 hurdles time, training age, previous weekly training frequency.
3. Basic tests:
   30m sprint from standing start without a starting signal (speed)—two attempts.
   Jump and reach (power)—two attempts.
   200m run with pulse recovery recording (endurance). Pulse rates are measured directly after the run, one minute and three minutes later.

4. Event specific tests:
50m sprint—as in the 30m sprint.
30m hops on right leg from standing start, aiming for a fast time with as few repetitions as possible.
30m hops on the left leg.
Hurdling technique—run over five hurdles, timed from the touch down of lead leg after the first hurdle to the landing of the trailing leg after the last hurdle (two attempts).
50m hurdles race—4 hurdles 84cm high and 8.30m apart. From start to first hurdle 13m (two attempts).

SHOT—MALE

1. Anthropometric measurements:
Height, weight, height/weight index, arm span.
2. Training information:
Best shot put distance, training age, previous weekly training frequency, best performances in other events.
3. Basic tests:
30m sprint from standing start without a starting signal (speed)—two attempts.
Jump and reach (power)—two attempts.
1000m run (endurance).
4. Event specific tests:
Three hops on one leg—two attempts for distance only.
Five double-leg hops—two attempts.
Standing long jump—three attempts.
Double-arm shot throw backwards over head (4kg)—three attempts.
Glides across the circle for technique evaluation, based on good, average, poor—three attempts.
Standing shot put—three attempts.

LONG JUMP—MALE AND FEMALE

1. Anthropometric measurements:
Height, weight, height/weight index.

2. Training information:
Best long jump distance, training age, previous weekly training frequency.
3. Basic tests:
30m from standing start without a starting signal (speed)—two attempts.
Jumps and reach (power)—two attempts.
1000m run (endurance).
4. Event Specific tests:
Five hops on the right leg for distance—two attempts.
Five hops on the left leg for distance—two attempts.
Ten steps from a five-stride approach, evaluated on distance and performance (explosive-reactive take-offs and horizontal speed).

DISCUS—MALE

1. Anthropometric measurements:
Height, weight, height/weight index, arm span.
2. Training information:
Best discus distance, training age, previous weekly training frequency, best performances in other events.
3. Basic tests:
30m sprint from standing start without a starting signal (speed)—two attempts.
Jump and reach (power)—two attempts.
1000m run (endurance).
4. Event specific tests:
Three hops on one leg for distance only—two attempts.
Five double-leg hops—two attempts.
Standing long jump—three attempts.
Double-arm shot throw backwards over the head (5kg)—three attempts.
20m continuous discus turning against the clock.
Coordination test of 360° turning right, followed by 360° turning left and completed with a normal discus turn.
Timed.

TABLE 1—RUNNING

Test or Measurement	Norms			
	Girls (10)	Boys (10)	Girls (11)	Boys (11)
30m flying start	4.2sec.	4.0sec.	4.0sec.	3.9sec.
60m standing start	9.2sec.	8.7sec.	9.0sec.	8.4sec.
300m	59sec.	57sec.	54sec.	50sec.
St. long jump	1.60m	1.75m	1.85m	1.95m
Half-levers*	6 reps.	8 reps.	7 reps.	9 reps.
Pull-ups	—	2 reps.	—	3 reps.
Push-ups	—	5 reps.	—	8 reps.

* = Lifting of straight legs in a hanging position to a 90° angle.

TABLE 2—HURDLING

Test or Measurement	Norms			
	Girls (10)	Boys (10)	Girls (11)	Boys (11)
Height	1.50m (4'11")	1.50m (4'11")	1.53m (5'¼")	1.55m (5'1")
30m flying start	4.2sec.	4.0sec.	4.0sec.	3.9sec.
60m standing start	9.2sec.	8.7sec.	9.0sec.	8.4sec.
300m	59sec.	57sec.	54sec.	50sec.
St. long jump	1.70m (5'7")	1.75m (5'9")	1.85m (6'1")	1.95m (6'4¾")
Half-levers	6 reps.	8 reps.	7 reps.	9 reps.
Pull-ups	—	2 reps.	—	3 reps.
Push-ups	—	5 reps.	—	8 reps.

TABLE 3—JUMPING

Test of Measurement	Norms			
	Girls (10)	Boys (10)	Girls (11)	Boys (11)
Height	1.52m (5')	1.52m (5')	1.53m (4'¼")	1.57m (5'2")
30m flying start	4.2sec.	4.0sec.	3.9sec.	3.9sec.
60m standing start	9.2sec.	8.7sec.	9.0sec.	8.4sec.
St. long jump	1.80m (5'11")	1.90m (6'3")	1.90m (6'3")	2.00m (6'6¾")
St. triple jump	5.50m (18'¼")	6.00m (19'8¼")	6.00m (19'8¼")	6.50m (21'4")
Half-levers	6 reps.	8 reps.	7 reps.	9 reps.
Pull-ups	—	2 reps.	—	3 reps.
Push-ups	—	5 reps.	—	8 reps.

TABLE 4—THROWING

Test or Measurement	Norms			
	Girls (10)	Boys (10)	Girls (11)	Boys (11)
Height	1.58m (5'2¼")	1.61m (5'3½")	1.60m (5'3")	1.65m (5'5")
Weight	42—48kg	48—50kg	45—50kg	50—55kg
Arm Span	1.60m (5'3")	1.63m (5'4¼")	1.62m (5'3¾")	1.67m (5'5¾")
30m flying start	4.5sec.	4.3sec.	4.3sec.	4.1sec.
60m standing start	9.8sec.	9.6sec.	9.6sec.	9.4sec.
St. long jump	2.00m (6'6¾")	2.10m (6'10¾")	2.10m (6'10¾")	2.20m (7'2¾")
St. triple jump	5.20m (17'¾")	6.00m (19'8¼")	5.60m (18'4½")	6.30m (20'8")
Shot throw**	10.00	10.00m	11.00m	11.00m
Half-levers	6 reps.	8 reps.	7 reps.	9 reps.
Pull-ups	—	3 reps.	—	5 reps.
Push-ups	2 reps.	6 reps.	3 reps.	8 reps.

** = Double-arm throw backwards over the head. Girls (10)—3 kg; boys (10)—4 kg; girls (11)—3 kg; boys (11)—4 kg.

TABLE 5—MULTI EVENTS

Test or Measurement	Norms			
	Girls (10)	Boys (10)	Girls (11)	Boys (11)
Height	1.53m (5'¼")	1.56m (5'1½")	1.56m (5'1½")	1.61m (5'3½")
30m flying start	4.3sec.	4.1sec.	4.2sec.	4.0sec.
60m standing start	9.3sec.	8.8sec.	9.1sec.	8.5sec.
St. triple jump	5.40m (17'8½")	5.90m (19'4½")	5.70m (18'8½")	6.40m (21')
Shot throw	9.50m (31'2")	9.50m (31'2")	10.50m (34'5½")	10.50m (34'5½")
Half-levers	6 reps.	8 reps.	7 reps.	9 reps.
Pull-ups	—	3 reps.	—	5 reps.
Push-ups	2 reps.	5 reps.	3 reps.	6 reps.

MIDDLE AND LONG DISTANCE TRAINING CONCEPTS

by Manuel Bueno, Switzerland

Swiss coach Bueno gives a quick overview of current European training methods and some practical advice on their application.

TYPES OF TRAINING

It is generally agreed that the development of aerobic endurance is accomplished either by the method of long continuous running at a constant speed, or by the method of extensive interval training (workouts of many repetitions at a reduced speed) (10,23,28). This paper will consider only the former.

Recently, in the literature on training, many examples are found which show the current trend is in the direction of different paces, all within the range of aerobic activity. It was not long ago that long continuous runs at a pulse rate between 120 and 140 beats/minute were considered appropriate for the development of aerobic capacity. Today the physiologists admit the use of different pulse rate aerobic runs, depending on the particular training task: the heart rate will rise above 170 beats/minute at times for well-trained athletes, after the level of conditioning and the particular characteristics of the athletes have been taken into consideration.

For the French, "fundamental" endurance is developed by steady long runs in the range of 150 beats/minute. If the intensity of the workout is about 80% of maximum ability and the pulse climbs to between 160 and 170 then the runner is doing "active" endurance and is improving his or her aerobic power.

The French also talk of the "critical zone" and of the "subcritical zone" depending on whether the athlete is close to or below his or her maximum level of oxygen consumption. The English share the same preoccupation and also recommend continuous running at different paces according to the desired goal, but never going above 160 beats/minute. Wilson (Ovett's coach) and Watts state that the rate of oxygen consumption is the main problem which the

runner must confront, a problem which requires a different solution for each individual.

Fred Wilt, an advocate of continuous fast running, feels that the pulse rate should at times approach 180. For the Soviets the classification is determined by the choice of different levels of pulse rates, based on the fact that the adaptation process takes place only when the intensity and the volume of the workout are specific. The West Germans also advise continuous running at well-defined degrees of intensity and with well-prescribed objectives: low intensity for recuperation, medium for maintaining, and high for improving the aerobic capacity. Schmolinsky (DDR) talks of efforts of average and long duration at different degrees of intensity: weak, below 80%; average, between 80 and 90%; and strong, at 90% or more of the individual's potential. All schools advocate a judicious use of the spectrum of pulse frequencies staying within the zone of aerobic metabolism.

PRACTICAL ADVICE

The most important priority for the coach and the athlete is to determine an *optimal individual intensity* of the workload in training necessary to improve the aerobic capacity. It is evident that the relationship between volume and intensity is essential: the greater the volume, the less will be the intensity that can be maintained.

Workouts of average intensity and large volume are good for *stabilizing* aerobic endurance but to *improve* it it is necessary to go up periodically to a higher level of intensity. Thus a long endurance run during which the heartbeat is in the aerobic zone can be used as a means of *recovery*, which is necessary after strenuous efforts lasting 30 to 60 minutes. If the duration is longer (1½ to 2 hours) the run may also improve the athlete's *mental* toughness. In

COACHES OF VARIOUS NATIONS DIFFER ON OPTIMAL PULSE RATE IN AEROBIC TRAINING.

the two cases the intensity is dictated by the feelings of the athlete, with the pulse oscillating in general between 130 and 160 beats/minute.

When the goal is to *improve* the aerobic capacity, prolonged efforts at increasingly higher intensities which approach the anaerobic threshold are advised. The heart should reach 170 beats/minute and faster (10-15 beats/minute more than for the recuperation/stabilization run) and the duration from 30 to 60 minutes maximum. The planning of the weekly microcycle must be determined by varying the effort, both qualitatively and quantitatively. Concerning steady intensive endurance runs, two or three workouts a week, maximum, suffices.

Given that determining the anaerobic threshold demands sophisticated equipment, which is not available to everyone, we can conclude by giving only some approximate indications of the speed and time span of a distance workout such as it is currently applied.

A long run at a moderate speed is advised to maintain the level of endurance and to allow for recuperation. The workouts should be long (including one of three hours) and the speed should be about 4:00 to 4:20 minutes/km for a well-trained runner, and from 5:00 to 5:40 minutes/km for the average runner. To improve the aerobic capacity, workouts of intensive endurance are best. The length of the effort can be extended to between 1 and 1½ hours if the speeds are in the range of 3:45 to 4:00 minutes/km for those moderately well-trained (with the pulse in the range of 155 to 165 beats/minute). A continuous run at a faster pace (3:15 to 3:25 minutes/km) for 30 minutes to 1 hour, is recommended for the better runners.□

SPEED TRAINING

by Frank W. Dick, National Coach, Great Britain

Speed is the capstone and essential aspect of every track and field discipline. Dick reviews the role of speed in the various events, the problems which can occur when speed is misapplied, and some possible solutions. Athletics Coach, *Vol. 15, No. 4, Dec. 1981.*

When we talk of speed in athletics, we are normally defining the capacity of a limb, or of the whole body, to move with the greatest possible velocity. In practical terms, however, it is used in reference to:

1. Speed of executing a technique; e.g., starting, hurdle clearance, throwing action.
2. Speed across the ground; e.g., sprinting.

Let me take these in turn.

SPEED OF EXECUTING A TECHNIQUE

Speed in this context should be seen as sophistication of technique. In a single technique event, say discus throw, the pattern of development is:

(a) Develop basic conditioning.
(b) Develop basic technical model.
(c) Develop specific conditioning.
(d) Develop advanced technical model (with speed/strength, etc.).

There is still further progression from the "d" specific to a given discipline. For example, there is development of the capacity to select one from several technical variants according to environmental demand (e.g., adjusting throwing or jumping technique according to surface, weather, etc.; adjusting running pattern according to race pattern, opposition, etc.). Here, we are involved in decision-making which requires:

(1) Recognition/reading of the situation.
(2) Selection of the correct solution.
(3) Execution of that solution.

Steps 1-3 require time, but this time can be reduced if:

— The athlete has mastered a-d.
— The athlete has learned to adjust his position to execute technique.
— The athlete has learned 1-3 through exposure to pressure practices.

This whole area might be thought of as "development of reaction." However, we must not lose sight of the fact that this—whether it be to a gun in sprint starting, to a cross-wind in vaulting, or to opponents' tactics in steeplechase—is based on having the ensuing technique mastered by the athlete.

SPEED ACROSS THE GROUND

Although, clearly, reaction speed is also involved here, it is more important that we consider the single technique of sprinting. Sprinting, as a technique, is built upon development of a strong pillar. The pillar is the trunk, from head to hips. If this is weak, then the arms and legs have nothing to work against, and no means of linking their respective contribution to propulsion. Within basic conditioning, then, the coach must include work to strengthen the pillar.

While the legs are obviously the principle source of propulsion, and must be developed for that role, no less important are the arms.

— To "pilot" the leg action for range of movement.
— To balance the leg action.
— To set the tempo for the speed of leg action.

In terms of practices, then, the following are used for development of basic conditioning:

Strength:			
	Chins	6 x 10	10 x 50
	½-squats	6 x 15	10 x 75
	Press-ups	6 x 5	10 x 25
	Treadmill	6 x 15	10 x 60
	Speedball	6 x 30 secs	10 x 3 mins.
	(6-8 weeks—6 days/week)		

Mobility: Various exercises for—hamstrings.

—hip complex.
—spine (rotation, flexion, extension).
—shoulder complex.

Endurance: Partly within strength work, partly via long repetitions (250m), partly via fartlek.

On this foundation, the basic sprint technique is built, working separately on arm action, posture, leg action. This sprint technique must, of course, be applied first slowly and deliberately then gradually progressing to trials and competition. As with all athletic techniques—only that speed which permits the technical model to remain uncompromised, must be employed. The motto, "If it isn't right show them it won't be right fast" should be followed for all techniques. Speed is a sophistication of technique.

The sprint race is normally considered as:
A. Acceleration.
B. Pick-up.
C. Holding form.

A. This is the leg drive phase, accompanied by a fast and positive arm action. For "specific conditioning" harness running, towing and weighted tire might be used. (3 x 30m ⟶ 6 x 40m).
In technique work, the distance covered in ten strides is measured (15.00m ⟶ 20.00m).

B. This is the "knee lift—fast strike" phase, accompanied by a full and positive range of arm action. For "specific conditioning," "high knees" (3 x 60 ⟶ 6 x 100m) and bounding (3 x 40 ⟶ 6 x 60m).

C. This is related to concentration, relaxation, and endurance capacity. "Specific Conditioning" involves 30-30-30 or 60-30-60 (2-3 x 3-4) of sprint-decelerate-sprint.

In terms of distances sprinters use in training, acceleration and faction work is done over 30 and 60. Seldom will such distances be raced more than 5 and 3 times respectively, in one unit, and a rule of thumb, 4.5 sec. and 7.25 sec. are reasonable starting targets, with 4.0 sec. and 7.0 sec. the "big barriers."

It is worth mentioning here that, although speed across the ground is a critical factor in the javelin and the jumps, such speed, unlike that of the sprinter and sprint hurdles is *optional*, not *maximal*. Nevertheless, the javelin thrower and jumper, like the endurance athletes, require a

SPEED IS THE ESSENCE.

high maximal speed, to offer, on the one hand, a range within which a high optimal speed is possible, without straining; and on the other, a large speed reserve.

Having discussed sprinting speed development at length, we should now consider development of speed in other disciplines. It should be stressed again that speed should not be pursued at the expense of technique. This is not to say that athletes should be content with slow techniques! Rather, pressure practices should be applied to equip the athlete to handle techniques at speed. Lack of strength has often been considered as the root cause of technical collapse as speed increases. This is not always the case. Coordination of movement and adjustment of body alignment to allow the technique to remain stable and efficient is equally—if not more—responsible.

By way of illustrating some speed problems and possible solutions, the following are offered.

Sprints:
— running at opposition

—opposition running at the athlete
(Practice—handicaps, downhill runs, etc.)

Hurdles:
— crowding the barrier at latter stages of the race.
(Practice—rolling start runs.
— broken/hurdles.
— shortening spaces.
— emphasize dropping the trail knee down off the hurdle).

Long/Triple Jump:
— exhaustion after 3-6 attempts in practice.
— being "past" the jumping foot before the jumping leg can extend.
— collapsing on landings (triple).
(Practice—downhill approaches.
— fast touch-off jumps.
— review conditioning work).

Pole Vault:
— striking pole with too great kinetic energy—pole breaks.
— shoulder damage.
— too low hold (easily altered!).
(Practice—plant in sand.
— make available 5-lb graduations in pole.
— make safe the surrounding mats.
— review conditioning work).

High Jump:
— collapsing of jumping leg.
— mistiming of free leg/arms..
— overshooting the take-off point.
— being "past" the jumping foot before the jumping leg can extend.
(Practice—fast approaches on to extended landing area.
— review conditioning work.
— work on isolation exercises for technique.

Throws:
— mistiming of contribution of arm/trunk/lower limbs.
— collapsing of front leg (javelin).
— misplacement of feet in turns/shifts.
(Practice—gradual acceleration into the throw.
— alter technique; e.g., point of entry for hammer.
— review conditioning work.
— work on isolation exercises for technique).

Only a few problems and practices are presented here. However, on the subject of reviewing conditioning work, it should be pointed out that the evolution of depth jumping and the various bounding routines were followed to meet this particular requirement.

In conclusion—and to stimulate thought on development of speed, the following are key factors in such development:
1. Innervation—selection and regulation of relevant motor units.
2. Elasticity—related to elastic component, reflexes, etc.
3. Biochemistry—Local energy supplies.
4. Muscle Relaxability—related to mobility, synergists, antagonists.
5. Willpower—capacity to concentrate.
6. Action Acceptors—selection of correct responses.

Practices focus in the first instance on making speed possible—then on obliging the athlete to learn to express his technique at speed. □

QUESTIONS AND ANSWERS IN THE DISCUS

by Kim Bukhantsev, U.S.S.R.

Bukhantsev, the senior discus coach of the Soviet team, answers some important questions on how to approach discus training. Soviet Sports Review, *Vol. 15, No. 3, Sept. 1980.*

Is it necessary, in the preparatory period, to throw the discus outdoors, or can one limit throwing to indoors, to throwing into a net?

At first glance it might seem that the answer depends on the climate during the preparatory period and that throwing into a net is a forced measure. However, many warm-climate throwers and coaches use a net, arguing that indoor throws do not impose great mental stress and that it is possible to accomplish more work than when throwing outdoors.

When throwing the discus in "natural" conditions, sensations arise that aid the formation of technical skills. The thrower can correct his actions with respect to the flight of the disc and the distance of the throw. Throwing indoors, a thrower concentrates on executing a specific technical element, and it is difficult for him to correlate his efforts, not seeing them put together in a regular throw.

The necessity of open-air throwing in the winter is evidenced by hammer throwers, who regularly throw during the preparatory period and are distinguished by their technical execution; on the other hand, javelin throwers, who don't throw outdoors during the winter, are technically inferior to their teammates in other events. Finally, a whole generation of throwers in the '60s answered this question: *they threw a lot into the net, and when they came out to train in the spring they began their technical training almost from ground "zero."*

A correct solution to this problem lies in the middle; indoor and outdoor work should be combined. But one thing is beyond dispute: Throwing in February should be conducted completely outdoors and the quantity should reach 1000 throws.

What should be the relationship between training and competition results?

Coaches and throwers often complain that

MYELNIK CAN HANDLE HIGH INTENSITY TRAINING: UP TO 100 THROWS AT "FULL POWER."

competition performance was below the level that was achieved in the last workouts. This is no accident. I am convinced that high intensity performance in the final training throws was the reason for the non-success in competition.

First, when making high-intensity throws

for distance, the thrower cannot work thoroughly on technique improvement; then, during competition, all the technical flaws will show up.

Secondly, a long training throw, done prior to the competition, excessively excites the athlete, often leading to insomnia and overestimation of his strength. This excitement is replaced by a state of inhibition during competition.

I know only one sportswoman—Faina Myelnik—who can tolerate a high training intensity fairly well, executing up to 100 throws at "full power." But even for her, such intensity directly before competition is ruinous: an example is her defeat at the 1971 Spartakiad, when she made several high-intensity throws before the competition.

In training, therefore, throwing should be limited to optimal intensity (five meters less than one's best result in the given period), concentrating on correctness of movement and not on distance.

Should voluminous technical training or work on throwing technique be executed when in a "fresh" condition?

Many throwers (especially men) feel that three work-outs a week are adequate for improving technique, and these workouts are to be conducted after a rest day. But only by an enormous number of repetitions can technically correct skill be developed. Olympic champion Wilkins, for example, works on technique six times a week in certain periods with the objective being "to throw not for distance, but for perfect technique."

Weightlifters are finding that improvement in technique is particularly successful in a state of incomplete recovery. That is understandable. The so-called "freshness" following rest is always accompanied by an elevated level of excitation, which may facilitate distortion of movement. It seems to me that in order to remove the mental fatigue from a large number of repetitions, it is necessary, during a period of technical work, to *vary the workout site and vary the weights of the training implements.* This helps to maintain mental freshness and to acquire a consistent, stable skill that can stand up even at the Olympic Games.

The problem of combining technique and strength: How does one combine development of physical qualities and work on technique?

There exists the opinion that at first a thrower should increase his level of necessary physical qualities and then try to parlay them into a specific technical "scheme." The words of a Brazilian soccer coach come to mind: "All technical skills of our players are grasped at an early age. In masters teams, however, we work on physical and tactical preparation."

Technique is an aggregation of skills which help one to realize his level of physical qualities. And all strength work should run parallel with progress in technical mastery.

One of the most effective methods for improving technique is imitation exercises (for example, "throws" without the discus), which are executed in conjunction with strength training. With rare exception, throwers do not include imitations along with barbell workouts. The reasons range from "fatigue" to "insufficient time." Another reason: lack of understanding of the importance of combining "imitations" with strength work.

What precedes technique training is very important. If technique work is begun after strength work (without imitations), then the background is negative. If imitation exercises are executed at the end of the preceding workout with barbells, then the background is positive for subsequent technique work. The same thing can be said with reference to periodization of the training load. If the thrower devoted the preparatory period to strength preparation, then in the spring he will experience certain difficulties in technical training, and vice versa.

Soviet women throwers execute a significantly greater volume of technical work than men. For some, the annual workload reaches 15,000 throws.

Does this mean that it is necessary to sharply and abruptly increase the training volume of men?

To be sure, some progress will be achieved very quickly. But with regard to a qualitative leap in mastery, it should be noted that only quality execution of each training throw leads to a substantial increase in performance. Concentration on each exercise, understanding of the necessity of the work, confidence in execution—these will bring about positive changes in performance.

Faina Myelnik is a good example. She concentrates thoroughly during every throw (be it in competition or in training), during every exercise. She does not spare herself in running, in jumping, or in heavy weight work. Her love for work has allowed her to develop the highest level of special qualities; an enormous number of repetitions and heavy workloads serve as a base for stability and reliability.□

SPECIFICITY IN TRAINING FOR THE RUNNING EVENTS

by Bernie Dare, U.S.A.

Bernie Dare, author of Running and Your Body, *updates some thoughts on specificity of training for the running events. Especially valuable for the coach who desires to design a detailed training program for a specific running event.*

The most important factors in constructing a training schedule are the proper combination of duration (time, distance, volume) and intensity (speed, effort). Both change as a season or even a training cycle progresses; and, both must be adapted to the demands of the event and the abilities (strengths) of the athlete to be most effective. It is my feeling that both of the latter are not always done as well as they could be.*

The more understanding that accrues about the operation of the neuromuscular system and its reaction to training, the more it seems necessary to carefully structure a training program to the exact demands of the event performed *and* the strengths of the individual athlete performing that event. Indeed in the more physiologically complex events (middle-distance), individuals can have quite different strengths and perform equally. This is creating an awareness that you cannot train an athlete's weaknesses effectively. An athlete has weaknesses (assuming a reasonably developed and experienced athlete) because his or her neuromuscular system** lacks certain factors, or contains them in insufficient amounts to ever make that weakness a strength. In this regard, it becomes very important for the coach and athlete to thoroughly understand the physiological demands of the event, the individual strengths and weaknesses of the athlete, and what sort of training meets those demands and strengths.

BASIC PHYSIOLOGICAL CONSIDERATIONS

Muscle cells differ in their qualities, manner of innervation (how they are caused to contract by the central nervous system [CNS], and thus the work they perform and how they react to training. Fast twitch (FT) fibers contract quickly, more efficiently than slower ones,

utilize ATP (the only muscle chemical energy source) quickly, can develop large glycolytic endurance (lactic acid resistance is therefore high), and have rather poor aerobic endurance. FT cells respond to fast, explosive work. They are not trained sufficiently by slow work.

Slow twitch (ST) fibers contract less quickly, perform slower contractions more efficiently, may utilize ATP less quickly (or in smaller amounts at a given rate), have lower levels of glycolytic endurance, but have many mitochondria and great aerobic endurance. ST cells respond to slower work of long duration. The muscle cells are coordinated (caused to act) by messages from the CNS (spinal cord and brain).

In explosive or fast work many muscle cells have to be called to work in a fast and often repetitive manner (field events are not repetitive, sprints are). This neuromuscular coordination probably has inherent factors—some individuals (the better sprinters) can continually produce large, fast muscular efforts without tension which would inhibit further contractions. In endurance work, the role of the CNS is to recruit new muscle cells as those being used fatigue, or general fatigue requires more effort. Fatigue may also require a greater nerve impulse to the working muscles to produce equivalent work. Some of these factors may be inherent and differ with the individual.

---

* In training younger athletes (high school), it is best to provide a good general training structure. It is not always as possible to individualize training at such a level due to team considerations, motivation problems, and lack of evidence.

** Neuromuscular system is being used as a catchall phrase here to include various factors of the central nervous system (CNS), muscle-nerve activation, and muscle cell function that have inherent qualities and differ from individual to individual.

Certainly, the most obvious individual differences are in the percentages of FT and ST muscle fibers, and thus differences in anaerobic and aerobic ability between individuals. In the simple events (sprints and long distance running, up to the marathon), where only one muscle type and energy source is used or is very dominant, there will be less individualization because success will demand a limited range of physiological factors. In the more complex events (long sprints, middle distance, distance), where more than one energy source or muscle fiber is making a significant contribution, there will be more individualization, because success can be achieved by different combinations of factors. This means that in the simple events, speaking physiologically, a certain type of work must probably dominate for all athletes. In the complex events, training factors should be combined to reflect the strengths of the athlete involved.

EVENT TRAINING CONSIDERATIONS

There is a general consensus that all the events require the same basic approach. The training season (year) should be progressive in nature and the athlete's career should be a progression from season to season (in general, each season should demand a little more from the athlete until some plateau is reached in the early to middle twenties, depending on the individual and event, later progress being made by experience, refinement, and taking better advantage of competitive opportunities).

The season should include a base conditioning period (U.S. fall pre-season), where the emphasis is on training basic event components and preparing for the more intense training to follow; a more specific conditioning period (U.S. winter—early spring) to prepare more specifically for competition; and the competition period, where the more important competitions occur, and which can be called speed with rest (reduced volume, increased rest intervals, reduced stress).

This rest allows for the highly stressed athlete to recuperate, compensate or super-compensate for any severe drains of the intense training period that preceeded it, and to perform better or peak. There are emotional and physical factors to peaking (emotional/mental and physical factors cannot be separated successfully; extreme physical fatigue causes emotional fatigue, and to some extent vice versa) which complicates the phenomenon, but such a period lasts from 2 weeks to 2 months, depending on the event, athlete, prior training season, and structure of the competitive season. There is statistical evidence to indicate that a middle-distance/distance athlete can effectively peak twice in a year (cross country, outdoor track—I recommend training through the indoor season). Athletes in the field and short track events may peak several times.

There are two factors that should be given consideration in all events. First, there is a staleness phenomenon that affects those events where repetitive practice of the same movement and intensity is common. The practicing of the

FALL TRAINING SHOULD EMPHASIZE BASIC EVENT COMPONENTS.

Cindy Brown

same movement pattern at the same intensity over a period of time creates a plateauing effect. To avoid this common occurrence in the field events and sprints, the training schedule should incorporate either continual, season-long varied activities, or complete turn-abouts every so often in the training season (e.g.: after a 6 week training session a week or two week period where volume and intensity is drastically changed). Many throwers, aware of this plateau effect, insert 1-2 week periods where they change their lifting patterns (i.e.: going from pyramiding or lifts of 3's say to lifts of 10's and inserting different lifts; or going from free weights to machines for a short period).

Second, there is evidence that a well rounded athlete may perform better, as well as being less susceptible to injury. This would mean that in all phases of the training season no one factor of conditioning should be totally neglected. For instance, in the aerobic background phase of the distance or middle distance runners development, anaerobic work should not be totally neglected, just de-emphasized. Some effort should be made to provide balanced training throughout the training year.

SHORT SPRINTS

The short sprints (110H, 100, 200) utilize FT fibers and the ATP-CP anaerobic energy system, with some use of the lactic acid (LA) energy system (200), and some use of the aerobic energy system (recovery). The primary consideration for success is speed and speed development. It should not be neglected during any phase of the training season. This means that the proper structure of the training year might be: establish speed with some speed endurance first; then establish speed endurance (ATP-CP as opposed to LA, here); then go to speed with rest for peaking. Also of consideration is avoiding staleness in the neuromuscular system, caused by repetitive practice. This can be avoided by repetitions where top speed is approached, ran at for a short period (10-20m) and then backed off or by ins and outs or outs and ins over 50-100m. Speed is trained by high speed runs from 20m-100m with adequate rest (3-4 min between reps). ATP-CP endurance is trained by repetitions of 20-100m with less rest (2-3 minutes between reps).

Volume suggestions: 6-10 early in year; 12-20 later on. Some LA training or longer training may be beneficial and is included in most programs, such. as repeats of 200s and 300s. Running short sprinters, who do not have the LA system talent, at distances above 300m is probably non-productive. Light aerobic training (2-4 mile runs) may be beneficial. Heavy aerobic training is probably counter-productive (to much decreased emphasis on FT fibre development).

LONG SPRINTS

The long sprints (200, 400, 400H, 800) utilize FT fibers and the ATP-CP and LA anaerobic energy systems, with some use of the aerobic system (recovery). The primary consideration in training is complicated by the fact that there are two types of successful athletes in the 400. The 200-400 sprinter basing his/her ability on speed and speed endurance (LA type). Therefore, speed development cannot be neglected at any part of the training season. The 400-800 sprinter basing his/her ability on anaerobic endurance, efficient running at high levels of LA build-up, and absolute speed may be a secondary factor.

For optimum success, I believe that attention must be given to these differences in the training schedule. Due to the observation that intense LA endurance training can reduce the ability to train for maximum speed, the first 400 athlete should bring his/her speed levels up before beginning the arduous LA anaerobic endurance training phase; follow that period with sufficient LA endurance training; and following that with the speed-resting phase, with only one speed (LA) endurance day per week. The second 400 athlete should emphasize the LA anaerobic background more in the early phases, though at reduced intensities and increased volumes. Doing extremely intense work early creates early plateauing/peaking and a loss of late season performance ability.

MIDDLE DISTANCE

The middle distances are the most complicated of the running events. They utilize both FT and ST fibers and anaerobic and aerobic factors to large degrees. An athlete can be successful bringing great anaerobic ability and only moderate aerobic ability to these events, or good anaerobic ability and good aerobic ability. The primary consideration for success is the proper blending of mostly aerobic and mostly anaerobic work. This is a subtle process, depending greatly on the individual athlete. The 800 runners who can run a good 400 and an adequate 1500 have great speed (relatively), great anaerobic endurance, and only moderate aerobic abilities. They can tolerate more intense anaerobic training than the 1500 runner who runs a mediocre 400, good 800, great 1500, and good 500. Because they do not have the anaerobic capacities of the former, they can be overfatigued by intense anaerobic training. In the middle, find the 800-1500 runner, who can run a reasonable 400 or relay leg, a great 800 and 1500, and an adequate 5000.

In the fall conditioning period these athletes can be trained nearly the same, except for volume considerations (30-80mpw; 2 x week fartlek, hills, or moderate intervals; 3 x week moderate mileage; 1 x week fast mileage (3-6); 1 x week long run).

In the pre-season anaerobic conditioning period (approx. Dec-March), they can be started on similar programs, but as the period progresses the 1500+ type should avoid the really fast anaerobic workouts, or not do race simulating workouts more than 1 x every 2 weeks (30-70mpw; 1 x week easy fartlek, hills, or intervals; 1 x week intervals 2-8reps of 400-1200; 1x week intervals 6-20 reps of 200-400; 1-2x week easy distance; 1-2x week moderate paced distance; 1x week long run). Generally, at the beginning of this period interval work should be at slower than ability levels and progress towards projected race pace (goal pace) levels at the end of the period. The athletes with less aerobic ability will not perform the longer interval workouts well (reps above 600), and a substitute workout towards their strength would be in order (high reps less distance).

It is not suggested that LSD runs be performed by any track athlete (and what good athletes claim is LSD is their 15 mile run at 7:00 or faster). To benefit middle distance and distance runners the aerobic system must function very well at relatively fast paces (near and above the anaerobic threshold*) and training must occur at those paces. This means most distance running where the last 1/3 of a run is moderately uncomfortable, and some where the last portion is quite uncomfortable (versus comfortable walk-and-run paces). Morning runs, for those who are poor morning runners should be an exception, for injury prevention purposes (morning paces male: 6:45-7:15, female: 7:45-8:00, based on reasonable ability—1-1:30 slower than normal).

A simple method of measuring anaerobic fatigue is heart rate (HR) monitoring. The

---

* The anaerobic threshold is that level of effort above which work is more anaerobic than aerobic, and below which is mostly aerobic. There is now some question to how definitive it is—that is, there is no extreme sharp break between aerobic training and anaerobic training. I have run and coached enough to know it is a good practical and theoretical construction.

athlete who does not recover within normal limits to 120 bpm or its equivalent is being overstressed (normal limits depend on the volume and intensity of the workout—The Gardner/Purdy *Computerized Running Training Programs* are good guidelines—generally, 3-5 reps allow 4-5 minutes, 6-8 reps 2-3 minutes, 9-12 reps 1-2 minutes).

Other factors to consider in middle distance training: these races are fast and require fast training, that is why workouts with reps over 10 (20 x 400) are probably not event specific enough; these athletes have great capacity to absorb anaerobic work compared with the distance runner and marathoner. Moderate track work will not cause over fatigue or overtraining, however, intense work too early and too much will.

DISTANCE

The distances (5000, 10,000—the 3000 is one of those in-between events, physiologically on the borderline between middle distance and distance) utilize the aerobic energy system and ST fibers as the primary movers with anaerobic energy sources as a strong secondary factor. The training should reflect this bias during all phases of development. To the distances athletes do bring differing abilities to withstand anaerobic track work. There are athletes who can be quite successful working on the track 2 or 3 days a week during the appropriate training period. There are also those who cannot tolerate more than 1 day a week on the track but thrive on fast distance runs. The physiological difference is that the latter can withstand a slow build-up of LA, as it occurs in the race or continuous type of run, but cannot tolerate the faster and heavier anaerobic loads of track training. Of course, the track work could be designed to accommodate this, but my preference is to keep them on the roads and trails, bringing them on the track 1x week.

With either type, the emphasis should be on fast distance running as a staple diet. There are successful athletes at 10,000m who train 65-75 mpw of fast mileage. Certainly, it may be hard to tolerate more than 90-100mpw of fast mileage, and there is little indication that it is needed (remember the track distance races do not require the mileage marathoners may require to facilitate fat metabolism or callous the body to the race). It can also be noted that young distance runners quite often cannot tolerate the same anaerobic loads that older runners of equal ability can. The younger athlete should train with less intense track workouts or more time off the track.

SUMMARY

• Make the training season progressive, and adapted to the specific demands of the event and the strengths of the individual athlete.

• Do not prescribe workouts that cannot be done—workouts should be tailored to the individual athlete's abilities—less capable athletes should not be saddled with the workouts of the star, or older more mature athlete.

• In skill events (hurdles, field events) to properly train the needed neuromuscular coordination requires full speed efforts. Lower speed drills do not properly train the needed muscle firing sequence.

• In the competitive season conditioning period, prior to the important racing season, properly condition for the specific demands of the event: sprints: speed, speed endurance; long sprints: speed endurance, speed; middle distance: anaerobic endurance, aerobic maintenance; distance: event fast aerobic-anaerobic mixture.

• Do not go to high intensity work too quickly, regardless of whether the athlete can do it. Ease into intense LA-anaerobic work. The faster work should occur later in the training cycle.

• Avoid long periods of LSD training for middle distance/distance runners (definition: slower than 7:00 for reasonable male athletes; 7:45 for female). LSD is recovery mode training, and does not train those factors needed in the track events.

• In the sprints and field events avoid long periods of the same repetitive work (more than 6-8wks), which causes staleness. Use a varied work structure or a complete change (for 1-2 weeks) as a major facet of the workout structure.

• If the athlete is allowed to adapt to the work (start easy, get harder later) and is supplied with steady progression in the work, the season's performances will reflect the same.

• Too much racing is the same as too much intense work, it reduces future season performance potentials. The American track season makes periodization and proper peaking difficult. To this end it may be beneficial to the athlete to low key early competitions and give the athlete some leeway in event choice and to skip a competition now and then. It depends on whether the goal is to maximize season long team performances, or individual athlete performance. If the program sides with the athlete, the reward may be a better year and performance.□

BIBLIOGRAPHY

Ariel, Gideon, "Movement," *Track and Field Quarterly Review,* Summer 1982 pp.58-62.

Dare, Bernie, *Running and Your Body,* Tafnews, 1979, 160.

Jarver, Jess, *Sprints and Relays,* Tafnews, 1978, 128; *Middle Distances,* Tafnews, 1979, 128; *Long Distances,* Tafnews 1980, 136.

Schmolinsky, Gerhardt, *Track and Field,* Sportverlag Berlin, 1977, 392.

Steinbach, Manfred, "Thoughts About Sprinting and Sprint Training," *European Sports Science Reviews,* #1, 1982.

GRADIENTS AND THEIR USAGE

by Jack Pross, Sydney, Australia

While hill running is not new—it was used effectively by Gosta Holmer in the late '30s—its applications have evolved somewhat since. Here Pross, Editor of the Birubi Newsletter, *summarizes the uses of various gradients. First printed in April 1981.*

Like other forms of training the use of gradients is but a segment of the total preparation and conditioning concept and should be used in conjunction with other work and with the end goal in clear sight.

The angle of inclination and the distance to be run is determined by the following training requirements:

Power and muscle strength.
Power and muscle elasticity.
Improvement in stride length.
Improvement in stride frequency.
Improvement in coordination.
Improvement in running posture.
Development of upper body effectiveness.
Regulation of physical effort.

Inclined gradient angles will vary from 5° (1 in 10) to 45° (1 in 1).

Declines (downhill) used for speed improvement will necessarily be of shallow angle. Experiments by the writer which have been confirmed by research indicate that the most effective angle is 2° (1 in 22). More acute running angles can contribute to muscle and joint disabilities.

Suggested applications for the various gradients shown in the attached sketch are:

A. 1 in 1 Leg strength, ankle development, hip rotation, close shoulder drive. 20-30m. Low reps. High intensity.

B. 1 in 2 Leg strength, ankle development, hip rotation, close shoulder drive. 30-40m. Low reps. High intensity.

C. 1 in 3 Leg strength, high knee lift, increased stride, extended shoulder drive. 40-50m Med. reps. Medium intensity.

D. 1 in 4 Leg flexibility, bounding with high lift and stretch technique. 40-50m. Medium reps. Slow tempo.

E. 1 in 5 Leg flexibility, stride frequency, bounding high-knee lift toe bounce. High posture 50-60m. Medium reps, surge tempo.

F. 1 in 6 Stride length and frequency, coordination, high and low knee action. Concavity posture. 50-60m. Low reps. High intensity.

G. 1 in 7 Stride length and frequency, bounding high and low for speed endurance. Improvement to upper body thrust. Concavity posture. 60-70m. Low reps, medium intensity.

H. 1 in 8 Leg speed, high lift, high hip movement, vigorous shoulder work, toe drive. 60-70m low reps. High intensity.

I. 1 in 9 Leg speed and endurance, stride frequency, stride length, alternate running and bounding. 60-70m. Reps and intensity vary in relation to preparation phase.

J. 1 in 10 Speed development—Low reps, high intensity
Endurance development—high reps, low intensity
Variations in stride length and drive, concavity posture practice. 70-100m.

In down hill training for speed development, the accent must be on above-normal speed with controlled arm and leg movement to restrict 'float' and ensure that normal stride length in flat running is maintained. The exception is when declines are used to increase stride length in a short-striding athlete. Any tendency to sit back and let the legs float should be eliminated.

The distance shown for incline runs A-J can be altered to suit the training requirement—shortened for high intensity and low volume, and lengthened for low intensity and high volume. A similar application can be made in respect to downhill work. An optimum downhill distance for 800 to 1500 runners is 300-400m.

Gradient training can be further adapted by the inclusion of level running before and/or at the end of the incline as practiced by Arthur Lydiard and others. □

REFERENCES

All About Hill Running: Ants Nurmekivi, USSR.
The Bounding Endurance Phase For Middle Distance Training, Nigel Leech.

C. 1 in 3   30-40 Meters

D. 1 in 4   40-50 Meters

E. 1 in 5   50-60 Meters

F. 1 in 6   50-60 Meters

A. 1 in 1   20-30 Meters

B. 1 in 2   30-40 Meters

G. 1 in 7   60-70 Meters

H. 1 in 8   60-70 Meters

I. 1 in 9   60-70 Meters

J. 1 in 10 70-100 Meters

K. 1 in 22. Decline.

2° for Downhill Speed Training.

TRAINING PROGRAM FOR THE SPRINTS

by Gary L. Winckler, Florida State University

The author, Women's Track Coach at FSU, stresses that training is not just what one does on the track, but an entire lifestyle, with all components working together. A part of training is a comprehensive workout program which exercises both the physical and mental faculties of the athlete, such as this one for sprinters.

Talent is a large factor in determining ultimate potential. However, how one trains determines how successful you become in achieving that potential. There does not exist any one or best way to train, but there do exist principles which must be adhered to if training is to become effective.

The basic laws in training which must be obeyed in devising any training program are:

SPECIFICITY
Adaptation is brought about by placing desirable stresses upon the athlete. Adaptation is specific to a stressor and the affect of a stressor is specific to an individual athlete.

OVERLOAD
It is necessary to provide a progressive increase in intensity and extent of loadings or stressors for the body to reach a higher level of adaptation.

REVERSIBILITY
When intensity or extent are reduced, the level of adaptation brought about by overload will decline. In general, the quicker the gains the quicker the losses and the slower the gains, the slower are the losses.

Other key characteristics to any training program are that it be:

SYSTEMATIC
Carefully combining all the components of training into a system.

SEQUENTIAL
Dividing the training year into specific phases each building upon the previous one to achieve a peak level of fitness and preparation at the desired time.

PROGRESSIVE
Building upon what has been previously accomplished.

VARIATIONAL
Avoiding monotony (without confusing the issue with too many extraneous activities and ideas).

IMITATIONAL
Simulating mentally and physically the conditions of competition with regard to terrain, time of day, type of facility, length of competition, etc. . .

THE PLAN

Planning is the start of control and consistency. It brings the future into the present so that you can do something about it today.

Begin by dividing your training into the categories or components of training which will blend together to devise a plan. Following each component is a short list of characteristics and/or examples of training units designed to develop qualities of that component.

MAXIMUM STRENGTH = The greatest force the neuromuscular system is capable of exerting in a single maximum voluntary contraction.
  a) Weights: 3-5 sets of 3-6 repetitions at 80-95%. 1 RM (Repetition Maximum).
  b) The role of maximum strength in the training program of sprinters plays a smaller role in the total training program than say for throwers.

ELASTIC STRENGTH = The ability of the neuromuscular system to overcome resistance with a high speed of contraction. This is accomplished through the coordination and involvement of reflexes and the elastic and contractile components of muscle.
  a) Plyometrics
  b) Harness work (20-40m)
  c) Weights: 4-6 sets of 6-10 repetitions at 75% 1 RM
  d) Exercises done at high speed and intensity specific to the event for which you are training.

STRENGTH ENDURANCE = The ability to withstand fatigue. It is characterized by the high ability to express strength over long time periods. For example, 400H, 400m, 800m-3000m are all events requiring a high degree of strength endurance.
  a) Hill running . . . 150-300m.
  b) Harness running . . . 50-80m.
  c) Weights: 3-5 sets of 50-75% maximum repetitions and 40-60% 1 RM with 45-60 sec. recovery between sets.
  d) Sprint drills over 60-150m.

BASIC ENDURANCE = The ability to carry out a given amount of work during a prolonged period of time without deterioration in the quality of such work.

a) A certain degree of endurance training is necessary to enable the athlete to do more work often.

b) Several intervals with short recovery.

MOBILITY = The capacity to perform joint actions through a wide range of motion.

a) Developed through passive and dynamic stretching.

b) Enhanced after 5-10 minutes of warmup activity (low intensity activity).

c) Mobility is a key factor in injury prevention as a sports move may cause the athlete to exceed his/her mobility range for a particular joint resulting in possible damage to muscle tissue.

d) Mobility exercises must be specific to the event and insure sufficient range of motion for all event movements.

f) Never use dynamic stretching (swinging movements) to increase mobility, but only to maintain present mobility. (The reflex contractions by muscle spindle complexes may result in injury to the muscle being stretched.)

g) Mobility is lost if the athlete discontinues mobility training.

SPEED = Moving a limb, part of the body's lever system, or the whole body with the greatest possible velocity. Speed can be improved through short duration work at 90-100% maximum intensity.

a) Sprint training at distances of 30-60m w/full recovery to 120 heart rate or less.

b) Technique work as in sprint drills, and harness.

c) Will power in training along with flexibility to accomplish muscle relaxability = the ability of the muscle to stretch and allow stretching at high speeds of movement.

d) Concentration on maximum voluntary effort to achieve maximum speed.

e) Reaction training = ability to make quick judgments and react appropriately.

SPEED ENDURANCE = The ability to produce high qualities of speed performance despite the presence of high oxygen debt and lactic acid buildup.

a) 30-60m sprints done in 3-4 sets of 3-5 minutes rest between sets.

b) Speed bounding over 30-40m.

c) Circuit training involving jumping exercises and relatively short recoveries.

TECHNIQUE = The capacity to perform an event with the most efficient biomechanical application under conditions of high physical intensity and mental and physical stress.

a) Harness work.

b) Sprint drills for sprint technique.

c) Starts.

d) Finishing techniques in sprint races.

e) Curve running.

f) Imagery.

RECOVERY = Allowing the body to recover from training bouts. This is where the real training effect occurs.

a) Active Recovery or Rest—any activity which involves physical movement of a light spirited nature and different from normal training.

b) Full Recovery—rest with no activity planned.

THE TRAINING YEAR

One of the most neglected facets of training athletes is the area of organization of the training year into progressive phases designed to get the best performances from all athletes during the biggest competitions. The term given for organization is PERIODIZATION. Periodization has three primary objectives:

1) To prepare the athlete for achievement of optimal performance improvement.

2) To prepare the athlete for a climax to the competitive season, (e.g., AIAW or TAC Nationals).

3) To prepare the athlete for the main competitions associated with the climax to the season, (e.g., major meets leading up to the championship event).

Periodization also helps the coach to plan effectively for recovery intervals to aid in the prevention of injury and excessive exposure to training stress.

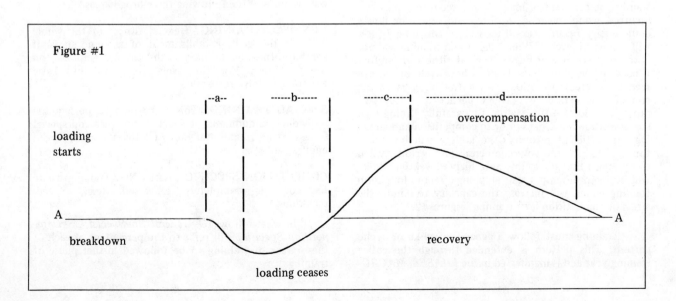

Figure #1

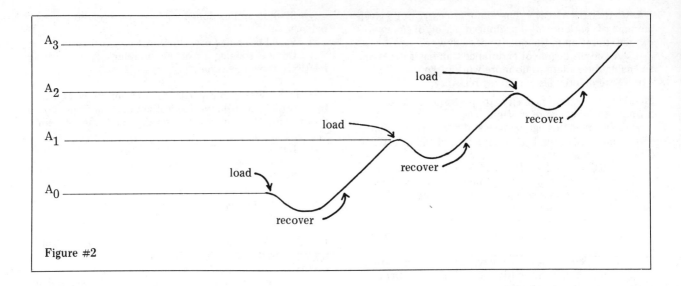

Figure #2

The organized planning of the training year can also help the coach and athlete prepare and plan more easily for long range competitions, (e.g., Olympics every four years).

Recovery is a very important aspect of periodization in training. To aid in understanding the role of recovery, see fig. 1. "A" represents the initial status of the athlete being trained, (i.e., where you are before training begins; your level of fitness). a, b, c, and d represent periods of time. During time period "a" the body is training hard and tiring; a breakdown of the physical components being trained is occurring. During time period "b" the breakdown has ceased and the body is at work recovering. Because our bodies naturally work to adapt to the stressors placed upon them we see that the greater the breakdown or stress placed upon the body the more it will compensate during recovery. In "c" and "d" we see this occurring. The body is overcompensating for the stress due to the breakdown during training. By the time "d" has passed the athlete will have returned to the original level of fitness.

From this model one can see the necessity for our training to follow a definite wavelike pattern. Should training be too hard or long without recovery, the stress incurred would become too high and injury or illness could easily occur. Also if recovery is too long fitness will return to level "A" once again and training will not have resulted in any higher level of fitness. Therefore what must be done is to begin a new cycle of "stress-recovery-overcompensation" when the body is at the end of time period "c". (This is particularly important during the competitive season. By carefully timing high stress workouts 3-4 days prior to competition and allowing for sufficient recovery, the athlete will be at top form, i.e., in the overcompensation period, when competing.) Starting at this new, higher level the athlete will begin to develop a stair stepping effect in long term training which will increase the capacity to handle the stress of competition level training. Figure #2.

Training must follow a general wavelike or cyclic pattern. This pattern is extended through the entire training year and is manifested in the *PHASES, MACRO-CYCLES*, and *MICROCYCLES* of the training plan in the form of:

PREPARATION—ADAPTATION—APPLICATION.

Following this pattern the athlete is sequentially prepared during each training session for what is to follow later in training.

Divide the training year into six major phases; each is explained below. Some definitions we will need are:

MICROCYCLE = A period of 7-21 days during which a specific training task is worked toward. Our microcycle will usually be 14 days and will follow the pattern of Preparation—Adaptation—Application.

MACROCYCLE = A period usually of 4-6 weeks composed of several microcycles. The macrocycle is used as a primary means of regulating intensity and extent of training loads and again follows the same general pattern expressed above in the microcycles.

All training components can be categorized into one or more of the following three broad areas.

GENERAL TRAINING: General fitness of the whole body is the goal. Establishment of a sound basis of aerobic fitness is primary with minimal emphasis on specific fitness for the event (e.g., mobility basic endurance, active recovery.)

SPECIAL TRAINING: This is training to perfect the individual components of sports techniques and special fitness (e.g., maximum and elastic strength, speed endurance.)

COMPETITION SPECIFIC TRAINING: Training where technique is completely rehearsed. (e.g., Speed, technique.)

In what follows *(G=General, Sp=Special, CS=Competition Specific)* will refer to the percentage of each of these areas of training to be followed in that phase of training.

The phases of the training year are developed as follows:

PREPARATION PERIOD

a)   Phase I "Training to Train" (G-25, Sp-55, CS-20)

1)   The longest phase in the annual cycle lasting around 4 months (usually September-December).
2)   Aim is to increase the athlete's ability to accept higher levels of work at greater intensity.
3)   Training is more general in nature and usually of high volume-low intensity levels.
4)   Endurance and strength are areas of emphasis.

b)   Phase II "Training for Competition" (G-15, Sp-60, CS-25)

1)   Usually lasts 2-3 months. January-March in a single periodized year. In order to achieve two peak periods during the year (Indoor & Outdoor AIAW), use Phase II in January and again in March. (Double periodized year.)
2)   Seeks to unite components of training into a whole.
3)   More specialization is used and General training falls off a bit.
4)   Technique, strength, speed, etc. are developed together so as to prevent injury and promote consistency in performances.
5)   There is exposure to competitions in the latter part of this phase.
6)   If training is progressing successfully the athlete should equal his previous best or be within 2.5% of his best after the first 3 competitions (spaced over 2-3 weeks).

COMPETITION PERIOD

a)   Phase III (G-10, Sp-55, CS-35)

1)   In single periodized year this will run from April-June. In double periodized year there will be an additional 4-5 weeks of this period in February and March.
2)   The main task here is to develop and maintain

competitive performance.
3)   More Competition Specific training and less Special and General work.
4)   Training extent will gradually drop and intensity levels will rise.
5)   Important to maintain the strength program.
6)   If training is going well the athlete should improve upon his/her lifetime best 6-8 weeks into this phase, (i.e., at major meet time).

b)   Phase IV (G-25, Sp-55, C-20)

1)   If competition is to continue beyond Phase III it is advisable to introduce a 4-6 week period where General and Special training increase once again. This is used to aid in recovery and to prepare the athlete mentally and physically for the coming competition in late summer.
2)   Athletes who have not peaked in Phase III may want to continue Phase III longer.

c)   Phase V (G-10, Sp-40, C-50)

1)   This is a period following Phase IV when 3-4 weeks are used to follow a pattern of competitions and Competition Specific training to reach peak performance levels again.

TRANSITION PERIOD

a)   Phase VI Sprints = (G-80, Sp-10, C-10)

1)   Usually during months of August and September.
2)   If the season was long and tough, 3-6 weeks of active recovery must take place before beginning Phase I again.
3)   General training is predominant here.
4)   Emphasis on physical and emotional relaxation.

The following are examples of how one might structure a macrocycle for Phase I, II, and III for an indoor season with a peak period in mid-March. For a continuation of training for a major peak in June one would once again return to Phase II for 2-4 weeks prior to Phase III work for the outdoor season.

TRAINING COMPONENTS		CLASSIFICATION		PHASE I % time spent in this phase	PHASE I Approx. # units/14 day micro cycle
Basic Endurance	(E)	General			
Mobility	(M)	General		25	5
Recovery	(R)	General			
Strength Endurance	(StE)	Special			
Maximum Strength	(MS)	Special		55	11
Elastic Strength	(ES)	Special			
Speed Endurance	(SE)	Special			
Speed	(S)	Competition Specific		20	4
Technique	(T)	Competition Specific			

Macrocycle I

Microcycle 1; Sept. 21-27
       Sept. 28-Oct. 4 —————————————————— Preparation

Sprints

Mon.	ES, E
Tu.	ES, StE
W.	MS

} Preparation

Th.	SE, T
F.	ES, E

} Adaptation

Sat.	AR*
Sun.	R

Mon.	MS, T
Tu.	ES, StE
W.	ES, T

} Adaptation

Th.	SE, T
F.	MS

} Application

Sat.　　AR
Sun.　　R.

Microcycle 2; Oct. 5-11 } Adaptation
　　　　　　　Oct. 12-18

Biweekly scheme above remains the same. Extent of loads rises.

Microcycle 3; Oct. 19-25 } Application
　　　　　　　Oct. 26-Nov. 1

Biweekly scheme remains the same. Extent remains constant and intensity rises.

TRAINING COMPONENTS		CLASSIFICATION		% time spent in this phase	PHASE II Approx. # units/14 day micro cycle
Basic Endurance	(E)	General			
Mobility	(M)	General	}	15	3
Recovery	(R)	General			
Strength Endurance	(StE)	Special			
Maximum Strength	(MS)	Special	}	60	12
Elastic Strength	(ES)	Special			
Speed Endurance	(SE)	Special			
Speed	(S)	Competition Specific	}	25	5
Technique	(T)	Competition Specific			

Macrocycle I

Microcycle 1; Jan. 11-17 } Preparation
　　　　　　　Jan. 18-24

Load intensity and extent remain constant.

Sprints

Mon.	MS
Tu.	ES, StE
W.	SE, MS

} Preparation

Th.	AR
F.	MS
Sat.	ES, SE

} Adaptation

Sun.　　R

Mon.	S, MS
Tu.	SE, StE
W.	AR

} Adaptation

Th.	ES, T
F.	T, S
Sat.	ES, T, SE

} Application

Sun.　　R.

Microcycle 2; Jan. 25-31 } Adaptation
　　　　　　　Feb. 1-7

Biweekly schedule remains. Load extent rises.

50

TRAINING COMPONENTS		CLASSIFICATION		% time spent in this phase	Approx. # units/15 day micro cycle
Basic Endurance	(E)	General			
Mobility	(M)	General		10	2
Recovery	(R)	General			
Strength Endurance	(StE)	Special			
Maximum Strength	(MS)	Special		55	11
Elastic Strength	(ES)	Special			
Speed Endurance	(SE)	Special			
Speed	(S)	Competition Specific		35	7
Technique	(T)	Competition Specific			

Macrocycle I

Microcycle 1; Feb. 8-14 ⎤——— Application
Feb. 15-21 ⎦
Biweekly scheme as below. Load extent levels and intensity rises.

Sprints

Mon.	MS	⎤
Tu.	ES, StE	⎬——— Preparation
W.	SE, MS	⎦
Th.	AR	⎤
F.	ES, StE	⎬
Sat.	T, SE	⎬——— Adaptation
Sun.	R	⎦
Mon.	S, MS	⎤
Tu.	T. SE	⎬——— Adaptation
W.	AR	⎦

Th.	ES, T	⎤
F.	S, T or AR	⎬——— Application
Sat.	T, ES, SE or Compete	⎬
Sun.	R.	⎦

Microcycle 2; Feb. 22-28 ⎤——— Adaptation

Level load extent, increase intensity, and follow scheme of last 7 days above.

Microcycle 3; Mar. 1-7 ⎤——— Application
Mar. 8-14 ⎦

Follow Scheme above, lower extent and increase intensity.

EXAMPLES OF TRAINING UNITS

BASIC ENDURANCE

1. Continuous runs w/o rest for up to 30 minutes. (Phase I)*
2. Fartlek up to 30 minutes.
3. Extensive interval work . . . 60-80% runs with worthwhile break and of 14-90 seconds duration. (Also known as Tempo Endurance running.) Worthwhile break refers to recovery interval allowing recovery to 120 heart rate. May use a recovery of 45-120 seconds or at least to 130 heart rate and perform fewer repetitions. (Phase I & II)

MOBILITY

1. Passive stretching in warmup.
2. Partner stretches of hamstrings, achilles, and hip flexors.
3. Medicine ball exercises.
4. Dynamic stretches done well within the limits of the range of motion achieved through passive stretches.

RECOVERY

1. General exercise.
2. Swimming.
3. Fartlek.
4. Easy distance runs.
5. Circuit training and games.
6. Light medicine ball work.

STRENGTH ENDURANCE

1. Weights
   a. 3-5 sets of 40-60% IRM and 50-75% of maximum repetitions using a 30-45 second recovery between sets.
2. Harness work over 50-100m. (Phase I & II)
3. Hill running over 180-200m. (Phase I & II)
4. Two each of A and B drills done for 60-120m. (Phase II & III)
5. Bounding done for 120m.
6. Elastic strength exercises done at lower intensity.
   a. 4-6 exercises done in 3 sets of 50m or 2 sets of 100m; e.g., Lunges, C's, harness, A's, B's. (Phase I & II)

[A's are forms of high knee marching and running. B's are forms of high knee marching and running with emphasis on active foreleg work (pawing).]

MAXIMUM STRENGTH

1. Weights

   a. 3-5 sets of 5-10 repetitions at 70-85% 1 RM with 2-4 minutes recovery between sets.

   b. Pyramid: (sprints); 8x75%, 6x75%, 5x85% . . . using 2-4 minutes recovery between sets.

   Pyramid: (jumps); 5x80%, 4x85%, 3x90% 2x95% . . . using 2-4 minutes recovery between sets.

2. Exercises using 3-5% body weight and involving whole technique. (Develops Maximum and Elastic strength components simultaneously.)

3. Plyometrics.

ELASTIC STRENGTH

1. Weights

   a. 4-6 sets of 6-10 reps and 75% 1 RM using 3-5 minutes recovery between sets.

   b. 4-6 sets of 10 reps at 30-65% 1 RM. (e.g., 10x30%, 10x40%. . . .)

   c. Alternate loads of 55-65% with loads of 85-100% 1 RM.

2. Plyometrics

   a. C's [These are forms of Driving extension work and bounding.]

   b. Depth Jumps, c. Jump Squats, d. Stair Hopping, e. Lunges, f. Standing long and triple jumps.

3. Harness work over 30-50m.

4. A's and B's with sandbags over distance of 20-40m (Phase I & II)

5. Medicine ball exercises (from standing or sitting positions)

   a. Chest passes, b. Shot put passes, c. Overhead pass, d. Discus pass, e. Squat throws (forward, backward, upward), f. Sit up passes, g. Push up passes

SPEED ENDURANCE (SPRINTS)

1. Series like the following: (Phase II & III)

SERIES I—4-5x30m sprints from crouch start and at medium speed. 1-2 min. rest.
SERIES II—4-30m sprints from crouch start and at sub-maximum speed. 2-3 min. rest.
SERIES III—4-5x60m sprints from crouch start and at submaximum speed. 2-3 min. rest.
SERIES IV—2-4x60-100m sprints from crouch start and at submaximum speed. 1-2 min. rest.

Make the latter half of the recoveries on these active. Recover to 120 heart rate between series. A pulse of 130 after 4-5 minutes rest implies the work load is too high.

2. *INTENSIVE INTERVAL WORK:* Runs at 80-90% intensity with recovery to 120 heart rate. (Phase I, II & III)

3. Stress loading at maximum and submaximum intensity over distances between 2/3 and 2 times race distance. (Phase II & III)

4. Stress loads at maximum race speed over distances 10-20% longer than race distance. (Phase II)

5. *VARIED SPEED RUNS:* (in-out-in. . . .)

   a. 100-250m for 100/200m types.

   b. 200-450m for 400m types.

6. Acceleration runs over 150-200m with last 60m at full effort. (Phase II & III)

7. *REPETITION RUNNING;* 3-6 repetitions of 90-98% intensity like those distances mentioned above in 5. or slightly longer. Use intervals of 3-10 minutes for recovery.

8. Split 500m or 400m. (e.g., 300m all out—rest 1 min.—200m all out). Use for 400m athletes. (Phase II & III)

9. 300m at race pace—200m jog—100m at full speed. Do sets of these for 400m types. (Phase II & III)

10. 200m in pairs; i.e., 200m at race pace—jog 100m—200m at race pace + 2 seconds. Do sets of these for 400m types. (Phase II)

11. Sets of 3x150m. From blocks sprint full effort for 60m—settle into 400m race pace for rest of 150. (Phase I, II & III)

12. *PURSUIT RUNS;* (Phase III)

    a. 150-300m for 100/200m types.

    b. 350-450m for 400m types.

13. *SUM RUNNING;* Number of times runner can run 1/3-1/4 their race distance at race pace using 15-20 sec. rest between each rep. (Ralph Tate-Oklahoma State)

14. *PROGRESSIVE INTENSITY RUNS;* e.g., 3x300m at 80%, 85%, 90%. (Phase III

SPEED

1. Series work as follows: (Phase II & III)

SERIES I—3-5x30m sprints from crouch start and at medium speed.
SERIES II—3-5x30m sprints from crouch start and at submaximum speed.
SERIES III—2-4x60m sprints from crouch start and at submaximum speed.
SERIES IV—2-4x30m sprints from crouch start and at submaximum speed.

Take 6-8 min. recovery between series and 3-4 min. recovery between reps. A pulse of 120 after the final recovery implies the workload was too high.

2. Flying start sprints over 20-40m. (Phase I, II & III)

3. Maximum acceleration over 30-50m followed by coasting. (Phase I, II & III)

4. 100m accelerations with 30-40m maximal speed section contained within.

5. Starts over 30m following the pattern of 1.

6. Hill work; 30-40m timed efforts for acceleration. (Phase II & III)

7. Downhill sprinting on grades less than 5%. (Phase III)

8. Diverging sequence: e.g., 4x20m, 3x30m, 2x40m, 1x50m. □

TECHNIQUE

1. A's, B's, C's.

2. A₃—Sprint stride progression. (30m-30m-30m)

3. ¼ turns in and out of turn.

4. Harness work.

5. Walk drill (arms).

6. Driving harness.

REFERENCES

Dick, Frank (1980), *Sports Training Principles,* Lepus Books, London.

Gambetta, Vern (1981), "Periodization", Paper presented at U.S. Olympic Development Camp, Florida State University, July 1981.

Mach, G. (1977), "Sprinting and Hurdling School", Canadian Track and Field Association.

Schmolinsky, G. (editor) (1978), *Track and Field,* Sportverlag, Berlin.

KINETIC ENERGY THEORY FOR DETERMINING WORKOUT TIMES

by James E. Thoma, Ph.D., Ohio State University

A technical, but thorough, discussion of a possible method of quantifying training for the sprints. The author also suggests possible adaptations to other running events.

I. Kinetic Energy Theory

It has been proposed that the kinetic energy equation can be useful for prescribing workout times for the 200 meter dash. The theory holds that if an athlete's mass (weight) and peak performance time are known, the kinetic energy expended at this peak performance can be calculated. From the kinetic energy value, a workout time that is a certain percentage (p) of the athlete's performance can be calculated.

athlete's mass = 50 kg
race = 200 meters
peak performance = 24.5 seconds

(1) $KE = \frac{1}{2} m(d/t)^2$

$KE = \frac{1}{2} (50) (200/24.5)^2$

$KE = 1660.0$

For example, as the coach you desire the athlete to train at 80% effort. By taking 80% of the calculated kinetic energy for the best time, the workout time is calculated

$80\% \ KE_m = KE_w$, where   m = meet
w = workout

$80\% \ KE_m = .80 (1660.0) = 1328.0$,   therefore

$KE_w = 1328.0$

Now working backwards through the equation,

$KE_w = 1328.0 = \frac{1}{2} m (d/t_w)^2$

$1328.0 = \frac{1}{2} (50) (200/t_w)^2$

$t_w = 27.4$ seconds.

Thus, for the athlete who has recently run a 24.5 second 200 meters, an 80% kinetic energy workout time is 27.4 seconds.

If the athlete maintains a relatively constant weight throughout the competitive season, which is generally the case, the calculations are simplified. The mass and the distance become constants in equation 1 and

$p \ x \ KE_m = KE_w$ reduces to

$t_w = t_m / \sqrt{p}$

Thus, given the athlete's best recent performance, a workout time for any percentage of the total kinetic energy to be expended is easily determined.

II. Other Theoretical Models

While this method of determining workout times is provocative, it has yet to be proven an effective training method. Except on paper the kinetic energy method has not been shown to realistically represent the percentage of the total energy expended.

To explore other methods, beside kinetic energy, to determine workout times, what if velocity, work or power were the determining parameter?

Velocity is the distance of the race divided by the runner's time.

Work is the amount of energy expended in a race. Thus, work is the equivalent of kinetic energy.

Power is the amount of work performed or kinetic energy expended by the athlete in the race divided by the race time.

Table 1

velocity	$t_w = t_m / p$	30.6 s
work (KE)	$t_w = t_m / \sqrt{2}{p}$	27.4 s
power	$t_w = t_m / \sqrt[3]{p}$	26.4 s

Table 1 illustrates the formulas for calculating workout times by each method, assuming constant weight and distance.

Included in this table are the calculated workout times for a 200 meter dash of 24.5 seconds at 80% effort using each method. These values indicate the discrepancy of workout times when using the three theoretical methods.

III. Discussion

Assuming that the kinetic energy theory is used to formulate workout times for the 200 meter runner, can this method be expanded for use in the other running events? In the investigation of this question, the following factors complicate the investigation:

1. According to Franklin M. Henry a significant increase in oxygen requirement occurs for velocities from 6.4 to 8.2 meters per second (7-9 yards per second) (1). For world record events this means men's events from 800 to 5000 meters and women's events from 400 to 1500 meters. Thus, these specified events do not show a relationship of oxygen consumption that would enable an expansion of this theory.

2. The 200-meter runner uses the anaerobic energy system almost exclusively. Expansion of this theory to running events of greater time duration necessitates ever greater aerobic use. Because there has been controversy about which energy system is more efficient and to what extent, the amount of work output measured per unit of work input (efficiency) measured during progression to the longer events is equivocal (2,3,4,5).

3. When the runner's lower extremity touches the track the muscles, bones and connective tissue is distorted to absorb the force. Soon the limb reaches full compression and begins to extend for the next stride. Generally, energy used in muscle contraction is the primary force for this next stride. However, propulsion is also provided by the elastic recoil of the compressed tissue and by the stretch reflex phenomenon. Fukunaga and Matsuo propose that the elastic energy of the knee and the ankle joints become a propulsive factor if and only if the athlete's velocity is at least 70% of his/her maximum (events up to 1500 meters for men and women) (6). This recoil effect could supply a 40% energy savings (7). Thus, the savings would distort the relationship needed for extension of the theory to longer events.

4. The kinetic energy theory disregards the effect of wind resistance. However, as the runner's velocity increases there is a non-linear increase in wind resistance (8). This factor is also affected by the wind velocity, direction, and density (altitude).

5. This theory is derived assuming that the athlete is one lump mass. However, because human locomotion constitutes movements of the arms and head as well as the lower extremities, the relative movements of these parts will individually vary. This translates into different kinetic energy expenditure for people of equal mass and event time.

This discussion introduces some of the problems that evolve by using the kinetic energy theory. Anyone extrapolating this theory to the longer events compounds the uncertainty. Stainbsy et. al. (9) summarize most of this section nicely:

"In most machines and exercising humans, energy is also expended to perform some other unmeasured work, which is necessary for the performance of the external work of interest. In exercise, this unmeasured work component is significant and very complicated. It includes energy required for accelerating and decelerating the limbs, for breathing, and for transporting ions against electrochemical gradients. It also includes the energy required to stabilize body parts, synthesize substrates, mobilize substrates, and circulate blood."

SUMMARY

The kinetic energy theory for determining workout times is a unique approach and certainly of value. The theory provides one of the few methods that a coach can use to systematically quantify workout times. However, there are still many questions that remain unanswered before its general use should be accepted. But a start has been made. Now is the time for a scientific study to be conducted that will identify and quantify the variables, test the theory or its offspring, analyze the results and systemize the components into a usable form for the coach and athlete. □

REFERENCES

1. Frankin M. Henry, "Time, velocity equations and oxygen requirements of 'all-out' and 'steady-pace' running," *The Research Quarterly* 25 : 164-77, May, 1954.

2. L. Bruce Gladden and Hugh G. Welch, "Efficiency of anaerobic work," *J. Appl. Physiol. : Respirat. Environ. Exercise Physiol.* 44(4) : 564-70, 1978.

3. Brian J. Whipp, Charles Seard, and Karlman Wasserman, "Oxygen deficit-oxygen debt relationships and efficiency of anaerobic work," *J. Appl. Physiol.* 28(4): 452-56, 1970.

4. P. Pahud, E. Ravussin, and E. Jequier, "Energy expended during oxygen deficit period of submaximal exercise in man," *J. Appl. Physiol. : Respirat. Environ. Exercise Physiol.* 48(5) : 770-75, 1980.

5. T.P. White and G.A. Brooks, "Lactate metabolism during rest and two levels of exercise," *Medicine and Science in Sports* 10(1) : 60, Spring 1978.

6. T. Fukunaga and A. Matuso, "Mechanical energy changes in sprint running," *Medicine and Science in Sports* 11(1) : 85, Spring 1979.

7. G.A. Cavagna, F.P. Saibene, and R. Margaria, "Mechanical work in running," *J. Appl. Physiol.* 19(2) : 249-56, 1964.

8. C.T.M. Davies, "Effects of wind assistance and resistance on the forward motion of a runner," *J. Appl. Physiol. : Respirat. Environ. Exercise Physiol.* 48(4) : 702-09, 1980.

9. Wendall N. Stainbsy, L. Bruce Gladden, Jack K. Barclay, and Brian A. Wilson, "Exercise efficiency : validity of base-line subtractions," *J. Appl. Physiol. : Respirat. Environ. Exercise Physiol.* 48(3) : 518-22, 1980.

The author wishes to thank Drs. Donald K. Mathews, Edward L. Fox and Wayne Armbrust.

UNDERSTANDING FLEXIBILITY FOR TRACK & FIELD ATHLETICS

by David E. Martin, Ph.D. and Marc Borra*

Many sport skills, especially the field events in athletics require excellent flexibility. The authors' in-depth discussion of the major muscle groups will help both the coach and athlete better understand how muscles function and how to stretch and maintain them for optimal performance.

GENERAL CONCEPTS

Flexibility implies suppleness, and refers to the ability to move joints through their complete normal range of motion. This is in part determined anatomically, with small individual differences in positioning of muscle origins and insertions as well as in joint tightness and bone configuration. It is also affected physiologically, by at least three phenomena.

One concerns the performance of various stretching exercises designed to lengthen muscles, thereby increasing flexibility. Another involves vigorous stretching of muscles beyond their normal resting length by bounding, sprinting, hopping, or jumping activities in sports. A protective neural reflex mechanism is activated by this quick forced stretch. This in turn promotes a protective generation of tension in the stretched muscle, resulting in subsequent shortening and decreasing of flexibility in the joints to which the muscles connect.

The third occurs when fast interval-type anaerobic running or long-term endurance running are not followed by adequate recovery via easy jogging to allow clearance of metabolic (primarily lactic) acid from the involved muscle cells. Entrance of water from the bloodstream into these cells, in an attempt to restore normal ionic relationships, causes cellular swelling. The muscle cells shorten as a result, reducing joint flexibility, often noticeable as muscle stiffness.

There is little positive correlation of body build, age, and sport skill level with joint flexibility. But there is good positive correlation between improvement in flexibility and the performances of exercises intended toward its development. Many sport skills, especially field events in athletics, require excellent joint flexibility; thus their participants devote considerable time to a systematic routine that provides such movement. Since neuromuscular transmission is facilitated at warmer temperatures, stretching is best done following brief mild exercise, and if performed in cool temperatures, with adequate clothing to maintain body warmth.

There are several benefits of good joint flexibility, developed and maintained through stretching. The incidence of muscle/tendon injuries can be reduced when the muscles are maintained and utilized well within their functional length limits. When athletes remain uninjured for long periods, they can train and progress in relation to their inherent excellence, allowing them to more closely approach their performance potential. Reduced muscle soreness allows a healthier and more positive mental attitude toward intense prolonged training.

It is the purpose of this article to: 1) identify some of the major muscle groups that require stretching for the performance of sport skills in athletics, 2) describe briefly their special functions in joint movements, and 3) suggest exercises that stretch these muscles in a manner related to skill performance.

Most of the described exercises are *static* stretches, that is, slow and gentle muscle lengthening. Examples are adapted in many instances from Hatha Yoga procedures, since they relate very well to body positions assumed in events of athletics. Other types of flexibility development have long been identified. One is *ballistic* (bouncing or swinging movements beyond the normal joint range of motion), another is *passive* (a partner aids in static stretching), and a *third* is proprioceptive neuromuscular facilitation (also called contract-relax, because isometric contraction of a muscle at its point of maximum length is followed by relaxation).

Current consensus suggests that a static stretching routine is as good as or better than the others. Its slowness prevents injury from the stretching act itself. Partners are not needed, which improves logistics. Continued muscle facilitation after the stretch is essentially nil. Multiple muscle groups can be stretched by the careful creation of exercises that not only reduce the total time needed for stretching but which stretch

---

*Dr. Martin is Professor of Physiology at Georgia State University, Atlanta, U.S.A.; Marc Borra is a member of the Belgian national athletics team and has a masters degree in physical education from the University of Louvain.

muscle groups in patterns related to the sport activity.

This is not to say that ballistic actions in sport are dangerous (in fact many vigorously performed movements in active sport *are* ballistic) or that vigorous swinging and bouncing of muscles should not be done. If these follow an effective static stretching program, the ballistic movements will be managed easily because performance demands placed upon the muscles are now more nearly within their length limits.

To understand the ensuing descriptions of muscles and their actions, the following very simple terms should be defined:

Directions in Space
   Anterior—toward the chest; forward
   Posterior—toward the spine; backward
   Proximal—toward the point of attachment closest to the trunk
   Distal—farther away from the trunk
   Plantar—toward the sole of the foot
   Dorsal—toward the back (or the top of the foot)
Directions of Body Segment Movement
   Flexion—bending
   Extension—straightening
   Abduction—away from the body midline
   Adduction—toward the body midline
   Medial rotation—anterior aspect turns toward midline
   Lateral rotation—anterior aspect turns away from midline
Muscles
   Origin—on the less mobile bone, not via a tendon
   Insertion—on the more mobile bone, perhaps via a tendon
   Antagonist—a muscle causing a movement opposite from the muscle acting as a mover (biceps is an antagonist of triceps)

MAJOR MUSCLE GROUPS
USED IN ATHLETICS

Posterior Lower Leg Muscles and Achilles Tendon
   The familiar word *calf* describes these important muscles. One, the *gastrocnemius*, is on the surface, and almost appears as two separate muscles because it has two proximal attachment portions to the back of the knee, and merges into the large calcaneal tendon (or tendon of Achilles) that inserts onto the large heel bone (the calcaneus). It has two functions: plantar flexion of the ankle (pointing the toes) and knee flexion. Another muscle, the *soleus*, is below the surface, not as bulky, and has an important role in posture. It is also a plantar flexor of the ankle. In running, this complex has an important role in driving the body forward (plantar flexion) and in helping the leg drive forward (knee flexion). Thus these are two-joint muscles. At takeoff in the high jump, long jump, and triple jump, strong plantar flexion helps the athlete literally run off the takeoff.

Our lifestyle predisposes us to problems with these muscle-tendon relationships. The wearing of shoes, especially those with well-padded heels, lessens the time during the day for this complex to remain optimally stretched. Perhaps we should walk barefoot more often. If we sat in a squatting position, Asian style, instead of

in chairs, the entire lower-back/ /hamstrings/gastro-soleus/Achilles chain would be passively stretched. One of the problems with endurance runners, logging many miles each week without accompanying stretching exercises, is that the constant increased tension in these muscles, being prime movers, also places constant increased tension on the Achilles tendon as well as the low back. Achilles tendonitis, plantar fasciitis, and low back pain are often the result.

Each step taken while running, especially when landing on the forefoot instead of the heel, tends to initiate the protective stretch reflex if the gastrocnemius or soleus are stretched beyond their normal limits. Weight training exercises involving the lowering of the body, loaded with weight, from plantar flexion, when the toes are well above the heels from standing on an elevated board, can also elicit this reflex. Adequate stretching exercises can be done prior to these training sessions to ensure proper muscle length relationships.

Posterior Upper Leg Muscles
   These are three long, strong thigh muscles collectively known as the *hamstrings*. They originate on the posterior portion of the pelvis known as the ischial tuberosities, which are covered by the buttocks—the gluteus maximus muscles.

The hamstrings group comprises the muscle bulk of the posterior thigh, and inserts into the upper portion of the lower leg bones, just below the knee. Thus, these are also two-joint muscles, with roles affecting both knee and hip. There is the *biceps femoris* (Fig. 25—B FEM), which helps to flex the knee and uniquely laterally rotates it; it also is a hip extensor. The *semi-tendinosus* (Fig. 25—SEMIT) and *semimembranosus* also extend the hip and flex the knee, but they are medial knee rotators as well.

When the rear leg pushes off during running, followed by knee flexion with the heel rising toward the buttocks (Fig. 1), this occurs due to hamstrings function. Then, as the leg moves forward during the stride, the hamstrings contract again to prevent excessive forward movement. Effective hamstrings stretching is thus essential to allow optimal striding patterns, especially for fast running and sprinting.

Hamstrings exercises are often integrated with exercises for the lower back and gastrocnemius. It is important to stretch all these groups, and not inadvertently underemphasize any of them. For the hamstrings, one should remember to bend at the hips, not at the waist (Fig. 25) to minimize the lower back component; this will become evident in the description of specific exercises.

Anterior Upper Leg Muscles
   There are five front thigh muscles. One is the *sartorius* (Fig. 28—SART), the longest muscle in the body. Originating from the anterior superior iliac spine of the pelvis, it continues diagonally over the thigh to insert eventually into the tibia. It is a medial rotator of the thigh and a hip flexor. The other four muscles collectively are termed the *quadriceps femoris*. The longest of these is the *rectus femoris* (Fig. 28—R FEM), originating near the sartorius. The other three—*vastus intermedius* (not visible externally, but just below the rectus), the *vastus lateralis*, and *vastus*

medialis—originate on the femur (Fig. 24—V LAT; 28—V MED). These all join together and merge into a common patellar tendon that inserts into the patella (kneecap) itself. Distal to this the tendon continues as the patellar ligament and inserts into the tibia. The entire quadriceps group extends the knee, and the rectus also flexes the hip joint.

It is the extensor thrust produced primarily by these muscles, coupled with gastro-soleus plantar flexion, that provides the takeoff mechanism in the jumping events. The sartorius helps to counteract lateral leg rotation during running, especially when turning. Also during running, the quadriceps muscles must absorb the effects of gravitational and momentum forces as the landing foot impacts on the running surface. These impact stresses become especially great during hurdling, when the lead leg plants just after clearing the hurdle. Stretching exercises for these muscles often take the form of a hurdler in mid-flight, so as to loosen the low back/quadriceps/hamstrings groups in a manner relating to the event itself (Fig. 2).

Groin Muscles

Three important movements—lifting the thigh (hip flexion), rotating the thigh (hip rotation), and thigh adduction/abduction—are controlled by muscles located partly in a region commonly called the *groin*, but partly in and around other parts of the hip (pelvis) and thigh. More than a dozen muscles allow these powerful movements to occur smoothly. For high jumpers, their function is crucial. Especially in the straddle, the strong lead leg lift is a thigh flexion, but the rotational components allowing the jumper to leap upward and over the bar, much as in leaping through a window, are generated by hip rotation and thigh adduction/abduction (Fig. 3). They are also important for hurdling, both traditional and that seen in the steeplechase, especially for the trailing leg (Fig. 2).

Most of the adductors originate on the pubic portion of the pelvis: *pectineus, gracilis,* and *adductors brevis, longus, magnus,* and *minimus.* All of these except the gracilis spread out to insert along the medial part of the femur. The gracilis is the most medial adductor and inserts far down on the tibia, along with the sartorius and semitendinosus. The small area of origin of these muscles renders them injury-prone, especially early in the season when they are not well developed, but also later on when they must help counteract movements initiated by the now very strong quadriceps and hamstrings. In order of importance for thigh adduction, we would list 1) adductor magnus/minimus, 2) adductor longus/brevis, 3) part of the gluteus medius, 4) gracilis, 5) pectineus.

Flexion of the thigh is accomplished by some of the adductors, but two other hip muscles as well as two thigh muscles. The *iliopsoas* arises in part from the sides of the 12th thoracic and first to fourth lumbar vertebrae as well as the large iliac portion of the pelvis, and then inserts on the proximal part of the femur. This is the most important muscle in the body for lifting the leg forward (hip flexion). When one is lying down it helps lift the torso and bend it forward. Another important muscle is the *tensor fasciae latae* (Fig. 24—TFL) originating near the anterior superior iliac spine of the pelvis and inserting into the iliotibial tract on the lateral side of the thigh. This wide but thin tract of connective tissue in turn inserts into the tibia. In order of importance, the hip muscles involved in thigh flexion are the 1) iliopsoas, 2) tensor fasciae latae, 3) pectineus, 4) adductor longus/brevis/gracilis. But two thigh muscles— the rectus femoris and sartorius—are also involved and would be ranked in the sequence between iliopsoas and tensor fasciae latae. It is these two muscles which, as they remain shortened from continued running with no stretching, help to tilt the pelvis forward, contributing to a lordotic posture.

Medial and lateral rotation of the thigh refer to rotation around its long axis, at the hip joint. As a hurdler's trail leg comes over the hurdle, that leg is under the influence not only of knee and hip flexion but also thigh medial rotation (Fig. 2). At footplant, the lead leg of a flop-style high jumper not only flexes at the hip and knee, but also medially rotates and adducts at the hip as it turns slightly to help impart rotation of the body for proper bar clearance. The relevant muscles for medial thigh rotation in order of importance, are 1) gluteus medius/minimus (Fig. 24—G MED; 2) tensor fasciae latae (Fig. 24—TLF), and 3) adductor magnus. For lateral thigh rotation, they are 1) gluteus maximus, 2) quadratus femoris (not visible externally, arising from the ischial tuberosity and inserting on the proximal femur), 3) obturator internus (similarly not seen externally, 4) gluteus medius/minimus, 5) iliopsoas, and 6) adductors.

Abdominal and Chest Muscles

The *abdominal* muscles (*rectus abdominis, internal* and *external obliques,* and *transversus abdominis*) are relatively weak muscles, especially among distance runners. Many hours of running strengthen the calf, hamstrings, and lower back muscles, and this great posterior strengthening (with accompanying shortening) should be balanced by exercises that strengthen the anterior muscles. Bent-knee situps are highly recommended, but seldom are done in sufficient quantity to maintain the muscle balance so important for preservation of spinal alignment.

Jumpers and those who do any form of hurdling almost universally include plenty of situp exercises in their training program, as well as strengthening exercises through weight-training for both abdominal and *chest* muscles (*pectoralis, serratus, intercostal* muscles). Stretching exercises are needed for such muscles by these athletes, to prevent tension generation in opposing or antagonistic muscles from stretching these beyond their functional limits.

Upper and Lower Back Muscles

The back muscles help support the body as it leans forward. The greater the amount of forward lean, as in sprint accelerations and hurdling, or in leaning into a hill while running up its length, the more these muscles are utilized, and strengthened. Weight training of course also demands strength in these groups. Prior to the use of these muscles in vigorous exercise, they must be stretched, again to ensure maximal functional performance possibilities in the event they are stretched by the action of antagonist muscles.

Good overall body posture is always important, and this involves an interaction between the spinal column and the muscles attached to it. This column has four slight curves: at the neck (anterior), the rib cage (posterior), the waist (anterior), and tailbone (posterior). Improper balance between the strength and length of the anterior and posterior chest, stomach, and back muscles predisposes to weaknesses which in turn can accentuate these normally gentle spinal curves. The end result is spinal malalignment, with its oft-occurring pains and injuries.

Proper posture should be maintained whenever standing: feet together, equal weight on both, heels slightly apart, quadriceps under slight tension, buttocks also under slight tension but lowered to induce a slight pelvic tilting, stomach relaxed, chest high, arms loose at the sides—just as if one were standing proudly on the victory stand, head held high.

ELEMENTS OF A FUNCTIONAL STRETCHING ROUTINE

Initially a few suggestions are appropriate to set a general philosophical tone for stretching exercises. The routine should be just that: a predetermined habitual pattern of exercises requiring little thought for actual execution. It should be accomplished in an unhurried relaxed manner, and done with care and sensitivity. The mind-body awareness continuum should allow one to assess the residual effects of the prior day's training or competition, to identify particular muscle groups requiring additional time for adequate stretch, and to detect asymmetries in flexibility that may suggest inflammation or injury. Thus, the time period for stretching is a period where physical relaxation, mental preparation, and body assessment occur. Not to stretch eliminates this important aspect of training.

There is a frequent tendency to compare one's flexibility to another's, or to attempt to achieve (or surpass) someone else's flexibility. This is both inappropriate and unwise. Inherent individual differences in flexibility have already been mentioned. One athlete's event specialty may be different from another's, creating different specific gains or losses in flexibility or emphasis on stretching certain groups. It is more important for athletes to assess their own changing flexibility over time, from day to day, and over longer periods. Then they know whether they are getting better, worse, or staying constant. That information has real value for them.

Most experts who design flexibility programs suggest that one begin with the head/neck region and gradually work down to the feet. In this manner, while smaller muscle groups are being stretched in the upper torso and neck, larger groups will have a more gentle initial stretch by being associated with these other movements. If possible, multiple muscle group exercises can be devised that mimic specific aspects of body positions achieved in the event itself. This is especially easy for field event athletes. Stretch should not exceed the threshold for discomfort, and should be maintained for a several-second holding period to allow muscle lengthening.

One good way to begin an exercise routine is with neck rotations, which can merge into rotation of the entire upper torso (Figs. 4-5). Initially there is stretch of two major supporting pairs of muscles for the head and neck. One of these is the *sternocleidomastoid* (Fig. 21—SCM). These cover the carotid artery, jugular vein, and vagus nerve on either side of the neck, originate on the sternum and collar bone, and insert on the mastoid process of the temporal bone. The other is the *trapezius* (Fig. 31—TRAP), originating on the occipital bone and inserting on the collar bone. The former muscles allow chin elevation, head movement toward the shoulder, and vertebral column flexion, the latter rotate the head, draw the head backward, and for the scapula can allow upward, downward, and rotational movement.

Other major muscles in this region are also stretched. The *deltoid* (Figs. 28, 31—DELT) originates on the collar bone and inserts on the humerus of the arm, helping to adduct, flex, and extend the arm, depending on how the muscle is utilized. The *pectoralis major* (Fig. 31—PECT) has the same body origins and insertions, but at slightly different locations, allowing it to flex, adduct, and medially rotate the arm. The *latissimus dorsi* (Fig. 28—LAT) covers the lumbar and lower portion of the posterior chest, but extends, adducts, and medially rotates the arm as well as pulling the shoulder downward and backward. As this rotation is increased in extent (but not in quickness) more muscles are activated, and more are stretched: the internal and external abdominal obliques, the hip rotators, and the adductor/abductor groups.

In Fig. 6 the deltoid muscles are being stretched. The right hand comes to the upper back from below, the left hand from above, and the fingers hook together. Then the exercise is reversed. A several-second pull of both interlocked arms is suggested by advocates of proprioceptive neuromuscular facilitation to elicit greater relaxation upon cessation of tension.

Moving to a sitting position (Fig. 7), and by alternating with right and left legs downward in the position illustrated, increasing stretch is applied to the combination of abdominal obliques, hip rotators, and quadriceps (on the right side illustrated here). The arms are used for support during the swing phase, when the hips are lifted and leg positions are reversed.

In Fig. 8, specific muscle groups on both sides of the body are stretched, and of course this reverses when the stretching position is reversed. Shown here, hand clasped behind the back, the stretched muscles include the right hip rotators, right abdominal obliques, and left-side back muscles. Turning the head to the right shoulder stretches, in addition, the left trapezius and sternocleidomastoid.

To complete this initial stretch of muscles with hip-related function, the hamstrings and gluteus maximus can be stretched (Fig. 9) by lifting one leg voluntarily, and then assisting in this lift with a gentle push upward on the calf muscle. The knee is flexed, and thus the gastrocnemius is unaffected.

The back muscles can be stretched in many ways. Two initial maneuvers are illustrated in Figs. 10 and 11. In Fig. 10 the athlete is simply hanging with his hands from a crossbar. He is looking ahead, relaxed, and will hold the position until his arms dictate termination. In Figure 11, the several groups of muscles positioned along the vertebral column for its stabilization are being stretched. Feet are on the ground, with hands grasping a nearby object; a gentle pull is exerted as if to slide the feet toward the hands.

It is now appropriate to implement a slightly greater stretch of the hip and lower limb muscles. In Fig. 12, with the right foot balanced on a railing (or hurdle, or steeplechase barrier), the left hamstrings and gastrocnemius are stretched. The adductors of the right leg, as well as its iliopsoas and gluteus medius, are all lengthened. By moving the right knee to the railing, the adductor stretch can be increased. As usual, this exercise is reversed, and comparison is made of bilateral flexibility.

In Fig. 13 the position of the raised leg now emphasizes stretch of its hamstrings/gastrocnemius/ Achilles tendon, with adductors included. Reaching with the near arm to apply stretch to the Achilles also stretches the abdominal oblique and latissimus muscles on the opposite side.

One could face the railing (or hurdle) instead of positioning at right angles to it, illustrated in Fig. 14. Placement of one leg on the railing, with the support leg well behind and with both hands grasping the railing on either side of the balanced leg, stretches the hamstrings and gastrocnemius of both legs as well as the upper back and intervertebral muscles. (This exercise can also implement a proprioceptive neuromuscular component as well.) Moving closer to the railing shifts emphasis to the hip flexors of the lifted leg, illustrated in Fig. 15.

Reversing the position assumed in Fig. 15, shown in Fig. 16, allows stretch of the plantar flexors (especially soleus), quadriceps, and iliopsoas of the lifted leg (here the right leg), as well as the rectus abdominis of the abdominal group and the sternocleidomastoid in the neck.

Figs. 17-18 complete this sequence. The gastrocnemius, hamstrings, gluteus minimus, and low back muscles on both sides of the body are linked together and stretched in Fig. 17 by use of the hands grasping both ankles to apply symmetric static stretch. Fig. 18 links the anterior muscle groups—quadriceps, abdominals, chest, and neck. In this manner, although previous exercises emphasized stretch of muscles on one or the other side of the body, symmetry is assured by subsequent stretch of the same muscle groups on both sides of the body simultaneously.

These kinds of exercises can be performed while sitting or lying on the ground as well as while standing. The difference in body support, however, alters the manner by which stretch is achieved and maintained. Thus, in Fig. 19 the soleus, quadriceps (rectus femoris and vastus, medialis), iliopsoas, abdominals (rectus abdominis) and pectoralis can be lengthened bilaterally and simultaneously. In Fig. 20, with gentle pull at the ankles, the iliopsoas and quadriceps are lengthened. The arched back stretches the abdominals especially rectus, the chest muscles, especially pectoralis, and neck, notably sternocleidomastoid. The relevance of this stretching position for high jumpers is considerable. Fig.

21 illustrates a standing vertical back jump, often used by floppers in practice. The similarity in the arch (from knees to shoulders) in Figs. 20 and 21 is easy to observe. A similar arch occurs when jumps are made using a normal several-step approach run.

Fig. 22 illustrates a related exercise for stretching extensors on one side, flexors on the other. Here, left quadriceps, right hamstrings, and right gluteals are lengthened as well as chest, neck, and abdominal muscles.

The hamstrings, gastrocnemius, and lower back are lengthened in Fig. 23, with emphasis shifted from gastrocnemius to gluteals as the knees are brought beside the head in Fig. 24. Some people find these exercises difficult due to prior neck injuries or a normally somewhat inflexible spine. The hamstrings, gastrocnemius, and Achilles tendons can be stretched with no back component, shown in Fig. 25. First one leg, then the other, can be stretched.

Greater emphasis will now be directed to the groin muscles, stretching them in concert with other lower limb and low back muscles. Fig. 26 depicts an exercise most familiar to hurdlers, since it imitates the position of a hurdler in midflight. Shown here, stretch is applied to the right quadriceps and groin muscles, and as well to the left hamstrings, gastrocnemius, and Achilles tendon. Reversal of leg orientation of course stretches the same muscles, but on opposite legs.

Additional groin flexibility can be achieved by the position assumed in Figs. 27-28 and 29-30. One can begin with legs outstretched, with an upright sitting posture, and then lean the trunk forward (Fig. 27) to add the low back component. By moving to the left (Fig. 28) and to the right, hip rotators are added as well as increasing emphasis on the hamstrings and gastrocnemius on the side toward which the trunk leans. In Figs. 29-30 an additional stretch of the lower back and sartorius occurs. Finally, in Fig. 31 the groin muscles are stretched as a somewhat isolated group, by placing gentle downward pressure on the knees.

We began with the head and neck; we end with the Achilles tendon and foot, although various foot exercises, such as rotation, inversion, eversion, and dorsi/plantar flexion are not illustrated. Figs. 32-33 do, however, suggest two additional stretching exercises for the gastro-soleus and Achilles tendon. Runners often are seen leaning against trees or buildings prior to a race, in the pose of Fig. 32, stretching their prime movers. Field event athletes more often perform the stretch shown in Fig. 33, using stadium steps or the inside curb of the track.

Hopefully this information has opened up 'the real world' of muscle function sufficiently that athletes understand better how their muscles function, and how to maintain them adequately lengthened for optimal performance potential.

FIG. 1

FIG. 2

FIG. 3

FIG. 4

FIG. 5

FIG. 6

FIG. 7

FIG. 8

FIG. 9

FIG. 10

FIG. 11

FIG. 12

FIG. 13

FIG. 14

FIG. 15

FIG. 16

FIG. 17

FIG. 18

FIG. 19

FIG. 20

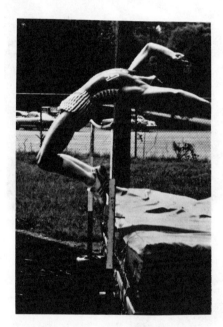

FIG. 21

FIG. 22

FIG. 23

FIG. 24

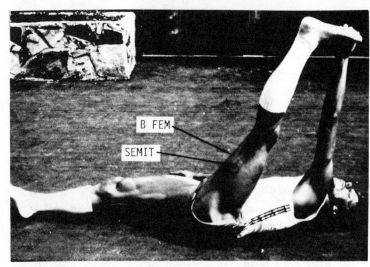

FIG. 25

FIG. 26

FIG. 27

FIG. 28

FIG. 29

FIG. 30

FIG. 31

TRAP.

DELT.

PECT.

FIG. 32

FIG. 33

RACING TO IMPROVED PERFORMANCES

by Bill Arnold, Great Britain

Racing is an important component of improved performance, as well as an end in itself. Arnold offers his thoughts on the approach to and frequency of racing in an athlete's schedule. Coaching Review, Vol. V, Jan/Feb. 1982.

Dependence on a sound competitive program, as part of an athlete's development, is probably the most important feature in scheduled planning. It is a time when the coach, athlete and administrators must work out a balanced program. With variations in types of athletes and their specific events there is not always identical planning for all runners.

Some generalities can be given, though, and many positive points made when assessing a sound competitive program for middle-distance running:

1. While competing regularly, the athlete maintains constant contact with the reality of his or her goals.

2. The coach can use race results to monitor the athlete's condition and make adjustments in the training program on a regular basis.

3. Low-key racing commitments at the club level can be fulfilled.

4. The athlete is able to run distances other than his or her racing specialty.

5. Regular competition relieves stress associated with regular heavy training. A different sense of enjoyment can be achieved by competing in non-pressure events (such as an 800m runner going out for cross country) without a strong obligation.

6. An athlete can experiment with strategy and tactical running in low-key races.

7. A build-up of racing will develop the mental toughness required in major meets.

8. Regular races expose the athlete to different types of runners and various racing situations, creating a wealth of valuable experience.

9. A good competition program exposes the athlete as a person willing to endure and fulfill tough competitive commitments.

10. The athlete will benefit physically from over-distance and underdistance races.

So, the advantages of having between 25 and 40 races per year are numerous and cover a wide range of satisfying reasons. The breakdown in types of races can be categorized as: road and cross country, indoor track preparation, indoor track major, outdoor track preparation and outdoor track major. If 32 races per year is an average, the following estimated breakdown could apply:

TYPE OF RACES	NUMBER
Road and cross-country	10
Indoor track preparation	4
Indoor track major	3
Outdoor track preparation	10
Outdoor track major	5
Total	32

Major races can be defined as championship meets, international team or individual meets and major games where the emphasis is on an ultimate (or very close to maximum) performance.

Some of what has been said so far needs more specific qualification to be better understood. An absolute racing program can only be attempted after several years of consistent conditioning build-up. There is a definite correlation between aerobic capacity, strength and the ability to sustain a full summer season of top level competition.

The ability to race and recover quickly and race again obviously promotes stronger motivation. An up-and-down season becomes nerve-racking and usually ends with the athlete becoming lethargic and losing the urge to run (a situation commonly called staleness).

Even the great stars of track falter under

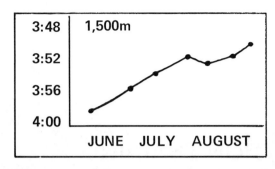

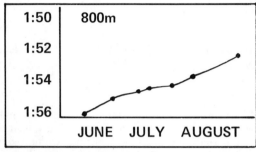

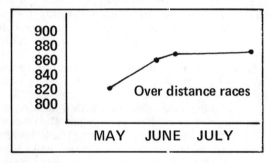

more relaxing atmosphere of road and cross-country racing. Some runners never get to feel the relaxed invigorating feeling of just going out and racing for run. Coaches should prescribe a good dose of this type of running even for the champions.

Coaches should constantly monitor their athletes' competitive potential through a thorough program of testing and plotting of performances. If the athlete is competing regularly, the coach can plot graphs and also relate these performances in terms of points using Gardner and Purdy's *Computerized Running and Training Program.* This monitoring will plot an athlete's current ability and progress in his or her speciality event and related areas—such as speed and general endurance. The graphical analysis of a 1500m runner's outdoor season indicates the following:

1. The over distance races in May indicated a good level of general endurance, while July's 3000m run confirmed that the runner had worked sufficiently to maintain the initial level.

2. The rise in performance from early June to mid July was satisfactory.

3. The flattening out of performance in late July needed some analysis and action taken to correct the problem.

Note: General endurance was good. 800m time had flattened out. 1500m time dipped.

Possible answers are:

a. Athlete is over tired and needs rest. This is most unlikely considering he ran a 3000m in 8:29.2 in mid July and looked good.

b. The more likely reason is a lack of speed and specific endurance. This can be claimed in light of the declining performance at the shorter distances.

c. There are many physio-metabolic and neuromuscular reasons for performance decline. Listed are some of the things which could affect these systems and hamper an athlete's progress:

1. Summer heat wave.

2. Summer job, especially if not compatible with athletics.

3. Too much swimming and suntanning.

4. A change in environment and routine.

5. Allergy symptoms and associated drugs.

6. More common things such as lack of rest and sleep, poor diet and personal problems can be factors.

With the injection of more specific training, the athlete's 1500-meter performance improves significantly. It was also evident that his 800-meter performance was more in line with the point score expected in this event. It is quite possible that the adjustment to achieve such a change is minimal, yet decisive, in producing the correct result. □

the pressure of over-racing. As we have read, Bill Rodgers stated he was too tired from the hard racing he had already put in to run the 1978 Fukuoka Marathon effectively. The other big racer that year was Henry Rono who as in the case of Rodgers, was not running as well toward the season's end. Both were able to run many high quality races due to several years of intensive aerobic conditioning. They were not able to balance their racing programs with enough recovery and low-key competition. Rodgers was always facing new fast opposition to beat, and Rono was expected to run world-class times everywhere he went.

There is a limit to the number of hard races a runner can have in one year. A young athlete should expect only three or four, while as the training base increases this builds up and ultimately could reach 10 or 15. However, I believe it is better to plan for no more than six to eight.

Of course, running must be enjoyable; and while enjoyment can be had from doing well in the track season, much can be gained from the

A DIFFERENT VIEW OF MARATHON TRAINING

by Frank Horwill, Great Britain

Famed British Coach Frank Horwill presents his views on marathon training, including his iconoclastic thoughts on achieving the two-hour marathon. Running Review, No. 8, Feb. 1982.

Sometimes the obvious in middle distance training thought stares us in the face but we do not see it until years later. For example, Ann Packer's 800 meters gold medal in the Tokyo Olympic Games did not greatly alter middle-distance thought in Britain. Many coaches viewed her success as a fluke, especially when the 800 meters was her second event and the 400 meters her primary goal. Coaches still trained athletes for the 800 meters with the majority of training being aerobic. However, Fiasconaro and Juantorena, caused some rethinking of contemporary methods and the hundred miles a week two-lapper gave way to the 100 miles a month runner, much of it being pure sprinting.

The same lesson faces us in the marathon and again we must go back to the Olympic Games of 1952 in Helsinki, when, in the course of seven days Zatopek ran a 10,000 meters, heat of the 5,000 meters and the final, and the marathon. He won the 5,000 and 10,000 finals, the latter in an Olympic record. There was much speculation before the marathon, it was Zatopek's first ever marathon; to run one's first marathon is strain enough to do it in the Olympic Games was thought a mad gamble.

Much interest was registered in Emil Zatopek's training and the conclusion of many British distance coaches was that he was yet another fluke who broke all the accepted rules of marathon training, which is a preponderance of long slow runs aimed primarily for the athlete to complete the course and not necessarily to complete it at a pre-determined pace never before attempted.

Zatopek's training formula was deadly boring and deadly effective. It was all repetition running with erratic pacing. His favorite session comprising 20 x 200m, 40 x 400m, and again 20 x 200m. Each repetition was followed by a 200m recovery jog. The times of the 200m reps, started at 34 seconds and the 400m runs started as fast as 56 seconds but through exhaustion slowed to 90 secs. towards the end. The total distance covered in his workouts was up to twenty five miles, of which half was faster than five minutes per mile pace. When asked if he found this sort of training soul-destroying, he replied, "I'm too busy getting fit to think about such things."

Asked what he did if he had to go away on army duties and no track was available, he stated, "I mark out

ZATOPEK SHOCKED THE WORLD IN THIS, HIS FIRST MARATHON, BY WINNING THE 1952 OLYMPIC TITLE

a 400 meter circuit and carry on the same." Questioned why he sometimes ran in army boots he stated that the snow rotted his running shoes. He always ran in his track suit and even in hot weather he only removed his top occasionally.

It is my considered opinion that the first man to run sub-2 hours for the marathon will be the man who emulates Emil Zatopek's training ideas and not the man who does spells of up to 200 miles a week considerably slower than race pace in the main.

Here is the **build-up** schedule for a two hour marathon, with explanations: Five minute miling is 2 hours 10 minutes. Four minutes forty seconds miling is near enough *two hours flat.* That pace is 70 seconds per 400m. The athlete should acclimatize himself to this pace, choosing 400 meters as the minimum distance in reps, and a total of 13 miles of running, and eight laps (3200m) as the maximum distance of reps. (9 mins. 20 secs.) The rest in the former (400s) should be 50 meter jog and in the latter (3200m), 400 meter jog, decreasing over a period of six months to 100 meters jog.

There is a case for one long run a week at the athlete's own choice of pace, lasting two hours or more. The distance covered is not too important at this stage. *The total time on the feet is the relevant factor.*

A hill session of running up and down a 1 in 10 hill for a total of six miles is also indicated—a will-power session, it is also a leg-strengthening workout and prepares one for hills on various routes.

A 1½ hour run is also indicated over a known route so that when the time has expired the total distance run should be calculated and strenuous attempts should be made over a lengthy period to run *farther* within that time phase of 1½ hours. If 15 miles can be run in 1½ hours in December, a reasonable target for March would be 17 miles in that time span.

A 45-minute fast run is indicated and this can be a measured 9xmile road run. The sub 2½ hour man would have an actual routine something on these lines:

Day 1—Build up to 40 x 400 in 70 secs. with 50m jog rest. First class athletes should be able to start with 20 x 400 and add four reps. per month. Do not add reps. if the times are not achieved. Day 2—6 miles of 1 in 10 hills. Day 3—2 hour run at own choice of pace, increasing time run by 15 minutes per month. Day 4—Day off. Day 5—45-minute *fast* run. Day 6—1½-hour run. Day 7—20 x 800 in 2 mins. 20 secs. with fast 100m jog rest. Start with 10 x 800 and add two reps. per month. Day 8—Day off. Day 9—1½-hour run. Day 10—As for Day 3. Day 11—45-minute fast run with 6 efforts of fast running for 4 minutes with 1 minute fast jog rest. Day 12—6 miles hill work. Day 13—Day off. Day 14—Race.

The cycle is repeated but the track sessions on Day 1 are changed to 12 x 1200 in 3 mins. 30 secs. starting with six reps. and on Day 7, 10 x 1600 in 4 mins. 40 secs, starting with five reps. The rest jogs are 150m and 200m respectively.

Every *fourth* day is off. Research has shown that the cortisone level of the adrenal glands becomes depleted within two months if athletes train every day at a high level. This will predispose the runner to *stress* and possible injury. Runners are able to increase the quality and quantity of their training more easily with every *fourth* day off. The statement by a now retired famous

runner, "I start the day off feeling tired and finish it even more tired.," is not to be taken as the yardstick to success. *The greatest challenge to world class runners today is to keep running without constant breaks from training caused by injury and ill-health due to over-stress*—the syndrome of every fourth day off or very easy, if universally accepted may be the greatest step forward to injury-free athletics. It is now known that runners are more likely to contract glandular fever than any other sportsmen. This is because the fatigued body is readily found in the runner. Rest, judicious rest, is now an important part of Russian women's training cycles and should not be viewed as a dirty word. The well-trained athlete can go five days off training before his endurance declines.

Now, it is quite obvious that the times given in the specimen marathon schedule is for the accomplished runner, but the principle of pace acclimatization applies to all marathoners of whatever standard. Here is a table of paces to fit into the training cycle which caters to most runners:

PACE

Dist. of Rep.	Advanced	Average	Novice	Rest
400m	70 secs	80 secs	90 secs	50m jog
800m	20 mins 20	2 mins 40	3 mins	100m jog
1200m	3:30	4 mins	4½ mins	150m jog
1600m	4:40	5:20	6 mins	200m jog

Two other factors must be given attention when embarking on the fast approach to marathon training: 1) Diet and 2) Weight. In the past I have been an advocate of the supplement for runners, this is because some runners find cooking their own food is tedious and tend to have snacks rather than meals. Well chosen food in sufficient quantity is superior to synthetic foods. The athlete must ensure he gets *the basic four every day.*
a) Three glasses of milk a day or equivalent, too much calcium interferes with iron, zinc and magnesium, absorption.
b) Two x 3 ozs. meat or equivalent (eggs, cheese, beans, peas, lentils, nuts).
c) Five full cups of vegetables and fruit.
d) Four servings of whole grains.

Three-quarters of the work performed in running is used to lift the body against gravity and a 2¼lb. reduction in body weight will decrease the work performed by 1-1½ percent. Ernst Van Aaken's height/weight recommendations are worthy of consideration in view of the foregoing facts.

Men	Ideal Weight	Women	Ideal Weight
Height		Height	
5 feet	88 lb	1.524m	2.551kg
5ft 6 ins	115 lb	1.676m	3.345kg
6 feet	141 lb	1.829m	10.433kg

The average height and weight of America's leading marathon male runners is: 5ft 10.3 inches (1.784m), height, and 132 pounds. □

Technique Analysis

ANALYSIS OF LINEAR AND ROTATIONAL JAVELIN TECHNIQUE

by Jeffrey Gorski, U.S.A.

An in-depth comparison of the technical components and physiological requirements inherent to each style of throwing. Gorski also presents specific training ideas for increasing strength, power and throwing ability.

In the United States the most popular technique in the javelin has been the linear, or Lusis style of throwing. Only recently has the rotational style of throwing, sometimes referred to as wrapping, been used by some athletes. Many American coaches are hesitant to use it with their athletes because many of the positive aspects of the rotational style are considered faults in the linear style.

Whichever technique is used, there are basic actions that must happen to produce good throws. These basic fundamentals are: 1. maintained or increased momentum from the run-up into the throw; 2. a noticeable backward lean; 3. initiation of the throw from the legs; 4. separation of the hip and shoulder axes; 5. a firm brace or plant from the front leg; and 6. a delayed arm strike. All these components are a result of the first, maintained momentum if the technique is executed properly.

In order for all the above to happen, it is extremely important that the thrower does not stop his forward momentum when the power leg lands after the cross-over. This "soft-step" or "deep-knee" position allows the back-lean, hip leading position achieved in the cross-over to continue into the front leg block with good speed (**Fig. 1**).

What the thrower is trying to do is achieve the longest possible power path for the throwing hand while maintaining as much forward speed, under control, as possible. These qualities are functions of the backward lean and soft-step, respectively. From this position, which is when the power leg begins to thrust the body forward into the plant, the athlete's aim is to generate as much velocity as possible at the point of release. This is accomplished when the legs initiate the throwing action, which causes the hips to lead the body as it drives into the plant leg.

This thrusting action by the power leg into the plant causes the hips to rotate around the vertical axis of the body. This hip rotation, while the throwing arm remains back, causes the separation of the hip-shoulder axes, which in turn develops torque from the stretch of the

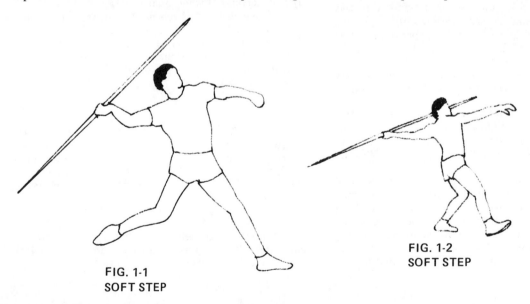

FIG. 1-1
SOFT STEP

FIG. 1-2
SOFT STEP

trunk and abdominal muscles. **(Fig. 2)** A great deal of velocity can be generated from this "taut-bow" position, because of the stretch-reflex action of the trunk muscles. This causes a much faster shoulder rotation, around the body's vertical axis, than a voluntary contraction of the same group.

The hip-shoulder separation maintains the backward lean of the body and the delayed arm strike, assuming the athlete has the needed mobility. This also places the muscles of the chest and shoulder in a stretched position similar to that of trunk and abdomen. The stretch-reflex will produce a much faster striking velocity for the entire arm than a willful contraction of that muscle group would.

From this description of the body movements, we can see the need for flexibility and relaxation of the muscle groups that oppose the throwing action. American throwers, in the effort to throw far would do better to stay relaxed and allow their technique to produce muscle stretch with the resultant contraction producing greater velocities and power. Americans are concerned with body position and alignment, while the Europeans advocate being relaxed. Most U.S. athletes stress strength and power training over technique and voluntary relaxation.

In observing the aspects of the linear and rotational throw we must remember the athlete's goals: long power path, highest controlled speed and the greatest release velocity possible. While the goals are the same, the means of obtaining these goals and the training priorities for each style differ substantially. Each style or variation will require different physiological qualities.

In the linear style throw, probably best personified by Janis Lusis of the Soviet Union, the athlete attempts to keep all of the components of the throw aligned with the path of the throw **(Fig. 3)**. There is a minimum of horizontal rotation of the body segments in preparation for the throw. The feet are pointed as straight ahead as possible, no more than 30 degrees out of the direction of the throw for the power foot. The hips also maintain a square up position, rotating, 45 degrees, at most, out of the direction of the throw during the crossover.

In many cases the rotation of the hips is between 20 to 35 degrees. The shoulders, throwing arm and javelin rotation 90 degrees to the throw, parallel to the approach run and throw direction, with the javelin directly aligned with the proposed path of the throw **(Fig. 4)**. The more the javelin is rotated past the 90 degree point, the chances of flight alignment and timing problems increases.

**FIG. 2-1
ROTATION TORQUE**

**FIG. 2-2
ROTATION TORQUE**

**FIG. 3-1
LINEAR STYLE**

**FIG. 3-2
LINEAR STYLE**

**FIG. 3-3
LINEAR STYLE**

While most U.S. throwers keep the javelin at the 90 degree rotation, it is interesting to note that Lusis rotated the javelin about 15-20 degrees past the 90 degree point, thus effectively increasing his power path. This is quite difficult for all but the most advanced throwers of the linear style.

This style of throwing is best suited to the more powerful, less flexible athlete. Because of the fairly straight-ahead position of the hips, a faster approach can be used to compensate for the limited range of motion. Also, because there is a more limited range to apply force to the javelin, the athlete generally has a higher quality of muscular development (e.g., Roggy, Kennedy,

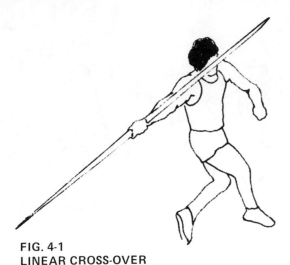

FIG. 4-1
LINEAR CROSS-OVER

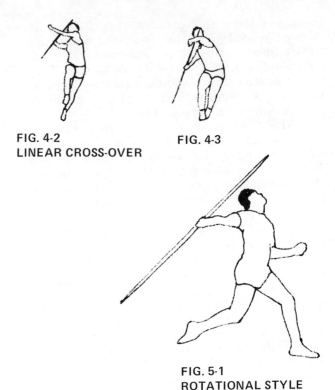

FIG. 4-2
LINEAR CROSS-OVER

FIG. 4-3

FIG. 5-1
ROTATIONAL STYLE

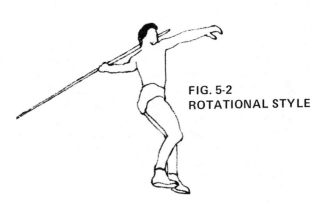

FIG. 5-2
ROTATIONAL STYLE

Murro). When using this style, the athlete must be careful not to over-rotate the upper body to the left (for a right-handed thrower) during the delivery. The shoulders must be square to the throw and stay over the hips; if they over-rotate to the left the thrower will lose much of the thrust and power generated by the plant. This will cause a break at the waist and a lean to the left, reducing the power generated by the body and putting undue strain on the shoulder and elbow joint.

The rotational style of throwing is typified by both hips and shoulders rotated well past the point of alignment used in the linear style, though the amount of rotation varies with each individual (Fig. 5). In most cases the feet are turned anywhere from 45 to 90 degrees to the right, with the hips between 60 to 90 degrees out of plane to the throw. The rotation of the shoulders ranges from about 120 degrees to extremes of 150 to 160 degrees to the right.

Hannu Siitonen of Finland was one of the first to demonstrate this technique successfully, which has been popularized by Hungarian Miklos Nemeth. Probably the most extreme rotation is demonstrated by Duncan Atwood of the U.S. (Fig. 6).

This style of throwing is used by smaller, more flexible athletes. The extreme rotation of the hips and wrapping of the shoulders and javelin dictate a slower approach than the linear style. However, the longer power path and strong hip and shoulder positions develop much more torque during the hip-shoulder separation phase. This results in a release velocity equal to or greater than that of the linear style.

It is an absolute necessity that throwers using this style have excellent strength and quickness in the legs, hips and the trunk muscle groups. Because of the side-ways body position and the slower run up, the last two steps prior to the throw must be extremely quick and

powerful. This puts the thrower in a favorable position to use the extreme wrap to produce more torque during the crossover and carry it into the throw.

Because of the rotational movements of this style, the classic, over the shoulder delivery is not possible. Even though the arm strike is taking place above the shoulder joint, it is seldom more than 45 degrees above the shoulder axis in either the linear or rotational style (Fig. 7). This produces a long throwing radius, with the chest and shoulder muscles contributing most of the final power. This is different from the linear style, where the arm strike is similar to a tennis serve action.

Even though the shoulders and javelin are not aligned in the direction of the throw, by the

**FIG. 6-1
ATWOOD**

**FIG. 6-2
ATWOOD**

**FIG. 7-1
ARM STRIKE**

FIG. 7-2

time the arm strike begins the shoulders have squared up to the direction of the throw. From here on the throwing mechanics are the same as in the linear style, except that the throwing arm's action is a bit wider.

Since the mechanical features of rotational throwing are different from the linear style, the points of greatest stress are also different. The areas that need the most strength and flexibility to avoid injury are the knees, groin, trunk, sides and lower back, and shoulder.

These comparisons of technical components show that the means by which velocity is generated in the javelin vary, even if the final result is the same. Similarly, the training of the two styles is different, with different priorities.

Too many American throwers work on improving general strength and forget about the specific strength development that will help them throw farther. Probably the best example of this is the importance that many throwers place on the bench press. The bench press is important to the development of basic, all-around strength for beginning and intermediate throwers. But once the athlete is past the stage of basic preparation, specific strength and power training should begin and bench presses should be an occasional supplementary exercise.

The final training goals are: the development of technique and the development of strength and power. The means of meeting these goals include various weight and implement throws with one and two arms, imitative exercises against resistance duplicating the throwing movement without release to improve technique, improvement of strength and power by various weight exercises, with loads ranging from light to heavy, as well as isometric and isokinetic exercises. Power improvement also comes from a variety of running and jumping exercises as well as different types of weight throwing.

The most important aspect of training is the development of correct technique. Without proper mechanics, no amount of strength and

power training will improve distances very much. It is best to consider strength training as a means of improving technique, by developing the muscle groups which contribute to certain aspects of the throwing action.

Technique training will be made up of throwing a variety of weighted implements, and imitative exercises against resistance. Early season training consists of a large volume of throws from moderate to high intensity against heavy resistances. Single- and double-arm throws with medicine balls, shots, and weighted javelins or stubbies from a stand and a couple of steps should make up the bulk of the early throwing sessions. The weights thrown should be as heavy as possible without causing a change in the throwing motion. Also, imitative exercises with pulleys, Exergenies and isometric rope drills should be done. In all throwing and technique drills the throwing movement should be initiated by the power leg thrusting the body forward into the plant.

As the year progresses, the volume and intensity of the technique training increases, while the resistance drops a bit. The volume of double-arm throws also drops. There is a greater number of throws with some approach run as opposed to standing throws. Again, the action of the legs should initate the throwing motion. Imitative exercises should still be done.

During the first training period, from Sept. to Dec., about 20% of all throwing is done with the regular-weight javelin, the remainder with overweight implements. Throws with the regular-weight javelin increase to 35-40% during the second training period, from Dec. to March. Training during the competitive period, April to August, is composed of 60% regular weight and 20% light javelin throws, with the heavy weight throws used only to maintain muscle tone and strength. The throwers aim during this technique training is to correct or improve delivery technique and to become comfortable with the movements so that he does not have to think about his technique or timing during the throw.□

A WOMEN'S APPROACH TO THE FIRST HURDLE

by Andrew McInnis, University of Western Ontario, London, Ontario, Canada

The trend in treating the women's hurdles race in the past has been to transpose data from research done on men, a practice which can lead to "random hypothesizing and subjective reasoning," according to the author. Here is a summary of the findings of studies dealing specifically with female hurdling subjects.

If one considers the variables between the two races (male vs. female), the relationship to each other is quite divergent, save the fundamental essence of the hurdle clearance action. **(Table 1).**

Aside from the obvious anthropometric differences relative to stature and stride length, the most outstanding variable between the two races is that of barrier height. Dick (1978), in an analysis of stature verses hurdle height ratio of both female and male Olympic hurdle finalists (1972 and 1976), concluded that women within the height range of 1.63m to 1.72m need to make little compromise to the path of the athlete's center of gravity (CG) in sprinting over hurdles.

This was significantly different from their male counterparts who must raise their CG over the barriers. It was suggested that the female athlete can attempt to maintain or even increase the downward pelvic tilt and increase lumbar curve (forward lean) associated with sprinting. This complied with previous studies by Riddle (1969) and Singh (1969). *With such an evident technical variation in clearance, the compromising demands imposed on men cannot be applied to women.*

It is a common point of focus for authors to discuss the value of speed and the generation of sprint forces in reference to hurdle success. In doing so, they invariably mention the importance of getting to the first hurdle first.

Due to the compromising nature of hurdling and sprint speed, the velocity (horizontal) with which the runner reaches the first hurdle coupled with speed endurance and technical economy, will determine race success.

It is virtually impossible to accelerate running velocity once the hurdler is between the barriers, as demonstrated in a comparison of top international competitive touchdown times by Ewen (1978). The tendency to show improvement in touchdown times is commonly a direct resultant of a technical correction effected in response to a previous hurdle clearance error.

Mitchell (1969) states, "The function of the sprint acceleration to hurdle one is to generate as much running speed (horizontal velocity) as possible in the confining distance, and to arrive at the correct spot on the correct foot for the most effective takeoff flight." A greater velocity at takeoff will afford the hurdler the ability to lower the trajectory of the CG over the rail, by increasing the takeoff distance and the horizontal forces applied.

The ability to effect a superior hurdle clearance would appear to be highly related to

Table 1: IAAF Hurdle Race Specifications

	Race	Hurdles	Height	Distance To First	Between	Run-In
Women	100 meters	10	84cm	13.00m	8.50m	10.50m
Men	110 meters	10	106.7cm	13.72m	9.14m	14.02m

the athlete's ability to generate and maintain sprint speed and visa versa. Dick (1978), Singh (1970), and Viaksaar (1979), indicate the ability of an athlete to exploit his/her natural sprint speed lies with the degree of compromise an individual must make within the confines of the standardized hurdle approach.

In examining female hurdle spacing and height ratios between 1972 and 1976 Olympic hurdle finalists, Dick (1978) indicated a need for little compromise to the natural stride length of women. He also noted, that the 100m women's sprint finalists fell within the same height range as that of the hurdlers. Such a similarity indicates no limiting optimal height range for hurdle success other than the wide range offered by sprint norms. This similarity continues to support the symbiotic references made between female sprint capacity and the women's sprint hurdle event.

The demands of compromise placed upon women in the sprint hurdles appear to vary significantly from those faced by the men. It would also appear that event success is dependent upon sprint speed in two forms: 1) acceleration from the starting blocks to the first hurdle; 2) velocity and its maintenance between hurdles.

A key variable to maximizing speed in hurdling is the ability to exploit fully an athlete's "natural" sprint speed. This ability is influenced by the degree of "unnatural" adaptation that the natural stride length must make to conform to the standardized spacing. Other variables that influence this topic of stride length alteration are the fixed item of physical stature (with the exception of growth), and the somewhat changeable parameter of sprint ability.

In summary, the female hurdler, within the height range of 1.63m to 1.72m and possessing a reasonable sprint ability, need make little (if any) compromise to her "natural" sprint ability when compared to that of men. Coaches should caution and question literature with specific orientation to the men's event in reference to its applicability to the female hurdler.

It is the intent of this paper to examine the degree of compromise exhibited by female hurdlers from the sprint start and acceleration phase of running to the first hurdle. The study will incorporate cinematographic analysis of the path of movement of the body's CG, stride length, and horizontal velocity under the two proceeding conditions:

1) The examination of variables from the crouch start and the first 8 strides from the starting line in a short sprint (no hurdle).

This condition will be the best

Paul Sutton/Duomo

WOMEN HAVE TO COMPROMISE MORE THAN MEN IN TERMS OF LEAN.

representative of the hurdler's "natural" sprint speed and accelerating stride length.

2) The examination of variables from the crouch start and first 8 strides from the starting line during the approach to hurdle takeoff (with hurdle).

This condition will represent any compromising or unnatural tendencies (if any) that are imposed upon the hurdler's natural sprint acceleration as compared to condition one.

A second purpose of this paper is to examine angular changes of the hurdler's forward placement of the CG in relation to the driving leg's point of support (forward body lean). This angular relationship over the period of the first 8 strides and the 8th stride (takeoff stride) in particular, will be examined in both conditions.

To achieve maximal acceleration, as much forward horizontal impulse should be striven for during the start. The facilitation of the horizontally applied sprint forces, acting linearly through the body's CG, is enhanced by the strong forward placement of the CG relative to its point of support. Wilt (1977), describes the degree of forward body lean as being proportional to acceleration.

A hurdler should therefore attempt to maintain a forward lean from the start to maximize acceleration, and yet by the 8th stride, consideration should be given to the level of the CG for an optimal path of trajectory across the hurdle. Consideration of the relationship between the degree and duration of forward body lean to the optimal CG height for hurdle takeoff for women has not been treated in literature. It is known that men must attain an upright position prematurely in their sprint approach, as the barrier height stands above the hurdler's CG.

It was hypothesized by Sipes (1976), that the female hurdler must come to an "erect" position sooner to negotiate the first hurdle, as opposed to her natural forward lean in a short sprint acceleration. However, the instituted demands of hurdle height in the women's event are minimal, and the female (dependent on stature), need make little adjustment in the path of her CG. As cited previously, a woman may even need to increase her forward lean to lower the path of the CG over the rail of the hurdle.

The previous use of cinematographic analysis in hurdling only incorporated male subjects, until a study instigated by Riddle (1969). Investigation at this time was prompted by the change of the international racing distance for women from the traditional 80m race, to the increase spacing, greater number of barriers, and higher hurdle height of the 100m race. She examined hurdle clearance and running between hurdles of two distinct ability groups.

However, she failed to consider any aspects of form in starting and acceleration to the first hurdle. Riddle indicated the takeoff angle of the CG, relative to the support leg in the sagittal plane, to be 60 to 65 degrees for the top performing group. Her definition and findings pertaining to the "better" hurdle group, however, exhibited several limitations which drew them towards much lower performance levels in study testing, than was their competitive norm. Therefore, interpolation of data as characteristic of better hurdlers (13.2 to 14.0 sec.) should be cautioned.

Four female hurdlers were used in the study, ranging in stature from 1.58m to 1.68m (5-2¼ to 5-6¼) in height. All the subjects had a minimum of one year specific hurdle training and event competition. Their athletic abilities ranged from one of international capacity, to that of junior national and provincial caliber.

The time of the film study (relative to their state of training) was conducted during the middle of the prepatory period for the winter (indoor) track and field season. Competitive results for indoor standards were attained within a one week period of the filming and used as a measure of current performance ability at the time of the study (Table 2).

These performance results indicated two subjects on standard with their outdoor performance level, and two subjects already potentially ahead of the past season's level as predicted by an extrapolation formula (50mH time + 0.2 sec.) + (part 1 time-1.0 sec.) = 100m hurdle time ± 0.2 sec.

TABLE 2

Subject Information/Performance Data

Subject	Height	Weight	Event Experience	1979 Best 100mH	100m	Ability at Testing 50mH	50m
1	5-2¼	113 lb	1 year	15.0	13.1	7.8 = 15.0	6.9
2	5-4¼	115 lb	3 years	13.2	11.8	7.0	6.4
3	5-6¼	141 lb	1 year	15.2	12.5	7.5 = 13.4	6.6
4	5-6¼	124 lb	1.5 years	15.1	12.7	7.6 = 14.6	6.7

IMPLICATION AND RECOMMENDATIONS

The female hurdler need make no (or only a slight) compromise between the forward lean and the position of her CG in the transition between that of a sprint acceleration and the first hurdle approach. This is influenced by the compatibly low height of the hurdle, relative to the female's rising CG by takeoff.

In the search for a means of utilizing an athlete's ability to accelerate to the first hurdle, this has significant implications. To be able to maximize the specific application of running forces horizontally (the direction of the finish line), the hurdler should accelerate from the start with a strong forward lean. It may be best not to concern oneself with rising to meet the hurdle, as there appears to be no need to differentiate between a sprint and hurdle acceleration for women, particularly the taller athletes (5-5+). If slight adjustments are required in the vertical level of the CG, they should be effected in the final 2 to 3 strides prior to takeoff. This detained transition will best exploit accelerating capacities until hurdle clearance necessitates change.

The angular relationship of the female's CG to the support leg of the 8th stride (forward lean) in sprinting need not alter in reference to the takeoff stride in hurdling. This is due to the sufficient vertical position for hurdle clearance attained in the sprint acceleration. The lower the hurdler can hold such a take-off angle, the more effective will be her ability to direct forces horizontally in rapid barrier clearance.

The larger percentage of female hurdlers will be and are subjected to compromise (increase) in their natural sprint stride length. It is known that the less compromise a hurdler is allowed to make, the more effective or greater will be her sprint speed (up to its natural ceiling). Research also implies that women of respective sprint ability and within a wide height range (5-4¼ to 5-7¾), need make little compromise in stride length.

Therefore, coaches carefully monitor the distance of hurdle take-off in respect to the problems evolved by an over-compromising stride length. Particularly for young and developing hurdlers, this implies a continual modification in approach distance and hurdle height. Such actions will encourage less compromise by promoting a correct gradual adaptation to stride length. It appears that the problem of an over-compromising stride length may stem from psychological and not physical barriers with women.□

REFERENCES

1. Corbett, Ken, Human Movement Center of Gravity Analysis, Computer Program, University of Western Ontario, April, 1977.
2. Dick, Frank, Biomechanics of High Hurdle Clearance, *Athletics Coach*, Vol. 17:3. 1979, pp. 3-5.
3. Ewen, Sandy, An Evaluation of the 1976 Olympic 100 meter Hurdles (Women), *USTCA Track & Field Quarterly Review*, Vol. 78:4, 1978, p. 6.
4. Mitchell, Les, Some Observations on the High Hurdles, *Track Technique*, No. 37, Sept., 1979, p. 1185.
5. Riddle, Patricia, Cinematographic Analysis of Women Hurdlers, M.S. Thesis, University of Illinois, 1969.
6. Salchenko, I., More Attention to Speed, *Yessis Review*, Vol. 10, No. 3, Sept., 1975.
7. Singh, Jagmohan, Forcast-Review of Women's 100 meter Hurdles, *Track Technique*, No. 38. Dec., 1969, p. 1221.
8. Singh, Jagmohan, The First Hurdle Attack, *Track Technique*, No. 41, Sept. 1970, p. 1316.
9. Sipes, Maurice, Hurdling Mechanics for the Female Athlete, *Track Technique*, No. 65, Sept., 1976, p. 2071.
10. Vaiksaar, Victor, Hurdling Technique, *Modern Athlete and Coach*, Vol. 17:3. 1979, pp. 3-5.
11. Wilt, Fred, *The Complete Canadian Runner-Theory and Training*, Canadian Track & Field Association Press, 1977, pp. 1-3.

FINAL STRIDES IN THE LONG JUMP

by Charles W. Armstrong, Ph.D., University of Toledo

Dr. Armstrong, of Toledo's Dept. of Exercise Science and P.E., has statistically analyzed the last two strides of national-class long jumpers to find the answer to several pertinent questions involving the ultimate and penultimate steps.

It is recognized that the approach in long jumping is a major factor influencing the distance of the jump. Particular importance has been attributed to the final strides of the approach immediately preceding take-off (Hay, 1980). While various authors have hypothesized what should occur during this phase, relatively little objective data exists. This study was conducted to provide data on several important aspects of this phase.

During the final phase of the approach, commonly termed the *gather* or *settle*, the jumper prepares himself for executing the movements involved in the take-off. This involves adjusting the body position so that the horizontal force produced by the approach can be directed at the desired take-off angle. Adjustment of body position permits the jumper to generate maximum force through the action of the arms and legs at take-off. Thus the final phase of the approach is instrumental in affecting two of the factors of primary importance to the actual distance jumped: take-off angle and take-off velocity.

To provide data about this phase of the jump, the trials and finals of the long jump competition in the 1979 NCAA outdoor championships were filmed. The camera was positioned to record a side view of the final two strides of the approach. The films were analyzed by computer-assisted digitization to produce accurate measurements of the length of each of the last two strides for every jump. The results were analyzed statistically to answer the following questions:

1. Do the final two strides differ from one another in length?

2. Does the last stride exceed the penultimate (next to the last) stride in length with greater frequency than when the penultimate exceeds the last in length?

Don Chadez

THE RATIO BETWEEN PENULTIMATE AND ULTIMATE STRIDES VARIES GREATLY FROM JUMPER TO JUMPER.

3. Does the relationship between these two strides relate to the distance jumped?

4. Does the variability of the relationship between the last two strides over repeated trials relate to the performance level of the competitor?

The mean of all last strides was compared to that of all penultimate strides. The results indicated that the two differed significantly, with the penultimate mean (2.434 meters) being longer than the last stride mean (2.194 meters).

The number of jumps in which the penultimate stride exceeded the last stride in length were compared with the number in which the last exceeded the penultimate in length. The results indicated that the greatest number of jumps were associated with a penultimate stride that was longer than the last stride. This was the case in ninety-two percent of the jumps.

To answer question 3, it was necessary to establish one value that would represent the relationship between the last two strides. This was done by forming a ratio, where the penultimate stride length was divided into the last stride length. This *"gather ratio"* was calculated for all jumps, and evidenced a range of 62.19 to 109.59 percent. The individual gather ratio scores were correlated to the related jump distances. The very low correlation ($R=+.24$) indicated that there did not appear to be a clear relationship between these two variables.

The variability of the gather ratio across all jumps was assessed to answer question 4. When the variability of the best jumpers was compared

to that of the worst, no difference was found. A summary of the data for each of the competitors is presented in Table 1.

It is quite clear from the data that the organization of the final two approach strides follows a consistent pattern, with the penultimate being greater in length than the last stride. This is consistent with data collected on similarly skilled jumpers by Popov, as reported by Hay (1980). Various authors have speculated as to why this occurs (Dyson, 1977; Hay, 1980; Tellez, 1979; Witt, 1975; Hempel and Klimmer, 1981).

Immediately prior to and during this phase the jumper's trunk is adjusted to a more upright position. Additionally, during the support phase of each of the last two strides knee flexion is increased, thus lowering the center of gravity. These two adjustments may interact to produce a lengthening of the penultimate and a shortening of the last stride. Conversely, these adjustments may be the result of such changes in stride length. Regardless, it is likely that the jump is influenced by what occurs during this phase.

One effect of alterations in stride length is a decrease in the forward tilt of the pelvis. This change would increase the tension on the hip flexors and knee extensors, thus facilitating contraction of these muscle groups. Given the importance attributed to these muscle groups in producing the forces necessary for jumping, such change would appear to enhance performance (Dick, 1974).

An additional benefit of the change in body position is that it may permit the jumper

TABLE 1
DATA SUMMARY
(MEANS)

COMPETITOR #	JUMP LENGTH	STRIDE LENGTH PENULTIMATE	STRIDE LENGTH LAST	PERCENTAGE LAST/PENULTIMATE
	(meters)	(meters)	(meters)	
496	7.952	2.379	2.099	88.30
516	7.927	2.332	2.215	94.97
220	7.815	2.284	2.285	95.60
864	7.747	2.249	2.204	91.20
27	7.680	2.379	2.242	94.48
256	7.678	2.664	1.967	73.86
611	7.660	2.455	2.119	86.33
68	7.658	2.431	2.277	93.91
512	7.594	2.858	2.154	76.15
176	7.510	2.596	2.423	93.44
800	7.495	2.235	2.439	109.19
660	7.438	2.535	2.328	90.94
772	7.320	2.171	1.996	91.99
700	7.000	2.510	1.971	78.61

to increase his take-off angle without a significant reduction in horizontal velocity. Normally, take-off angles in the long jump fall well below the theoretical optimum. Beyond the range of approximately twenty to twenty-two degrees, increases in take-off angle occur at the expense of take-off velocity. To increase the take-off angle, the jumper's center of gravity must be repositioned relative to the take-off foot, such that the distance between the two is increased. When this occurs as part of the take-off action in the last stride, horizontal velocity is sacrificed. When the penultimate stride is lengthened, however, the center of gravity is repositioned in a similar fashion. As this occurs prior to initiating the take-off action, it may be that optimum horizontal velocity is maintained.

One might have expected to find greater consistency in the gather ratio from trial to trial among the better jumpers. This did not appear to be the case. However, it does not seem to be due to a lack of consistency by the good jumpers, but rather a high degree of consistency among all of the jumpers. This may reflect an intuitive awareness on the part of the jumpers as to the importance of the last two strides. It may be that regardless of what accommodations are made in the strides preceding this final phase, the penultimate and the last stride always remain the same.

Based on these findings, it is premature to suggest anything conclusive about the final phase of the long jump approach. While the data certainly indicates important trends regarding the gather ratio, it would be improper to suggest that an absolute ratio exists, one that all jumpers should attempt to achieve. It is much more

likely that further study will reveal a range of acceptable ratios, dependent on the physical characteristics, technique, and skill level of the jumper. Coaches should not tamper with their jumpers' gather ratios, unless the variability from one jump to the next is great, or the ratio is excessively out of line with the range presented in this paper. In either case it would seem that the effects of such problems on performance would be severe enough to warrant serious attention from the coach. It should be recognized, however, that jumping is like any fundamental motor skill in that it is overlearned. That is, as a result of repeating the skill thousands of times, the motor pattern is quite firmly established. This makes it very resistant to change, which would complicate the task of altering an undesirable gather ratio.

It is clear that further information of this phase of long jumping technique is needed. Of particular value would be information about the variability in the magnitude and direction of the forces produced at the moment of take-off as a function of changes in the gather ratio.□

REFERENCES

Dick, F., "Biomechanics of the Long Jump," *Track and Field Quarterly Review,* Vol. 74 (2), June 1974.

Dyson, G., *The Mechanics of Athletics.* New York: Holmes & Meier Publishing, 1977.

Hay, J., *The Biomechanics of Sport Technique.* Englewood Cliffs, NJ: Prentice-Hall, Inc., 1980.

Hempel, K. and H. Klimmer, "Last Strides in the Long Jump Run-up" (abstract). In: *Track Technique,* Vol. 82, Winter 1981.

Tellez, T., "Tom Tellez on the Long Jump," *Track Technique,* Vol. 79, Spring 1980.

Witt, E., "Coaching the Long Jump," *Track and Field Quarterly,* Vol. 75 (2), Summer 1975.

ANALYSIS AND REVIEW OF THE POLE VAULT

by Kevin McGill, from H. Czingon and D. Kruber

McGill provides a handy technique checklist for analyzing various phases of the pole vault.

EXERCISE PHASE	EXERCISE CRITERION	# of jumping trials									
		1	2	3	4	5	6	7	8	9	10
APPROACH	Maximum pressure in approach										
	No upper body lean-back										
	Stride frequency increases until the pole plant										
	Relaxed carry of the pole										
	Employ a pole angle of about 70 degrees in the first step										
	Middle of the pole before the middle of the body (see from the front)										
	Continuously lower pole point										
	Both elbows close to the body										
PLANT	Stride frequency picks up										
	Complete hip, knee, and foot extension in last stride										
	Third final ground contact: left arm extended ahead (on left foot)										
	Second to last ground contact: right arm extends past the face										
	Last stride: perfect extension of right arm before the head, and above										
	Shoulder axis in the last stride parallel to the mat										
	No discernible loss of speed										
	No discernible upper body lean back										
TAKEOFF, SWING, AND LONG PENDULUM	Under arm fixed at 90 degrees in the elbow										
	Upper arm remains extended										
	Scissor action with takeoff leg and swing leg										
	Dynamic takeoff point vertically under the upper hand										
	Takeoff explosion straight ahead										
	Vigorous penetration with the chest into the pole										
	Push causes the pole to bend immediately										
	Natural head position										
	Swing leg in takeoff direction fixed for a short time										
	No pushing of hips and jump legs before the lower hand										

EXERCISE PHASE	EXERCISE CRITERION	# of jumping trials									
		1	2	3	4	5	6	7	8	9	10
ROLL UP TO L-POSITION	Steady acceleration of roll motion with increased pole bend Upper arm still long Under arm still fixed at over 90 degrees Natural head posture Jumping leg tries to get to swing leg Both knees achieve a strong bend Upper body parallel to the ground even with the bend of the pole										
SWING UP TO I-POSITION	Dynamic knee and hip extension Upper arm still stretched Bending of the arms under allowed here, as you bring the upper body to the pole Quarter turn about pole along body's axis Center of body (navel) next to pole Head kept in natural position										
PULL	Good coordination of pull-extension motion of both arms during the last phase of pole recoil Maintain the body pressure as long as the vaulter climbs										
CROSSBAR CLEARANCE	Body gets round Swing the arms together as the hip passes the bar Landing at least one meter from the box, and certainly not more than one meter from the center of the mat										

THE LONG JUMP, DEMONSTRATED BY CARL LEWIS

by Dorothy Doolittle, University of Houston

The author, Assistant Track Coach at Houston and herself a world-class marathoner a few years back, analyzes the long jump using Carl Lewis's 28-7¾ windy leap at the 1981 TAC Championships as her model.

THE APPROACH

The greatest determinator of distance in long jumping is horizontal velocity. Therefore, much time should be spent on sprinting mechanics and developing an accelerating pattern over the longest possible distance. Lewis's approach is twenty-one strides at a distance of 147-6. Lewis has an odd number of strides because he starts his approach with his left foot, but takes-off of his right foot. The length of his approach was designed around his running mechanics, ability to accelerate, strength, speed, and experience.

Empirical evidence indicates that the success of the entire approach, and the entire jump, will depend on the consistency of the first two or three strides in the approach run. At the beginning of the run, force is applied downward and backward to set the body in motion and gain more ground per stride. The strides are short in the beginning followed by longer strides as acceleration increases. Gradually, the body obtains an upright running position as maximum controlled acceleration is met at take-off. The last few strides of the approach is of a cadence to allow for an active take-off.

A coaches' check mark is placed four strides from take-off. The check mark for Lewis is about 32-6 from the take-off board. This check mark is vital in helping the coach evaluate the approach and determine where a mistake, if any, has been made.

PREPARATION FOR TAKE-OFF
(Next to last stride)

There should be no physical change in the jumper's sprinting position until the *penultimate stride*, the next to last stride (Fig. # 1, 2, 3, 4, 5). Due to the acceleration curve, the penultimate stride is the longest.

The penultimate stride is actually where the jumper "sets up" his take-off. By slightly flexing the ankle, knee and hip joints, and planting the foot flat with a minimum loss of horizontal velocity, the jumper adopts a more erect position. This causes the hips to lower. Therefore, as the jumper leaves the penultimate stride, the hips begin to rise and continue to rise throughout the take-off.

TAKE-OFF (Last stride, Figures 6-9)

The extensor muscles of the ankle, knee, and hip are tensed before impact. This impact force works briefly to stretch an already tensed muscle (stretch reflex) like an elastic band. The greatest degree of flexion at the knee for Lewis during the last stride appears to be about one-quarter (about 140°—see Figure #8).

It appears that the pattern of good long jumpers favors a shorter last stride, when compared to the penultimate stride. In a study by Haven and Smith at the National Sports Festival in 1978, out of eight jumpers, six jumpers' last stride ranged from 2.52 to .06 feet shorter, while two jumpers were .37 and .06 feet longer than the next to last stride. In Lewis's 28-7¾ jump, his penultimate stride is approximately 8.01 and his last stride seems to be 7.71. (It must be noted that the

measurements are taken from a panned film therefore, the measurements are approximate.) One should realize that the stride length of the last two strides is effected by results of the total run. If an acceleration pattern is smooth and consistent, the last stride will probably be very close to the same length as the penultimate stride. It should be noted that Lewis was over his check mark, which influenced the length of his last two strides.

Aided by an erect body position in the penultimate stride, the jumper places the take-off foot *flat* and ahead of his center of mass (occurs between figures #7 and #8). The foot placement is commonly thought to be "heel-ball-toe" because of the deceptive appearance in figure #7. However, a "heel-ball-toe" action will cause a jumper to spend too much time on the board, hindering horizontal velocity at take-off. The position of the body remains erect throughout the take-off. With the trunk upright, the forces act through the center of mass, thus creating a vertical velocity component. This is contrary to popular opinion of the line of force directed from the take-off foot through the trunk. Such a position at take-off would create too much forward rotation. (Figure #10).

The free leg—in Lewis's case, the left leg—is well flexed at the knee, so the thigh comes through quickly. It decelerates at take-off, along with the left arm The right arm decelerates on the backswing, simultaneously. This combination of actions aids in horizontal and vertical forces and lightens the load from the take-off foot. The applicable principle is that deceleration of any body segment produces a force in the direction of acceleration before the segment is decelerated. *This is not a coaching point, but a natural result of running off the board.* Note that the lower free leg does not pass the thigh before lift-off. (Figures #10 and #11.)

When the take-off foot contacts the board, the rest of the body pivots over and past the foot as the support phase of take-off occurs. The tendency for forward rotation becomes evident. Once the jumper is in the air, nothing will change the parabolic path of the center of mass. Technique in the air aids the jumper's balance in the air and prepares him for an effective landing.

The hitch-kick method can absorb and even counteract forward rotation to a small degree. By cycling the legs when airborne, the athlete creates a secondary axis of rotation. When the leg is moving in a backward direction of the cycle, the knee should straighten (Figure #11-14). The difference of the moments of inertia of the legs in this action results in the lower body moving forward and the trunk rotating backward (Figures #15-22). The movement of the arms produce another secondary axis which also aids in the backward rotation of the trunk (Figures #15-22).

Delaying the extension of the legs as long as possible inhibits forward rotation. Therefore, Lewis continues his cycling legs and arms to complete a double hitch-kick.

Landing efficiency is increased when the distance between the heels and center of mass is extended as far as possible. A common misconception among coaches and jumpers is that failure to get their feet up high enough upon landing is a sign of weakness in the abdominals. Actually, it is a result of forward rotation. By bringing both arms forward then back (Figures #23-27), an equal and opposite reaction of the legs occurs. Thus, the landing point of the heels is extended.

It should be remembered that good technique in the air automatically follows a well executed take-off. They are interrelated. Once the athlete is in the air, his aim is to prepare for an optimal landing position, primarily by counteracting forward rotation. Correct flight in the air and a good landing is totally influenced by the approach and take-off. □

A RUSSIAN APPROACH TO WEIGHT TRAINING

by Toni Tenisci and Rolf Ubel, Washington State University

A synthesis from Dr. W.W. Kuznyetsov's published volume on weight training in athletic preparation.

MUSCLE STRENGTH & DEVELOPMENT OF THE MOVEMENT FUNCTIONS

Muscle strength is related to the physiological diameter of the muscle. This muscle strength may be regarded as *POWER*. Power can be measured in 2 ways:

Absolute Power: Here the measurement of power is done purely on the weight lifted for one maximum repetition regardless of body weight and muscle diameter.

Relative Power: Here the measurement of power is done by the weight lifted (1 max repetition) with regard to the diameter of muscle in proportion to the body weight.

Two ways of developing muscle strength or power:

Relative strength (power) done by activating maximum muscle fibers with a maximum muscle tension in each contraction. Through a maximum effort, a complete synchronization of the muscle occurs—therefore the muscle develops coordination. The maximum loading helps develop the white fibers of the muscle tissue, which are the strength fibers of the tissue.

Absolute strength (power) is developed through increased repetitions. The increased repetitions break down the white fibers of the muscle tissue, which are the strength fibers of the tissue. The increase in anaerobic work leads to greater white fiber breakdown, therefore increasing the muscle mass development.

The development of relative power therefore does not mean the muscle mass will develop in size, whereas, the development of absolute power requires the breakdown and building up of muscle mass.

TWO WAYS OF TRAINING

Maximum loading to a 1 repetition max load.

Repetitions with weight done to the point of muscle exhaustion. Each preparation is chosen for the specific sport the athlete is doing and the time variable needed for that sport performance.

The maximum loading preparation should be done for an athlete who is not on a high level of preparation and who needs to be developed (brought up) at a quick rate. There are benefits and problems associated with this development.

Benefits:

Power is increased *quickly*.

Good *coordination* is developed in the muscle groups used.

Problems:

There can occur a *quick loss of strength* if an injury occurs and/or if *time is spent away* from the weight work done. The base foundation of strength is not laid down firmly and can be lost quickly.

The increase in power is significant, but *plateauing occurs* frequently and lasts longer.

It is recommended that *weight athletes* should work on *absolute strength*, rather than on relative strength. It is cautioned that the increase of repetitions done in absolute strength work not be over-done, because of the decrease in muscle coordination that occurs as fatigue sets in. As fatigue builds up in the assisting muscle groups, a process which occurs faster than in the main muscle groups, there is a decrease in loading occurring on the main muscle groups used. It is recommended that the repetitions chosen for each exercise allow for *proper concentration* of the *fine, smaller, assisting muscle groups that aid the main groups.* The assisting groups therefore, should not be allowed to fatigue excessively in any exercise. The key factor to remember is not to neglect the coordination factor and still maintain repetition for strength.

Absolute strength for a weight athlete means increase in power, more than their relative strength, where absolute strength improvement becomes the most significant factor (as well as personal weight increase). Relative strength may increase for an athlete, but the absolute strength may not.

Gymnast body weight 70 kg.

absolute increase of strength:
70 kg.

relative increase of strength:

$\frac{140}{70}$ = 2 kg/kg body weight

$\frac{210}{70}$ = 3 kg/kg body weight

Throwers body weight 100 kg.

absolute increase of strength:
70 kg.

relative increase of strength:

$\frac{200}{70}$ = 2 kg/kg body weight

$\frac{270}{100}$ = 2.7 kg/kg body weight

i.e., Strength increased by lifting maximum weight single time.

Although both athletes improved their strength by 70 kg., the gymnast improved better in relative strength because this refers to his body weight. But in throwing events we have to look for the absolute strength because this is the force we can utilize to accelerate the implement.

WEIGHT TRAINING

Average training (common):
— The goal is the development and conservation of the whole body. *Body conditioning*

Multiple and directed training:
— Special aims but ones which are away from the specific goal. The aim is to train *the main and assisting muscle groups*, but in a form different to the actual, specific event.

Specific Training:
— Specialized and specific *exercises that are unique to the event.*

An Example:
Weight-ball throwing or weight javelins. A certain weight cannot be chosen for all athletes to throw. Each athlete must be considered with the following criteria.
    a. speed of muscle contraction
    b. power of muscle contraction
    c. special characteristics (the visual performances)
    d. the time characteristic of when these adapted implements may be used to enhance the throwers performance—age, maturity, level of performance, physiological background.

Two individuals were tested. The first two tests used only the speed and power criteria, where the second two tests used only the spacial and time criteria. Each test was with different weighted implements. Noting these results, it was concluded that each individual must have their own level evaluated before using adapted weights. It is recommended in the javelin, therefore, that the weight of the adapted javelin be no lower than 1.4 kilos to a top weight of 2.2 kilos/no lower than 600 gms (also including 650-700 gms wt). *A point to note:* Increase and/or decrease of weight used can cause serious damage to the technique and development of the athlete, and the choice of weight must be carefully planned and observed before used in the athlete's development.

DYNAMIC POWER

Explosive power—maximum acceleration.
Fast power—less acceleration than maximum, but fast.
Slow power—acceleration is zero, which is slow movement. A constant speed is held, but no acceleration.

Explosive Power: The amount of strength that an athlete has on release of the implement is related to the level of explosive power the athlete has.
Explosive power can be measured by:
    a. EEG
    b. Alpha and gamma rays produced by the activity. Alpha rays must stay at special frequency. When frequency drops, adjustments in the technique occur which indicate too little or too much weight compared with the competition weight (this alpha wave indicator can give a coach a better idea if a higher or lower weight should be used by the athlete).
    Exercises for the testing of explosive power for leg strength:
    a. squats—1 repetition
    b. jump and reach
    c. standing long jump, standing position
    d. triple jump, standing position
    A pre-testing is done to calculate the top performance of each athlete. Training of these exercises for explosive power should be done at the amount of repetitions that the top performance can be achieved. *Once the top performance drops, the exercise should not be continued.*

280-300 jumps in a six week period were done on exercises b, c, d leg exercises, therefore only *quality performance* and *high level of work* is done by the athlete.

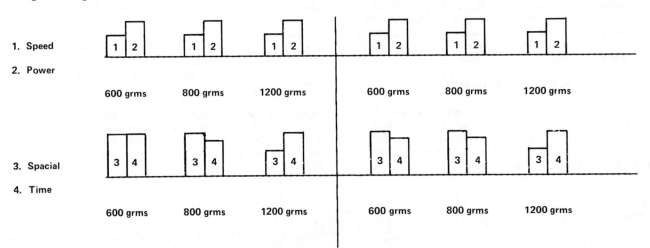

THE DYNAMICS OF THE AVERAGE, DIRECTED AND SPECIFIC TRAINING OF ATHLETES

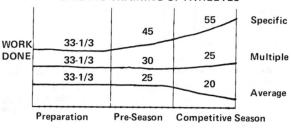

			55	Specific
WORK	33-1/3	45		
DONE	33-1/3	30	25	Multiple
	33-1/3	25	20	
				Average

Preparation	Pre-Season	Competitive Season

Average athlete	Upper class athlete	TIME	International athlete

Athletic Strength Development—Two methods may be chosen by the coach in the development of the strength level of the athlete:

Maximum loading—one repetition for maximum weight.

Muscular exhaustion—

a. One exercise done till exhaustion. The exhaustion occurs through continuous repetitions, not in the amount of sets done. This exhaustion approach should be done at a moderate five to six sets overall.

b. Moderate weight chosen for high sets. Exhaustion does not occur through singular reps, but through lengthy sets; i.e., 12-15 sets.

c. A combination of (a) and (b) where max *reps.* and max *sets* and high *weight* is used. The athlete works at reps until they are exhausted. No set number of reps, only until exhaustion. (The athlete governs the level of work done, because the exhaustion level is individual to each athlete.)

d. Explosive power—An athlete should be fully prepared and conditioned before beginning a program for explosive power.

For explosive power development with athletes in the throws and jumps, a weight should be used that is 80-90% maximum/three-four reps should be repeated until exhaustion. For athletes in the sprints, decathlon and middle distance, a 70-80% maximum weight, with a 5-8 repetition till exhaustion is recommended.

What type of approach in training should be chosen by the coach for his/her athlete:

First, the *level of the athlete* must be defined.

a. Average level

b. Upper class level

c. International level

Second, choose exercises that *best help suit the development* the athlete is at, as well as *the event* the athlete does.

An example: (Refer to chart diagram).

1. International Athlete

55% — *Specificity* of training to the event

Training — Throwing and related drills that do not change the actual technique used in the event.

25% — *Multiple* activities

— these activities work on the major muscle groups. Heavy weight throwing is a part of these activities.

a. Olympic Power lifting—squats, cleans and snatch, etc.

20% — *Average* (level of) activities

a. 10% minor and supportive muscle groups

b. 10% conditioning, running and jumping

Upper Class Athlete—Training percentiles:

45% — Specificity of training

30% — Multiple activities

25% — Average activities

Average Class Athlete—Training percentiles:

33-1/3% — Specificity of training

33-1/3% — Multiple activities

33-1/3% — Average activities

These percentages are only an approximation of the training percentiles for each level of athlete. A coach should continually evaluate the percentage emphasis chosen for their athletes and observe whether those percentages are being effective towards that athlete's development. Continual process of evaluation is necessary for development.

Planning and continual evaluation of the set plan is the most important point in developing the athletes potential. The discovery of the weak points and improving them is the main emphasis of the coach. There is no need to continually repeat or work on points that are already good. *Planning can increase the work level of an athlete up to five-six times if carefully done.*

TWO WAYS OF PLANNING EXERCISE FLOW AND/OR STRUCTURE:

a. A singular exercise, done one exercise at a time.

b. Circuit style exercises, where two or more exercises are done.

Within these two structures, the main training points may be implemented for strength training.

a. Maximum loading—one rep for max.

b. Increase reps, five sets done till exhaustion.

d. A combination of high reps, high sets and high weight till exhaustion.

Two ways of developing the different needs of specific events. Every event needs the following characteristics:

a. Correct technique

b. Explosive power

c. Agility

d. Speed

e. Coordination

f. Summation of movements

The first way to develop these needs are: *Whole-Part-Whole method* of training.

— the whole-part-whole method is not applicable all of the time.

Holistic Training Method

Specific training must meet the requirements of the technique, therefore the whole-part-whole method does not meet these requirements because by separating sections of the technique away from the whole, these requirements do not develop exactly as the technique requires. The holistic method is more closely aligned to the totality of the specific events and the specific requirements needed can be correctly developed.

But — There are variables within the holistic approach.

a. Individual needs required by the athlete.

b. A whole-part-whole method must be used at sometime. Here is a crucial point for coaching, in that, once an exercise is chosen to help develop the technique in a whole-part-whole manner, then that exercise must not interrupt the holistic foundations too much. There is a trade off that occurs here; i.e., increased weight can cause a decrease in neural-muscular sensitivity to the specific event, but increased strength occurs. The coach must therefore know how much weight to use and how long to proceed along with that exercise and still keep the holistic feeling intact.

Whole-part-whole is a valid training method for technique, but not for the specific development and the overall needs of the technique. Speed, explosiveness, co-ordination, etc. are altered by having them adjusted into a technique that does not represent the full technical execution. Imitating a section of the technique does not improve the demands of the technique because different power is used, and the muscles are used in a less specific manner, as well.

The holistic method should be used as much as possible in the consideration of improving the specific technique. The neuro-muscular pattern must be trained as specifically and as closely to the technique as possible in order to get the best training effects.

A coach must be able to analyze the event and determine the: 1. Speed required. 2. Strength required. 3. Explosive power required. 4. How accurate the technique is for the event (i.e., gymnastics has basic fundamental techniques which provide optimum performance, where throwing may have ten technical variations to provide the same distance). Once these points are analyzed for their importance, the coach must then construct the best suited program to develop them properly.

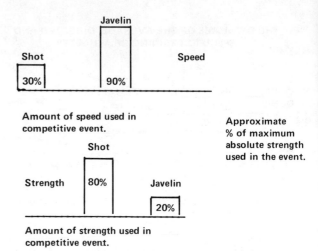

Amount of speed used in competitive event.

Approximate % of maximum absolute strength used in the event.

Amount of strength used in competitive event.

The shot put has an 80% maximum strength and a 30% speed requirement, whereas javelin throw has a 20% maximum strength and 90% speed requirement. These percentages would suggest that an increase in strength will help improve the shot put because an increase in strength adapts well to the needs of the technique. The short confinement of the technique and the weight of the object held close to the power source, would require more strength over speed.

The javelin throw, on the other hand, allows the athlete to apply only 20% of their maximum strength, therefore suggesting an increase in strength would not always increase performance because only so much strength can be utilized in the technique. Increased speed (90% requirement) plus technical work is more advantageous than increased power for the overall execution of the javelin throw. □

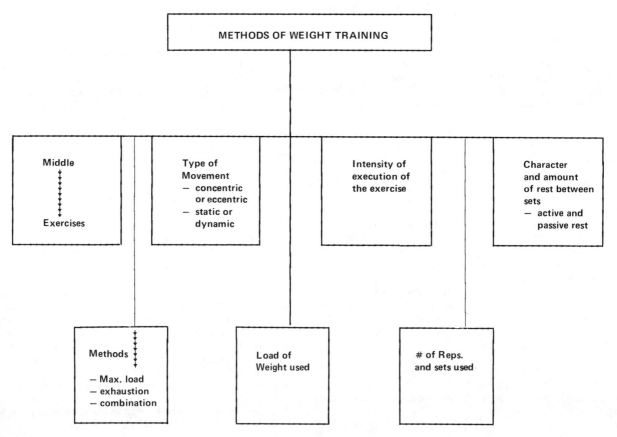

OVERVIEW OF COE'S NON-TRACK TRAINING

by George Gandy, Lecturer in Physical Education, Loughborough University.

George Gandy, coach at England's Loughborough University and training advisor to Sebastian Coe, offers a detailed overview of Coe's non-track training. Originally appeared in the British publication Running *(No. 1 July/August 1980).*

How can one can achieve incredible success in the ferociously competitive world of top international athletics? What qualities make it possible? How are they developed?

When Sebastian Coe first came to Loughborough University at the age of 18, he was already a successful runner. Under the sole guidance of his father, Peter, he had won a European Junior Bronze medal at 1500M, recording 3:45.2. His 800M best, though, was only 1:53.8. His natural advantages—suitable shape, exceptionally long legs and mobile hip joints—had been developed to a marked degree in cross-country running and hill work in his home town of Sheffield. He moved like a gazelle.

But don't assume, just because he's now the best in the world, that his background and attributes were all ideal. When I first met him and joined the father-son team as training advisor, I became aware of several deficiencies in his frame (now 5-9¾/119). His arms and shoulders were very thin and lacked strength. His abdominal and back muscles were also weak and, most important of all, he lacked power in the main locomotor groups—the quadriceps and the gluteals. The length of his running stride already approached 6½ft but it tended to decrease noticeably as he tired, and his leg cadence was not impressive. Furthermore, an imbalance between upper and lower-body development and function was evidenced by excessive contrarotation of the arms.

These deficiencies have been eliminated or reduced during the recent years by a carefully-planned program of exercise routines, some of which are further on. This was Seb Coe's "secret training" in the sense that it took place far from the gaze of the media and the attention of the crowds: it took place indoors and well away from the track. At the same time he was undertaking a reasonable volume of low-intensity running—starting in 1975 at 35 miles per week and building up to 70+ miles per week in the past two winters—plus sprint drills and repetition runs on hills, road and track. But he carried out the indoor exercise routines - the non-running conditioners so many runners ignore - relentlessly.

To compete at world level today, a runner must possess suitable natural endowments as reasonable cardio-respiratory and cardio-vascular systems and muscular coordination; highly developed physical attributes in the three S's"—stamina, suppleness and strength; and an appropriate level of fitness. Only then can fringe qualities such as determination, tactical awareness and the right mental atittude be of any benefit.

Putting it another way, a potentially world-class runner needs the strength to produce sufficient force in the propulsive muscles and to tolerate the stresses created with the help of equally strong non-propulsive muscles. There must be a range of movement in the appropriate joints and planes of actions so as best to apply these forces, and enough stamina to allow the process to be repeated over a period of time at the required rate.

Encouraging the development of these qualities is the main job of the out of season training program. Both coach and runner must choose and balance the types of training necessary to produce the desired effects. In the last analysis, there is no substitute for quality running but I think that a gradually progressive running program is likely to be more effective if combined with appropriate conditioning and development work. Such a combination is the key to Sebastian Coe's success.

EXERCISES WITH WEIGHTS

Weight training is the best training method for controlling levels of resistance, allowing isolation of specific muscle groups and promoting effective standardization of movements. As such, it can be of tremendous value in building a level of strength with which to ensure that the dynamic activities of the gymnasium and track - to which it ultimately gives way - are safer and more productive.

All exercise programs are viewed as a long term commitment with long-term objectives. This is particularly so in exercising with weights. The ultimate aim is maximum strength gain in the major propulsive muscle groups - the quadriceps on the front of the thighs and the gluteals at the rear - and good all-round development of other body parts. In the end this demands use of very heavy weights and with the number of repetitions at a premium. However, for safety and full benefit, the high quality lifting must be built upon a background of many repetitions over a long period at lower loadings.

The exercise with weights employed at Loughborough over the last few years by Seb Coe and other successful athletes have emphasized full front squats and cleans (for propulsive strength); split squats (for range and strength endurance in the legs); bench press and bicep curls (for upper body strength) and short range sit ups and over grasp pull ups (for trunk stability and postural control).

I believe front full squats to have been particularly beneficial in the development of my athletes. This is contrary to some medical opinion, but in some 6000+ injury free person-sessions are strong arguments on my side. I am not suggesting that this exercise is safe, per se but I am confident in my own ability to make use of it without inducing injury. Full squats make it easier to achieve overload, as the back and trunk of the average runner are not usually capable of safely supporting the necessary weights for overload in half-squatting. Full range movements also appear to be better from the point of view of maintaining range of movements.

A front hold in this exercise assists in more nearly permitting isolation of the quadriceps and in allowing the weight to be dropped the instant the athlete senses trouble. Thus front squats are a better and safer exercise for the quadriceps than back squats.

Nothing else about the weight exercises are particularly noteworthy. It is worth noting, though, that we have moved towards a short range movement in sit ups as we believe a decrease in mobility in the stomach muscles in conjunction with strength increase to be desirable both for posture and ultimately, for running technique.

These exercises are performed twice weekly each year from September/October to March/April. In the first couple of years, my main concern is always the establishment of good technique, although there is invariably some progress in weights used. More recently, pre-Christmas workouts have given way to maintenance of upper body strength (2 sets of 6), with rapidly increasing emphasis on legs and stomach (more sets, fewer reps and progressively demanding weights. Since 1977 both Sebastian Coe and international 400 sprinter Steve Scott have increased their tolerance of weight in front squats by over 100%: from 85 lbs to 175 lbs in Seb's case and from 120 lbs to 245 lbs for Steve. This has provided a very good foundation for other more dynamic aspects of training.

EXERCISE ROUTINES FOR ALL RUNNERS

Long mileage and high quality repetition work on the track are often insufficient for a runner looking to realize his full potential. To use the popular motor car analogy: given a model with defective steering, poor suspension and worn tires, few would risk driving it for thousands of miles or merely concentrate on super tuning its engine. Why then do so many runners treat their inadequate vehicles (their own bodies) in just this way? Exercises other than running alone should be used to remedy physical deficiencies.

Exercises with weights do require expert guidance and supervision if they are to be fully effective but the other routines could be performed by virtually anyone with no control other than personal common sense. *Stretching exercises are, in my view, an absolute must.*

The number, duration and regularity of repetitions will depend very much on personal condition, objectives and time available; the whole program must be regarded very much as a long-term investment. I cannot be too specific in my recommendations, but you should initially err on the side of doing too little and being too gentle. But do it regularly and be persistent. It is not where you start that matters, it is where you finish.

Sebastian Coe, his father and I believe in the extreme importance of 'background training' as a foundation for running at all levels. There is probably nothing in our routines which could not be obtained in some other way, but the exercise routines described here have been a convenient and effective conditioning method for us and could be of value to any runner if programmed carefully and appropriately. Every runner has different problems, different strengths and different weaknesses. But common to all runners is the fact that improvement will only come by looking up from the mileage chart and doing more than just running.

GYMNASIUM EXERCISES

The exercises described here are the sort which played an important part in his early winter build up for the Moscow Olympics. The weekly gymnasium training sessions are rarely the same for 2 weeks in succession. Progression in quantity and/or quality is built in and exercises are modified to ensure improvement in specific areas.

After a warmup jog, athletes do one continuous lap of the circuit with work on each acitivity restricted to a few repetitions (max. of 10, less in some cases) and only one rope climb. After this comes 15 minutes of personal stretching under direct instruction, before we embark on two complete laps of the exercise circuit, spending 30 seconds on each exercise and aiming for good quality and continuity. Fifteen seconds are allowed between stations and a 10 minute pause for further stretching occurs after one full lap.

Although only a part of the total picture, Seb's circuit training program has developed to conform with alterations in his physical makeup and aspirations. The session shown here includes, for example, more leg work and fewer general exercises than those of two or three years ago. It is more fragmented, thereby allowing a greater volume of good quality work than even a year ago.

Exercise 1,2 and 3 assist the development of biceps, triceps and muscles of the chest and upper back. Although not of primary importance for running, they are included because of Seb's commitment to the removal of all deficiencies and the achievmeent of top all-round body condition. Exercises 4 - 9 concentrate on the propulsive muscles of the legs (especially the quads and gluteals). They contribute to speed and power on the track.

EXERCISE 1. ROPE CLIMB—Using a 15' rope, some athletes manage with the arms only, Seb, although a competent rope climber, prefers to grip with his feet as well.

EXERCISE 2. INCLINE PRESS UPS—Make sure your feet are supported at a point above shoulder height then lower your chest to the floor and push up.

EXERCISE 3. DIPS—It is important to go down far enough to break the plane of elbows, below right angle level.

EXERCISE 4. BURPEES—Starting with a squat thrust movement, Seb continues by leaping upwards in start jump style, extending as far as possible. Then he reverses the process back to the starting position.

EXERCISE 5. DEPTH JUMPS—A barrier course which Seb negotiates double footed for stability (others opt for single foot takeoff but lower heights). After the third box he sprints back to begin again.

EXERCISE 6. BEAM JUMPS—From balancing with his hands on the beam, Seb drops to the ground without releasing the beam and attempts to immediately bounce back to starting position. Main aim to promote maximum leg drive.

EXERCISE 7. LOW THRUSTS—Mimicking a sprint start, drive horizontally forward off the front foot to cover as much ground as possible before landing again in the start position with the legs reversed. Very good for the gluteals and a strong horizontal drive.

EXERCISE 8. STEP - UPS—Any stable surface about 18" off the ground will do for this exercise. Seb repeatedly drives with a straight leg from the floor, dropping back onto the opposite leg.

EXERCISE 9. REVERSE SPLITS—A strengthener of the upper leg. Start with the front leg at right angles and the rear as far back as possible, then reverse their positions rapidly.

EXERCISE 10. LEG RAISES—Hanging from the wall bars, Seb repeatedly raises and lowers both legs. It is important to reach at least a horizontal position. Sit ups on the floor exercise the same abdominal muscles.

EXERCISE 11. BOUNDING—The closest Seb comes in the gym to ordinary running—but in an exaggerated form. Used to assist in the development of strength, resilience and coordination.

STRETCHING EXERCISES

Unfortunately, life's natural processes seem to set strength gains against mobility losses. Crash programs for strength may therefore accentuate a decrease in the range of movements you are capable of. This can be so detrimental to a runner as to negate completely progress in other aspects of fitness. Lack of mobility may also predispose an athlete to injury.

Sebastian Coe's program of stretching exercises has included work on all main joints. The emphasis, however, has been on ankle flexion and extension, hamstring extensibility, hip extension and low back mobility. The locations most relevant for a runner.

All routines involve static positions with a feeling of slight stretch - discomfort beyond a minimal level is considered counterproductive. Generally each position is held for 30 seconds at a time, or, with progressive decreases in joint angle, for three consecutive periods of 6 to 10 seconds. The exercises are advised for at least one hour every day.

Once or twice per week, for 20 minutes or so, partner-assisted stretching is carried out. This is mainly aimed at improving the flexibility of the hamstrings on the back of the thighs.

EXERCISE 1. LOWER BACK STRETCHING—Lie flat on stomach with feet outstretched. Space hands apart and push trunk upwards to maximum range maintaining contact with hips to floor.

EXERCISE 2. GASTROCNEMIUS STRETCHING—Body in a split position, rear leg stretched to maximum with heel on ground, front leg flexed in like position. Lean against upright and bend trunk to upright. Change legs.

EXERCISE 3. SOLEUS STRETCHING—Body in semi split position. Back leg relaxed. Front heel on ground. Lean against upright. Lower body to upright maintaining front heel on ground.

EXERCISE 4. HAMSTRING STRETCHING—Body in sitting position on floor. Reach forward to grasp ankles, pull torso towards feet maintaining locked knees.

EXERCISE 5. ASSISTED HIP EXTENSION—Lie flat on stomach with chest flat on floor. Raise one leg for coach to support at about 70° angle. Coach pressure is static, athlete forces down against coach's hold. □

COMPARISON OF WATER JUMP STYLES

by John Gartland and Phil Henson, Indiana University

The authors kinematically studied the conventional method of clearing the water barrier—by landing on top of the barrier and pushing off—used by Bill Lundberg with the unconventional approach of 1980 NCAA Champion Randy Jackson, who hurdles the barrier completely and lands directly in the water.

The two steeplechasers were filmed at the USOC National Sports Festival. The meet was held at 7,200 feet altitude, which affected the times in the distance events, but this did not affect the technique employed or relative performances. Despite running about 40 seconds slower than their best times, Jackson and Lundberg finished first and second. Their times were 9:01.3 and 9:04.0, respectively.

This study analyzed and compared the two subjects in three areas: (1) Time, (2) Velocity, and (3) Center of gravity.

TIME

Naked eye observation of Jackson in the steeplechase competitions has lead many coaches to believe he gains on his competitors in the water jump. The results of comparing the two subjects seem to confirm these observations.

Jackson was faster through the water jump on five of the six water jumps compared. Jackson's mean time through the water jump was 1.23 seconds while Lundberg's mean time was 1.37. Carrying out the mean times over all seven water jumps showed that Jackson gained .98 seconds during the race. This would appear to be a very significant gain since Jackson won the race by only 2.7 seconds.

Lundberg only surpassed Jackson on the second water jump (the first one compared). This may be due to the fact that Jackson appeared to need more room to utilize his style. At the beginning of the race, Jackson was surrounded by other runners. He may have had difficulty in not wanting to land on someone early in the race when there was congestion.

Lundberg became progressively slower in the water jump throughout the race. This was

RANDY JACKSON IS UNIQUE AMONG TOP-LEVEL STEEPLECHASERS IN TERMS OF WATER JUMP TECHNIQUE, AS HE HURDLES THE BARRIER DIRECTLY.

true, despite the fact that he was still improving his position in the race. Jackson, on the other hand leveled off and remained almost exactly the same throughout the race. It appeared that Jackson's style, at least in this race, was much faster at the point in the race where fatigue had affected all the runners. Lundberg may have been adversely affected by the altitude of the race site, and this may be why he slowed towards the end of the race.

Jackson's style seemed very effective in this race when he was out ahead or by himself as he approached the barrier. However, when he was in a group he did not come through the water jump as fast. Difficulty in crowds could be a limiting factor in the hurdle style technique.

Time Through Each Water Jump*

Water Jump	RJ	BL
1	NT	NT
2	1.29	1.27
3	1.17	1.23
4	1.20	1.31
5	1.20	1.39
6	1.20	1.42
7	1.33	1.58
X	1.23	1.37

*Time determined from the point where the subject's knees are together before take off until the torso breaks the plane at the right edge of the film.

VELOCITY

Comparing the velocities of the two runners, the hurdle style does not have the advantage it did in the time comparison. Jackson's velocity appeared to be faster off the ground at take-off throughout the jump until he landed in the water. As Jackson landed in the water, his body absorbed the shock of the landing and his velocity was lowered greatly. Lundberg, on the other hand, had much less velocity at take-off and on top of the barrier. However, Lundberg, probably because of the push off the barrier, had more velocity than Jackson coming out of the water.

The key point is whether Jackson lost velocity out of the water. If he lost velocity at this point and Lundberg gained velocity, this study should be replicated so that each runner is timed to a point two strides out of the water. This type of study may more clearly show which runner is actually getting through the water more quickly. By measuring to a point two strides after clearing the water it can be determined whether Jackson is losing velocity or not.

Jackson's range of velocities were from 6.33 feet per second to 9.75, or a difference of 3.24 fps. Lundberg, on the other hand, had a range of 6.23 to 7.67 or a difference of 1.44 fps. Jackson's large difference in velocity may mean he is using more energy because of slowing and speeding up. Energy cost was not a subject of this study, but it would seem to have some affect on Jackson's style.

CENTER OF GRAVITY

The curves formed by plotting the centers of gravity of both subjects were virtually the same. Jackson's curve, as would be expected began lower and stayed lower than Lundberg's throughout the curve. Jackson's center of gravity stayed lower because he did not have the period of support that Lundberg had on top of the barrier. Jackson did land lower in the water, as evidenced by his lower center of gravity.

It is interesting to note that Lundberg's center of gravity lowered on top of the barrier for a brief time. This is the point where the steeplechaser bends his knee to let the weight of his body roll over his foot. This maneuver was very evident in Lundberg's center of gravity curve.

Jackson's center of gravity reached a high point of 5.25 feet and a low point of 3.59 for a difference of 1.66 feet. Lundberg's extremes were 5.44 and 3.71 for a difference of 1.73 feet.

It is difficult to determine whether Jackson had an advantage by keeping his center of gravity lower throughout. The fact that Lundberg's center of gravity is almost identical would seem to show that neither runner gained by their center-of-gravity position.

SUMMARY AND CONCLUSIONS

From this limited, descriptive study it is difficult to conclusively declare that one water barrier clearance technique is superior to the other. In each of the areas studied—time, velocity, and center of gravity—both styles seemed to have some advantages and some disadvantages. It is very clear that more research is needed to determine the efficiency of the hurdle style water barrier water clearance.

The following conclusions were drawn from an evaluation of the results of the present investigation:

1. The hurdle style water jump clearance technique appears to be faster when compared strictly on a time basis with the conventional style, using subjects Jackson and Lundberg.

2. The conventional style water jump clearance technique appears to be more efficient based on its more constant velocity throughout the entire clearance.

3. The conventional style water jump clearance technique appears to be more efficient because the runner lands in a shallower part of the water and therefore does not have as much of a center of gravity lowering. □

EUROPEAN APPROACH TO THE HIGH JUMP

by Pat Reid, Canada

The author—one of Canada's foremost jump coaches—spent much time in Europe studying the latest approaches to high jump training. All aspects of the different European systems are covered, with emphasis on points which can be incorporated into North American training programs.

DIFFERENCES BETWEEN EUROPEAN AND U.S. TRAINING METHODS

The main difference is the **Schedule and Seasonal Goals/Objectives** and **Total Flexibility** in carrying out the program. The schedule is planned out starting with the **Main Focus** which is the Olympic Games, World Cup or European Championship Meet. Working **backwards**, the program is built up depending on the **Strength** base, the **Speed** base, the **Technique** base, the **Post-Injury** status and the level of overall ability. (Europeans plan on 4, 6 or 8 year cycles and annual increments are sought—but not total success in one year to the point of injury or exhaustion; i.e., Seb Coe turns down races and money if the plan gets too intensive. That's flexibility.)

Europeans test (with field tests) the athlete's level of development. Records are kept, training is monitored. So when the new year is on the horizon, the *coach*, and in later discussion with the athlete, maps out the year. The coach knows from experience what it takes to reach certain performance objectives. These are the keys to success.

In the U.S., by contrast, the schedule is very traditional and consists of too many compulsory events. There is really no assessment comparing the *strength*, *speed*, *technique*, etc. bases left over from the previous year to plan the next (other than straight performance against the watch, how high you can jump, etc.). Consequently, the plan becomes subjective and is fraught with potential hazards (i.e., over-achieving, under-achieving, etc.) This approach, over time, will allow a certain number of intuitive, "instinctive" coaches to develop a winning program—but not everyone does, and it's tough to copy.

The objective in the U.S. scene is to win every time out (duals, tri's, state finals, NCAA, AIAW, conferences). The #1's are on the team record win-loss and not the **individual** athletes' rank. This makes it virtually impossible for the athlete and coach to plan *peaking* or to work on areas of weakness or even experiment with changing techniques or technical points. The athlete as an individual is sacrificed for the *team.* The Europeans have a concept of dual-jump meets, or tri-sprint meets, not full team duals all of the time. This helps enhance development of the individual events.

THE MAJOR EMPHASIS IN WEIGHT TRAINING

In West Germany, we trained with Dragan Tancic, the national jumps coach and Mogenburg, Thranhardt, Schneider, Nagel, Meyfarth, Holzapfel, and the throwers under national coach Christian Gehrmann. Gehrmann did not allow weight belts in the weight room. This led to an analysis of approaches to strength/weight training. They use weights for specific strengthening of weak areas, but more so for *total* body toughening. Rather than strictly emphasizing leg strength in jumpers for instance, equal amounts of time are spent on lateral (trunk) pelvic girdle strength, low back strength and strength in the positions the athlete is in when performing the event. They use free weights and assume ranges of motion that are event-specific; i.e., high jumpers do toe raises with a weight plate under one arm and on the take-off foot, with the other leg bent at the knee similar to a take-off position **(Fig. 1).** The

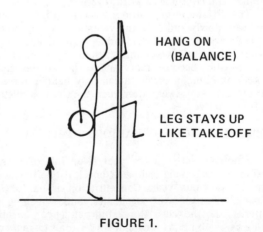

HANG ON
(BALANCE)

LEG STAYS UP
LIKE TAKE-OFF

FIGURE 1.

exercises are specific to the *force application* positions so that when an athlete is trying a performance exceeding his/her previous best the limiting factor won't be an injury to these key areas.

Another example is toe raises on an incline board or step-ups on wooden ramps, etc.—very simple, very applied, very effective. Lastly, Europeans adjust weight programs so that heavy cycles flow into speed cycles, (fast reps, medium weights), and they aren't so concerned about big max's, like boasting a 700 lb half squat or 400 lb bench press.

As far as women in the weight room in Europe they are introduced to it early, and aren't inhibited by the folklore that women can't push big weights. European women are very strong and it is not uncommon to find 16-year-olds doing ¼-squats and half squats with over 200 and 300 pounds.

A REALISTIC GOAL EMPHASIS

An analysis of the individual athlete's current state is done first, and then meets are plugged in. Early in the year, there are experimental meets where high jumpers try all heights and strive for consistency at the higher heights. Emphasis is on lots of audio-visual analysis, feedback, and "hands on" monitoring by the coach, often on a 1-1 basis and at the most 1 on 3.

Training is built on audio-visual analysis and also experimental training and performance in training at high and low intensities. Dwight Stones once was written up as the world record holder who never jumped high in practice. Ackermann told me that she tried the world record over 200 times in practice before setting it in a meet. The point is, if an athlete is not very consistent at high heights then he/she should spend a day a week correcting this weakness. Again, this means there must be flexibility in the *training* and a *competitive* schedule. The key factor is a totally individual program.

HOW MANY YEARS FOR DEVELOPMENT OF HIGH PERFORMANCE?

The answer is approximately 8 years as a national team member. This is about 6 years beyond the university in many cases, so the key ingredient is the coach-athlete relationship. The coaches and athletes are in "units" and continue to work together.

The difference in philosophy is that in Europe you build more slowly and fully and you stick around longer. The U.S. system is so demanding and of such high intensity, that it's all-consuming; then after university, other priorities become important so the athletes move on. Also, the human organism can only handle so much high intensity stress year after year. So, the U.S. system is self-destructive.

EMPHASIS PLACED ON VARIOUS COMPETITIONS

Emphasis *early* in the year is on lots of jumps, working on surpassing technical (check list) efficiencies from the previous year. Concentration is on lots of feedback, discussion of mechanics, and screening of competitions. *Midyear*— More independence to the athlete, big increments attempted (2.10-2.15-2.20-2.25-2.30, or for women 1.75-1.80-1.85-1.90-1.95). If the technique is not honed

and repeatable at all heights then the maximum height won't be attained. Many athletes jump well "low" and even "medium" heights, but "high" heights cause inconsistency.

Experiments are tried where the athlete does only six jumps. After six jumps even if leading, they must drop out. Even more unusual is having athletes take a recorded fourth attempt, just like weight lifters do. Simeoni, the world record holder, is one who does this often.

Athletes who normally go 1.75-1.80-1.85-1.88-1.91 will pass 1.85 or even 1.88 to put tremendous pressure on themselves but also, from the positive point of view, strengthen their options for the big meets, when such a move puts tremendous pressure on opponents.

I can't stress enough the consistency factor of first-attempt jumping as exhibited by the 1980 women's Olympic final:

GOLD: 1.80—1st, 1.85—1st, 1.91—1st, 1.94—1st, 1.97—2nd (Simeoni).

SILVER: 1.80—1st, 1.85—1st, 1.88—1st, 1.91—1st, 1.94—1st, 1.97 out (Kielan).

4th: 1.75—1st, 1.80—1st, 1.85—1st, 1.88—1st, 1.91—1st, 1.94 out (Ackermann).

Of the top 12 (women finalists) if you look at their jumps (*all* jumps at *all* heights to see how many were on first attempts, how many 2nd and how many on 3rd):

1st attempts—36 (This is phenomenal, considering this is so *high.*)
2nd attempts—8
3rd attempts— 2
TOTAL   46

A quick look at the top 16 men (all finalists, 16 made final qualifying height, 7-3):

1st attempts— 45
2nd attempts—13 (2 athletes with injuries)
3rd attempts— 4
TOTAL   62 (including world record)

HOW IS TALENT SELECTED AND DEVELOPED?

Selection is like anywhere else—an athlete performs well at a young age and gets recognized. The big thing is the reporting and centralization of *statistics*, so that everyone knows what everyone is doing and where they are coming from.

Athletes and coaches stay together—the system totally supports the relationship and encourages it. The Eastern bloc, and places like Italy and Britain, want to keep the athlete-coach units alive. In some cases there are "event" centers (Perrin for PV in Paris), but the rule is more: athlete and coach together, a strong club system and a *lot* of *nationally* paid coaches who can afford to stay on the case over time.

TESTING

The following is my list compiled from sources in: E.G., W.G., Hungary, Italy, Britain, U.S.A., Canada.
1. Flying 30 meters *SPEED*, stopwatch.

2. Ablakov test—Take-off on one foot, land on one, and then long jump. Land on 2 measure "x." Forms strong basis for leg power.

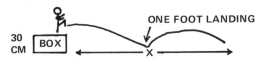

3. Three stepper and one foot take-off jump and reach. Like sergeant jump only applied to high jump. Measure difference to standing stand and reach up.
4. Back-overs to maximum height—use a pit and a two foot take-off. Tests power, quickness, conversion, aerial control.
5. Put bar up and have athlete do 3 steppers, 3 strides, driving the knee to bar height. Keep raising the bar and within 5 total jumps (approximately) try to reach your maximum knee drive height. Coach or recorder stands back and eyeballs whether the knee did reach bar height.

*COACH

6. Three-four stride approach and do scissors—land on feet (standing) in pit—no falling down—that's a failure. Go to maximum height, which means 3 misses in a row and out.
7-8. The last two tests are from jumps decathlon and since there are ten, they can vary.
7. Hop (one foot) 25 meters for time.
8. Distance covered in 3 hops from stationary start on take-off foot.
9. Measure best of 3 distance. (Simeoni's favorite)

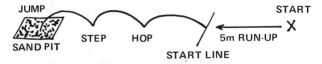

10. Six hurdles at lowest height, spaced 5 footsteps (use athlete's footsteps) apart from each other; time how long it takes from two-feet start to hop (2 feet) over all six hurdles. Move up to 3rd height (4 ft. hurdles) for women: 1-2-3 increments up starting from lowest. Men start at 2 and go to 3 and to highest height—Some experimenting. . .3 warm-up trials, then perform at highest height increment possible. Go for a time with 2 (3) trials.

MAJOR TECHNIQUE EMPHASIS

The **APPROACH**: The rhythm is critical. Europeans spend hours in winter perfecting their running skills (tall, relaxed, upright, hips slightly

Don Chadez

BETTER JUMPERS—LIKE DEBBIE BRILL—TAKE OFF FROM FARTHER AWAY.

forward—opposite to sprinting—not speed, not sprinting, per se) but high jump approach running. Sprinting, then high jumping, tends to make one lean forward too much initially, and when leaning back on the gather, athletes tend to slow down to get the hips ahead, which is incorrect. Hips should be above the center of gravity and the lean a fluid effort.

One technique used in Europe is timing the approach. From a fixed start to take-off is a reproducible measurable time (about 2.5-3.5 seconds—depends on start up and length oftentimes). However the BEST are very consistent, within 1/100 second, while the "lower" jumpers (non-world top 25) tend to be erratic. Fast, then slow, always inconsistent. I have timed Mogenburg, Stones, Huntley, Woodard, etc. Huntley's attempts at her world record in New York were within 1/100th of a second on *every* attempt until the world record height in 1981.

A few weeks later, Jeff Woodard was trying for 2.36/7-8¾ at the TAC Championships. Former WR holder John Thomas—who was officiating—told Woodard he was too slow, so Woodard sped up and wasn't even close. I showed him the times afterwards (I didn't realize or know what J. Thomas had said) and when he saw the times I'd recorded he then told me Thomas told him to speed up and he was sorry he had! So you see the eye, even of a world-class retired jumper, is deceiving and destructive. Subjective instinctive vs. objective coaching!

TAKE-OFF DISTANCE FROM STANDARD

A jumper starts a minumum of 3½ feet away, and the better jumpers (Mogenburg, Wessig, Brill, Meyfarth) are up to 5 feet away. *Distance is time.* The further away, the more time you have to do the aerial mechanics (like holding the vertical and waiting for the knee to rise to bar level . . . remember the knee drive test. . .) is the key.

The biggest mistake that coaches make on this event is having athletes spin or twist the free leg knee across the body and throw the head over the bar. Some athletes are more kinesthetically aware and can do the "gymnastics," but higher heights are never attained.

Speed floppers are basically all that exist in Europe. Though some are *faster* than others, the idea of *power* floppers enforces the idea of being slow and strong, but that was because of the Soviet Sapka and he's gone! The idea of *speed* is the only one in top coaches' minds in Europe.

CLEARANCE TECHNIQUE

Clearance technique is very individual, from the outside arm (on take-off) of Brill to Spencer's and Huntley's inside arm to the double arm action of Stones, to the up and down again knee of Jacobs and Wszola to the straight lead leg of Simeoni. (She's the world record holder and she really exemplifies the vertical knee drive to the added extra point of straightening that free knee-drive-vertical-leg when the knee approaches bar height.)

The key is efficiency and comes from relaxation after take-off and being in the proper position during take-off. Errors in the air are *reactions* to positions on the ground and relaxation must be experienced using a mini-trampoline, for instance, and by trying PR heights, and experiencing the vertical lift of the knee and relaxation at PR heights. The mini-trampoline allows for minimal effort—lots of awareness and a "slow motion" type of time frame to let kinesthetic activities become familiar.

LENGTH OF APPROACH AND ANGLE

The 45 degree angle (flop) is pretty standard. The parallel or more-narrow-than-45 angle tends to lead to problems with the body twisting (back) to the bar too soon, making it difficult to drive the knee vertically, which in turn leads into the head throw.

The length has increased from the 8-9 stride traditional approach *back* to 10-12 strides. Athletes are using more of a jog-into-it, or moving start (e.g., Simeoni, Huntley, Mogenburg, Wessig, etc.). This may mean 8-9 strides but with 3-4 tacked on to get up to approach speed. This allows for full concentration on running with rhythm as previously stressed.

PLYOMETRICS—TYPE AND FREQUENCY

The European schedule includes hurdle hopping early in the year, a jumps decathlon early in the season, then moving to small boxes and double leg take-offs and landings, then, in the pre-competition period, moving to single-leg work and reducing the time of the exercise from fifteen minutes down to about eight minutes. The higher box work is left to triple and long jumps.

Volume, progression and intensity is built into the preceding basically like this:

Sept/Oct: hurdles and two-feet work—
            45 minutes, 2 times a week.

Nov/Dec: hurdles and one-foot work—
            45 minutes, 2 times a week.

Jan/Feb: hurdles and one-foot work—
            15 minutes, 2 times a week.

Mar/Apr: hurdles and one-foot work—
            8 minutes, 2 times a week.

May/Sept: hurdles and one-foot work—
            15 minutes, once a week.

The key is these are done in sprint spikes and *not* in flats and *done on a carpet on top of synthetic surfaces.* If done directly on a synthetic surface, athletes will have shin splints within three weeks. *That's trouble (only can get rid of them by taking time off since they are caused from pounding in this case, similar to high jump forces).*

RUNNING AND TYPES USED

The jumper, in the end, will be performing at *efforts* beyond his/her maximum which is how records are set. To do this, the body requires ruggedness at all the joints which contribute to the extension positions, at take-off particularly. Therefore, some *general* overall fitness is required as well as the *speed* component that comes later.

Due to the high intensity of speed exercises, the speed work is closely monitored and built into a progression which follows aerobic (endurance) running, and then becomes a balance of anaerobic alactic (high intensity speed which is short in duration and has adequate rest between intervals) and anaerobic lactic (high intensity speed which is a little longer in duration with a bit shorter recoveries).

Sept-Nov: endurance up to five miles, fartlek (not on track), woods, X-C.

Dec-Feb: speed—longer, less intense intervals like 300m x 3 at ¾-speed two times a week, work up to sets of 250s, 300s, 350s (350 is maximum distance).

Mar-May: speed—shorter more intense, but less often, vary: 10 x 30s, 10 x 50s, 10 x 80s. The key is controlled rhythmic running—a bit upright, not straight sprinting.

Jun-Jul: lots of meets, so program phase depends on program components. Definitely, speed work is reduced in quantity.

Aug-Sept: Same. The "raw" running is reduced to a Sat/Sun 2-mile fartlek and one speed workout tacked onto a workout as a 15-minute session.

The indoor running (winter phases) are all controlled sessions where the coach stands at right angles to a 50m or 75m strip of carpet on tartan and watches the athlete run tall, upright and relaxed. *This is not easy*—it is almost not normal—it's not a sprinter's (center of gravity ahead) pose and it's not flat out like traditional sprint work. These develop quickly into acceleration runs of 30-60-90-meters in length. The key is *not* to do it on a track per se where you really tax the legs, rather to do it on a solid cushiony surface so that there isn't a cumulative strain on muscle, tendons, etc.

All speed work is done in sprint spikes and emphasis is on fast foot movements—but since the shoes are thin for fast foot movements, a carpet (astroturf roll out) over either boards or tartan is used.

There are lots of "fast foot" drills which are like race-walking on your toes (heel, toe contact but right up on toes)—hard to describe but used for *fast* movements, since kinesthetic internal speed as a concept is worked on and not sprint speed for 100m, etc. (Remember sprint speed testing is a flying 30m only.)

Then there is a lot of curved running which is scrutinized. The big difference between Europe and the U.S. is that in Europe the coach puts less emphasis on the stopwatch and more on the mechanics *done to perfection.* Mass workouts just are not done—too much margin for error. Jumpers work on things one-at-a-time under scrutiny, as opposed to supervision. The coaches are event specialists and that's why exercises are done over and over until "perfection" of desired body positions is attained.

EXERCISES FOR REHABILITATION OR INJURY PREVENTION

Athletes are tested and known weak areas are areas that the program will specifically cater to. If hamstrings have slipped in the quad-ham ratio then exercises are done to bring them back up. Strength-to-body weight is another ratio and tells how much base pre-season work is needed. Tests are few, simple, reproducible and even athlete-specific. They are done monthly and are received as motivators and assurances to the coach and athlete that the program is working.

Weight belts aren't used all that much in the weight room and monitoring again is the key—the coach attends with the training diaries and jots things down—observations of fatigue, etc. are all part of monitoring.

In rehabilitation, electrical stimulation is alive and well and used extensively. If injury occurs, then electrical stimulation is used to strengthen specific areas and fine muscles.

In Europe the coaches are familiar with modalities like ultra-sound, short-wave diathermy, electrical stimulation, even the use of ice. Since units are more 1-1, the coach can follow through and follow up, whereas in the U.S. schools and clubs, the coaches are forced to rely on the school physio, paramed, trainer, etc. and there's room for slippage.

MENTAL REHEARSAL, IMAGERY, RELAXATION

This is specific to the athlete; however, there is some generalization. It is planned into the program. Imagery is based on audio-visual work which is done extensively early in the year. Often coaches lose the essence of observation by watching and then translating. Too much room for error. A video recorder is used and is the focal point. The coach relates the progression checklist (athlete-specific) of things the athlete should be doing to the video of the jump. Both focus on the before, the actual, and the result of the mechanical error, and technique is worked on at low heights, medium heights and high heights.

The video then gives you the perfect jump. I've seen coaches film on a super 8 camera, their athlete from behind with the bar at medium height and measuring board set to read say 1.95 (for a 1.85 jumper) or 2.30 (for a 2.20 guy). The athlete is seen captured on film as doing the proper approach, explosive take-off and a proper bar clearance and being successful. The high jump measuring monitor states 2nd attempt, 1.95. It is all done in slow motion.

When you have this recording of a good jump by your athlete, you show it to them. They can visualize what they look like, as if they had left their bodies and are watching from behind. They also unconsciously see themselves clearing a personal best height. This forms the basis for mental imagery.

When attempting quality jumps, either in practice or meets, they observe themselves as on the film, being successful and they try to duplicate the feat. It is a point of focus and eliminates a lot of the pressure of seeing only "the bar" and panicking.

Mental rehearsal can be done in the classroom or in the change room or in the bathroom. The East German bobsled coach told me at Lake Placid that their athletes mentally rehearse the run—with all turns, anticipating the leans, acceleration points, mid-line of the total run *100* times for every practice run!! Even if exaggerated threefold, the point is well-made.

Many elite athletes mentally rehearse best the weekdays prior to the meet, particularly in bed, when the mental processes are uncluttered by information (visual, auditory, olfactory, etc.) and concentration on "the big meet Saturday afternoon" is keyed upon. One secret—it's one of the reasons why sex is frowned upon prior to big meets—it interferes with the possible mental rehearsal opportunities since it is so powerful (sex) on imagery itself.

Relaxation techniques are athlete-specific. Have the athlete *after* a meet write down when he/she was the most anxious at different times during the meet (i.e., at registration, trying to warm up, when jumping in warm up, watching when Leo Williams was jumping or Tyke Peacock, etc.) and then you know *when* he needs to focus on a relaxation item. Deep breathing and thinking of how well he does knee drive (think of a positive aspect of *his* jumping) is an applied approach.

Relaxation must be 1) Discovered as a need (post-meet talk to find out when); 2) Talk to the athlete about focusing on something else at that time so then the athlete can be in better control; 3) Practice it in early meets or in quality jump sessions (staged). The key is telling the athlete that *his* mind is very powerful—so powerful that sometimes, on its own, it will try to think negative thoughts, putting you down. The athlete has to get a grasp on his independent mind and turn that around to positive statements "Those guys are big, but wait until they see my knee drive" or "Wait till they see how I have improved technically," etc.

MEN AND WOMEN TRAINING

In Europe, there is less of a women-men (macho resulting) approach. Women's liberation is not a big deal, not an impacting thing on attitude. Women are not excluded from workouts when men are training. They use the same field equipment and there is much more equality. This is definitely not the case in the U.S. and I don't want to say more—let's just say it's an attitude difference.

In Europe, the top coaches work with women on an equal basis with men. (Tancic-West Germany, Azzaro-Italy, Eros in Hungary, etc.) The U.S. has more distinct *men's* coaches and *women's* coaches—this is not very progressive.

ARM ACTION

There are three basic arm actions: inside arm, outside arm, and double arm. European coaches stress the *knee drive* and the *vertical* (holding the vertical). Consequently, the arms are *ignored* since arm action will accommodate leg and body positions. The arms are worked on *last* and only two principles are stressed: 1) Not reaching in on take-off, which pulls you in toward the bar—the reach must be *up*, not *in* and when *up* bends toward the bar, it is at a point about a meter (3') above the bar—not 6" above the bar (i.e., Huntley style). 2) On the 2nd and 3rd to last steps, no double-arm wide action. That slows you down, a la Sapka. You must accelerate the last three, not decelerate. The key being, for correction purposes, to work on accelerating the legs and the arms will follow. Focus on legs. To eliminate wide arm circles, have the athlete do small circles (like hurdles) with hands and arms (i.e., change the focus).

LENGTH OF LAST THREE STRIDES

Personal preference is indicated here, but the last stride is shorter than the previous two. The plant foot is consciously brought down *and at the same time*, the rear leg is performing a push-off and pull-through initiating the powerful knee drive. KEY: Accelerate the last three strides, *particularly* the last one.

FOOT PLACEMENT ON TAKE-OFF

It's a curved approach. The lean away from the bar toward the center of the circle is critical. The radius of the curve is a function of the speed of the approach. (Thus no cookbook approach to measuring approaches—it depends on trial and error and how fast you are, how strong you are, so you can handle the curve and speed, etc.)

The last step on take-off, the foot leaves the *arc* path and initiates the tangent-to-the-arc leading to take-off. **Fig. 3.** The angle is 45 degrees approximately and only gradually leaves the arc. A more important key is the last step—it must be curved and not straight ahead. *Many* jumpers break the curve there and try to "2 step" straight at the bar—this 3rd step must stay curved to keep the body lean in.

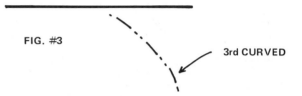

FIG. #3   3rd CURVED

COACHES CHOSEN AND TRAINED

University programs *in coaching* are offered. Not "Mickey Mouse" but very technical with exercise physiology, human anatomy and biomechanics being key components. Many coaches are paid *higher* than engineers and professors. That's the second key, it's a profession.

Paul Eros (a Hungarian national high jump coach and personal coach and new husband to Andrea Matay, world record holder, indoors) decided to go back to part-time coaching of Andrea and return to teaching (he's a remedial expert at the elementary level) and he took a substantial cut in pay to do so.

In Italy, Erminio Azzaro (a national high jump coach and fiancee of Sara Simeoni) is one of 200 national, state paid, full-time professional coaches. He's at a training center full-time and coaches a handful of athletes. He can work in administration or not (with the Federation). He can move around to other centers or stay put. He's a professional.

WHAT THE COACH CAN IMPLEMENT

This goes back to two key points: 1) the ability to plan objectively and stick to it and, 2) the ability to monitor your athletes and keep coming up with the innovative drills and points of emphasis to ensure *progress* and no *injuries*.

EUROPEAN WARM-UP
AND FLEXIBILITY RATIONALE

High jumpers take 30-45 minutes to warm up. It's gradual, it's necessary and no one cheats on it. It's attitude again—European athletes know what they have to do for injury prevention so if they show up late for a workout, they warm up on their own. They don't just do a few strides and jump in on drills. The warm-up is methodical and is a series of jogging, stretching, running, stretching, specific flexibility, even a change in a damp T-shirt and more intense stationary range of motion stretching and then right into drills. The coaches in Europe are very organized and workouts just flow. □

FREE WEIGHTS FOR STRENGTH AND POWER

by John Garhammer, UCLA

Dr. Garhammer, of UCLA's Dept. of Kinesiology, makes his case for the use of free weights in strength training for track & field over the various "weight machines" in strength training for track & field. Excerpted from the National Strength Coaches Association publication, Vol. 3, No. 6, Dec. '81/Jan. '82.

One of the obvious advantages of free weight exercises over machine exercises is the ability to perform free standing total body lifts which require the maintenance of balance and coordination of many major muscle groups during execution of the lifting movement. Exercises such as the squat, power clean or snatch, standing overhead press and jerk are among many common examples.

Free standing total body lifts result in the training of one's neuromuscular system, not one or two joints in isolation, and the result is excellent transfer to the neuromuscular demands of athletic competition. The reason for this derives from a principle in exercise physiology called "specificity of training."

It simply states that the body adapts to the specific demands made upon it. This principle agrees with other physiological theories of adaptation, such as that developed by Selye (15).

There have been arguments presented by Jones (10) that strength training must either be exactly specific or not specific at all to the event to be contested. As an example to support his contention he relates the difficulty in maintaining shooting accuracy when changing from one long time used rifle to a new one. However, this example really supports the specificity concept. If someone had hunted with a bow and arrows for years and then switched to a rifle it would take a longer time to develop consistent marksmanship with the rifle than if they merely changed from one rifle to another. So it is also with the transfer of strength and power developed with free standing total body free weight exercises to free standing total body competitive events.

It takes some careful thought to properly blend strength training with technique and other components of an athlete's overall program during a training cycle to achieve maximal results. However, the transfer of strength and power will be easier and more beneficial if the strength program is based on free weight multi-joint exercises. It is unfortunate that the results of a few short-term, limited scope motor learning studies have been misinterpreted and extrapolated inaccurately to be used as evidence for complete specificity in exercise.

There is another very important reason why total specificity of exercise is unacceptable. It is the need for variability in exercise if progress is to be made over long periods of time. We know, for example, that a 1500 meter runner does much more in his yearly training than just run 1500 meter races as fast as he can. A weightlifter does much more during the training cycles than attempt maximal weights in the competitive lifts. Such a course of action for these or any athletes would rapidly lead to stagnation, overtraining and decreased performance.

We know from practical experience that runners train at distances above and below their competitive distance and at various paces (in addition to other exercises). Weightlifters do most of their training lifts with 75% to 85% of maximum and frequently do partial lifts with various hand spacings and initial bar heights. Shot putters throw 15 and 18 pound shots as well as the 16, they run sprints and do power cleans.

These examples are meant to emphasize the fact that training for any sport involves exercises with varying degrees of specificity to the competitive event. This variability of training methods is of paramount importance for continued improvement, especially for the advanced athlete. The neuromuscular similarities of the major free weight exercises to the neuromuscular demands of athletic movements make transfer of strength easy while permitting ease of varying the strength exercises.

Objective measurements have shown that Olympic-style lifters produce greater power outputs than are found in any other human activity (6, 7).

Russian weightlifters are by far the world leaders in their sport. The writings of their top coaches consistently stress the importance of variability in training. NOTE: Two recent papers summarize and reference many of their key concepts (references 2 and 21.) in addition to the empirical knowledge of need for variability, as examplified by the Russian literature, there is a physiological basis for its importance as indicated in Selye's "General Adaptation Syndrome" (see references 8 and 15). Another advantage of free weights involves the ease by which variability may be injected into a strength and power program. One may, for example, squat with various foot spacings or to different depths, or do high pulls with various hand spacings and/or from various initial bar heights (using boxes or small platforms). The variety of ways to execute a given free weight exercise, and the variety of

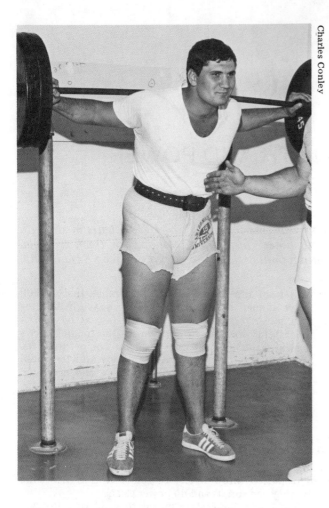

WITH FREE WEIGHTS, SQUATS MAY BE DONE WITH VARIOUS FOOT SPACINGS OR TO DIFFERENT DEPTHS.

exercises possible with free weights are almost limitless. A far cry from the monotonous few exercises possible with even a complete set of any machine company's products.

It is interesting to note that the vast majority of those who emphasize machines in a strength program have little or no competitive experience in strength or power oriented sports and have not spent countless hours in the weight room striving for the improvements so critical to these types of competition.

Thus far arguments have been presented for the superiority of free weight training based on the multijoint, multi-muscle group nature of total body free weight exercises and the resulting neuromuscular specificity and transferability to sport activities. The ability to easily add variation to the strength program was another important point. The following are but a few of many additional considerations which favor the emphasis of free weight exercises in the strength and power programs of athletes:

(1) Acceleration: Lifting free weights is not isotonic exercise as commonly stated. Isotonic means constant tension and this is never the case in lifting free weights. The reasons are many but acceleration or changing bar velocity is a major factor. While passing through strong leverage positions an athlete can exert a larger force on the bar and it accommodates this effort perfectly by accelerating at a greater rate. This perfect accommodation is perhaps the greatest advantage of free weights when coupled with reasonable total body full range joint movement exercises, rep after rep, as fatigue develops the athlete can always make the maximum possible effort and the barbell accommodates it by the appropriate acceleration.

Variable resistance type machines, including some cam machines, restrict acceleration severely by increasing resistance through the movement range. The resulting velocity profile therefore deviates severely from what is common to athletic movement: that is, periods of high acceleration. Other cam devices permit so much momentum to be built up in the linkage mechanism during a movement that the movement must be done slowly or no resistance is felt near the end of the movement range. In fact, if done too fast these machines continue to move on their own for a short distance after the trainee has reached full joint extension or flexion.

(2) Eccentric Movement: When giving in to the weight, such as lowering the barbell in a squat or bench press, muscles undergo a lengthening or eccentric contraction as opposed to the normal shortening or concentric contraction. This is another type of valuable stimulus for the development of muscle strength. Studies reported in the Russian literature indicate that a combination of both types of muscle contraction is superior to either separately. Some types of machines, especially isokinetic devices, do not permit eccentric movements. With free weights and spotters one can do a variety of supramaximal eccentric movements (too heavy to reverse via concentric contraction). These, however, must be done with caution and should be a very small fraction of the total training volume. The eccentric movements that occur with normal lifts, such as returning the barbell to the floor in a controlled manner after a power clean, are the preferable way to mix both types of contraction.

(3) Counter Movement: When muscles and connective tissue are forcefully and rapidly stretched elastic energy is stored and can be utilized in an immediately following concentric contraction. This energy recovery is very important in many sport movements, such as running, jumping and weightlifting, in terms of power output and efficiency (1,5, 11). This counter movement effect is found in many free weight lifting movements, such as direction reversal in the squat (11), dip for jerking a barbell overhead (5), and shift of the knees and hips when executing a snatch, clean or pull using the "double knee bend" technique (4,6). A "stretch reflex" facilitation of the concentric contraction may also occur. The speed and force of the stretch and lack of delay or unloading prior to the subsequent concentric contraction are critical factors. The presence of counter movement effects in training is very important. Connective tissues are viscoelastic in nature. This means that they resist elongation (stretch) differently depending on the rate of loading. If never exposed to high and rapid loading in training one cannot expect these tissues to be conditioned to withstand them without high risk of injury when encountered in competition. High loads and rapid loading are the rule rather than exception in sport competition.

Machine exercises can play a meaningful role in an overall strength and power program but still a minor one. The vast majority of world class strength and power athletes do more than 95% of their lifting volume with free weight exercises. The contribution of machines to improved strength programs for athletes has been small.

In many cases the "machine influence" has hurt progress in strength training in the United States by making coaches and athletes think that the best way to train is the machine way. If this continues our athletes will be at a major disadvantage in international competition since foreign athletes from the world sport powers use the best means to train rather than the easiest or most novel way. The lastest fad to appear in strength training is "Computerized exercise machines." These have many of the faults already given for other machines, especially constrained movement patterns and very limited exercise choices, in addition to basing one's effort on a single force-position or time measure for each subject in a given exercise. It is well known that such a measure will vary from day to day, change frequently during an exercise program, and vary due to fatigue during a single workout session and with repetition in a single set. What about variation of the load (ie., light, medium, and heavy training sessions)?

Major advances in strength and power training will come from better educated athletes and strength coaches, better training programs with productive exercises, and not from money making gimmicks. □

REFERENCES

1. Cavagna, G.A. "Storage and utilization of elastic energy in skeletal muscle". Exercise and sport Science Reviews (R. Hutton, ed.). Journal Publishing Affiliates, Santa Barbara, California, Vol. 5, 1977. pp. 89-129.
2. Charniga, A. "Variability incorporated into the training of a qualified athlete". Master's Thesis, The University of Toledo, Toledo, Ohio. 1981.
3. Edington, D.W. and V.R. Edgerton, "The biology of physical activity". Houghton Mifflin Company, Boston, Massachusetts, 1976.
4. Enoka, R. "The pull in Olympic weightlifting". Med. Sci. Sports 11(2): 131-137, 1979.
5. Garhammer, J. "Force-velocity constraints and elastic energy utilization during multi-segment lifting jumping activities". Med. Sci. Sports Exercise 13(2): 96, 1981. (Abstract)
6. Garhammer, J. "Evaluation of human power capacity through Olympic weightlifting analyses". Ph.D. Dissertation. University of California, Los Angeles, 1980.
7. Garhammer, J. "Power production by Olympic weightlifters". Med. Sci. Sports 12(1): 54-60, 1980.
8. Garhammer, J. "Periodization of strength training for athletes". Track Technique 73: 2398-2399, Summer 1979.
9. Garhammer, J. "Muscle fiber types and weight training". Track Technique 72:2297-2299, June 1978.
10. Jones, A. "Specificity". In Nautilus advertising brochure. 1976.
11. Malone, P.E. "An investigation of the sticking point phenomenon in the parallel squat". Purdue University, 1980. (personal communication)
12. O'Shea, J.P. "Scientific principles and methods of strength fitness". Addison-Wesley Publishing Company, Reading, Massachusetts. First edition, 1969, p. 62. Chapter 22, pp. 800-801.
13. O'Donoghue, D. H. "Treatment of injuries to athletes". W.B. Saunders, Third Edition, 1976. Chapter 22, pp. 800-801.
14. Pipes. T.V. and J.H. Wilmore. "Isokinetic vs. isotonic strength training in adult men". Med. Sci. Sports 7(4): 262-274, 1975.
15. Selye, H. "Stress without distress". J. B. Lippincott, New York, 1974.
16. Swimming Technique, August 1980, pp. 14-25. "Scientists talk about strength training".
17. Starr, B. "The strongest shall survive—strength training for football". Fitness Products, Ltd., Annapolis, Maryland, 1976. Chapter 18.
18. Stone, M. and J. Garhammer. "Some thoughts on strength and power". NSCA Journal, Vol. 3. No. 5. 1981.
19. Turner, G. "More about free weights vs. machines". Muscle, Vol. 40. No. 7, July 1979.
20. Wilmore, J. H., Letter to the Editor, Med. Sci. Sports 11(3): iii, 1979.
21. Yessis, M. "The key to strength development: Variety". NSCA Journal, Vol. 3, No. 3 pp. 32-34, 1981.

Motivation

A SEASONAL PSYCH PLAN

by Eugene F. Gauron, University of Iowa

Prof. Gauron, a sports psychologist at Iowa, has worked with swimmers, gymnasts, wrestlers and other athletes on the mental approaches to their sports. In this article, from Swimming Technique, *Vol. 18, No. 4, Feb/Apr. 1982, he presents a program with ready application to track and field.*

MENTAL TRAINING PROGRAM

The format of the program involved twice-weekly meetings (approximately 45 minutes per session) with the entire team. The blend of the average session was approximately one-third didactic and two-thirds experiential, with the swimmers being led in exercises related to each skill being practiced.

The mental training program focused in sequence on nine major topic areas. Each will be discussed in turn.

Team building & team unity
Key Concept: "We are one." (4 weeks)
Focal activities:

a. Team members getting better-acquainted through talking to a partner about assigned personal topics (e.g., what is your major, why did you come to this school?). This type of conversation continues with different team members and different questions.

b. Evolving a team code of conduct concerning behavior directed toward coaches, team members, opponents and the general public. (The key concept is, "We conduct ourselves like champions at all times.")

c. Communicating within the team about team-related or sport-related topics (e.g., how to cope with pain or the pressure of winning, what are the qualities of an ideal coach, is it important to be cohesive as a team?).

d. Orienting to the approaching season.

Although swimming generally is regarded as an individual sport, our intent has been to emphasize the team aspect and to develop a support system whereby team members rely on each other. We start our program with a large dose of team building and this focus continues throughout the season as sessions are devoted to increasing team unity. Cohesiveness assures not only higher quality performance but also increases the likelihood of member satisfaction and fulfillment with being part of a strong team.

Motivation—goal setting
Key Concept: "I can do anything I really want." (2 weeks)
Focal activities:

a. Clearing up each individual's motives and reasons for participating in the sport.

b. Discussing time management and how to be more efficient in the use of time.

c. Setting team goals for the season through discussion.

d. Establishing goals for the year for each team member.

e. Following through on team and individual goals through developing action plans.

F. Developing will (want) power through discussion of what is meant by determination, persistence and desire, and how these are manifested in behavior.

In order to continue an activity that is as physically taxing and time-consuming as swimming, it is necessary for each athlete to have a clear notion of why he is participating and what personal need are met through participation. The understanding of individual motivation is translated into more effective coach-athlete interactions in that the coaching staff knows specifically how to aid each individual with motivational issues. By the end of this segment of the mental training program, the entire team knows exactly what they intend to accomplish during the season and what will be required individually and collectively to make it happen.

Attention control
Key Concept: "I keep myself in the here and now." (2 weeks)
Focal activities:

a. Discussing elements in concentration, including being in the here and now and handling distractions.

b. Practicing mind control and concentration improvement via exercises such as meditation, focusing on a specific object for a period of time, expanding and contracting awareness, learning to focus on external as well as internal processes, and focusing on visually rich designs while attending to different aspects of the design.

c. Learning to deal with distractions; observing the mind at work.

Concentration involves the ability to focus one's energy, attention and intentionality. Literally, it means bringing all personal resources to bear on exactly what one intends to accomplish. Skill at concentration

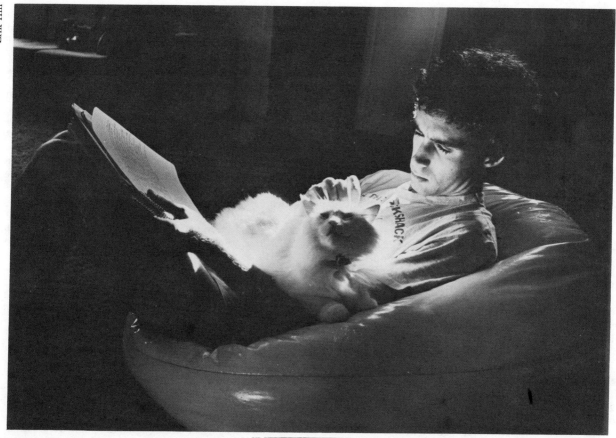

"I REMAIN CALM AND IN CONTROL" IS A KEY CONCEPT.

definitely increases with consistent practice. Improved concentration ability pays off in other areas of life beside athletics.

Emotional Control

Key Concept: "I remain calm and in control." (3 weeks)
Focal activities:

a. Considering the relationship between arousal and performance. An optimal level of arousal is almost desirable for peak performance, while too-low and too-high arousal are to be avoided.

b. Experiencing a variety of relaxation training techniques including centering, breathing exercises, progressive muscle relaxation, autogenic training, meditation, passive progressive relaxation and visualization for relaxation purposes.

c. Devising individual arousal control strategies and personalized cue words and cue images. The emphasis throughout the program is on individual differences and knowing oneself.

d. Learning how to energize the body to become keyed up or activated when needed.

Relaxation is not presented as a panacea. However, the importance of knowing how to manage stress, tension and nervousness is emphasized. The literature suggests that no relaxation technique is preferable to another. Each athlete is encouraged to develop his own perferred relaxation technique for later use, to develop his own key relaxation words; e.g., "calm down" or

"relax," and his own key images which he associates with being relaxed. Through repeated practice, swimmers acquire the facility to calm the body at will.

Body awareness

Key Concept: "I move with self-awareness." (1 week)
Focal activities:

a. Discussing differences between moving with awareness and moving without awareness and advantages of the former in terms of maximal use of energy and effort.

b. Understanding the relationship between body awareness and arousal control. In order to effectively use emotion control procedures, it is necessary to know through body scanning when one is overly aroused and where one is feeling tension.

c. Developing awareness of individualized stress-reaction profiles. Each athlete is encouraged to know his own body and his own reactivity to stress, to know where to look to determine if he is feeling stressed.

d. Experiencing body awareness training exercises such as that developed by Israeli physicist Moshe Feldenkrais.

The benefits to be derived from this portion of the training program include: increased body awareness; more efficient, graceful, effortless use of the body; relearning the art of how to use the body (many of the ways in which the body is used were arbitrarily or randomly acquired); being more in touch with oneself; a broadened range of choices about how to act and how to move; discovering pleasure in movement; and cutting down on injuries resulting from misuse of the body.

Cognitive psychology and intervention

Key Concept: "I am what I think I am." (2 weeks)

Focal activities:

a. Demonstrating the power of thought, the influence of thought on feelings and actions; establishing the subjectiveness of reality.

b. Learning about cognitive distortions and irrational fears.

c. Acquiring the skill to manipulate personal perceptions and cognitions in more self-beneficial directions.

d. Applying cognitive manipulations to arousal control, stress management and pain management.

What one thinks and what one says to oneself are critical in terms of what one is able to do. Feelings are affected by thoughts. What one is able to do is affected by thoughts. Changing thoughts changes feelings; changing thoughts liberates other possible behaviors. It is essential that an athlete know how to recognize his self-defeating thought processes and how to go about changing them.

Self-confidence

Key Concept: "I believe totally in my own infinite power." (2 weeks)

Focal activities:

a. Establishing that self-confidence is a critical element in peak performance.

b. Discussing internal dialogue and how self-talk affects self-esteem.

c. Becoming aware of the internal dialogue and changing as necessary individual self-talk from negative to positive.

d. Building and maintaining self-confidence through creating and repeating personal affirmation statements individualized for each athlete.

e. Generating a team affirmation, which is repeated daily as a team activity.

Many studies investigating differences between elite and non-elite athletes in a variety of sports have shown that self-confidence is a critical factor, even overriding talent. The athlete who believes in himself performs at a higher level than a comparable athlete who is lower in self-confidence.

Unfortunately, how an athlete feels about himself is greatly affected by recent performances. Athletes tend to determine their self-worth by how well they are performing. The battle of self-confidence is one that is never totally won. It is important that athletes be taught techniques that can regularly be used to bolster and maintain self-confidence.

Visualization

Key Concept: "I program my body through mental pictures." (3 weeks)

Focal activities:

a. Understanding the difference between the functions of the right and left halves of the brain and how use of mental imagery instructs the body.

b. Developing and expanding imagination, clarity and control of mental imagery through training exercises.

c. Presenting and practicing uses of visualization in athletics. Possible applications include mental rehearsal, relaxation and rejuvenation, preprogramming desire or anticipated outcomes, self-healing, replaying past outstanding performances as a boost to self-esteem.

Training in visualization assists athletes in recapturing a skill (through imagination and creative mental imagery) possessed at an earlier time in their lives which has since fallen into disuse.

Swimmers are presented with the premise, "Your body is your servant and will do what you want if you know how to go about instructing it." One instructs the body through mental pictures.

Mental preparation for competition

Key Concept: "I mentally prepare myself for each competition through an established and practiced routine." (3 weeks)

Focal activities:

a. Putting the psychological skills together and developing a comprehensive individualized mental readying program prior to competing.

b. Having a carefully prepared and effective countdown of what to do and when, from one week prior until the moment competition begins.

c. Engaging in strategy planning and development of solution banks so that the athlete has prepared for all eventualities which can be anticipated.

Obviously, skills must be applied in pre-competition and actual competition situations in order for maximal benefit to occur. Much of this portion of the program is individualized work, with the sport psychologist meeting with athletes to construct mental preparation programs for competition. The total program has been successful when each has his own program for getting himself mentally ready for peak performance.

It should be emphasized that this aspect of the program is ongoing and cumulative. Athletes mentally prepare themselves for competitive events, such as dual meets during the season. After each performance, the athlete examines how well his mental preparation program worked and what modifications or improvements need to be made prior to the next competition. Athletes are presented the proposition that there are always additional ways of increasing readiness.

The more athletes practice the skills described in this program, the more adept they become. Obviously skills increase with use. The most effective routine involves commitment to a daily mental workout of 15 to 20 minutes. The mind deserves at least this much exercise because of the uncontested importance of mental factors in performance. Truly the mind is the limit and represents the remaining athletic frontier to be advanced. □

Physiology

SHIFTING THE ANAEROBIC THRESHOLD IN DISTANCE RUNNERS

by Scotty Powers, Ph.D. and Ralph E. Steben, Ph.D., school of Physical Education, Louisiana State University

A brief overview of the concept of anaerobic threshold and its application to the training and middle- and long-distance runners.

Many training studies have attempted to define just how "hard" a distance runner must work in order to obtain improvement in cardiorespiratory performance. There may be a threshold below which the athlete can work without getting any physiological benefit. The time honored procedure of knowing when the athlete has stimulated himself has been monitoring of heart rate immediately after a workout. If the predetermined target of 70% of the maximum heart rate possible has been reached, there should be a training effect that brings about an improvement in the runner's maximum aerobic power (VO_2 max). (Fox, 1981) High values of VO_2 max are associated with outstanding performances in middle distance and distance events.

There is no doubt something has happened in the past few years regarding training and performance. In the late 30's, Don Lash ran 4:07.2 and 8:58.0, while Jim Ryun, in the mid 60's, ran 3:51.1 and 8:25.2 with the same aerobic capacity (81 ml/kg-min). Recent investigations with Snell, Prefontaine, and Shorter post 73, 80, and 71 ml/kg-min respectively. Isn't it interesting that Shorter ran so well with a comparatively low capacity?

The names and data cited suggest that, while one of the goals of any training regime for distance runners would be to improve VO_2 max, people with similar values often perform quite differently in events greater than the 1500 meters. Several studies have shown that performances will continue to improve even after an athlete's VO_2 max has reached a plateau (Davis, 1979; Costill, 1973; Astrand, 1977). This suggests there are other measures involved in successful performance.

One such measure is the "anaerobic threshold", *which is the greatest VO_2 max beyond which lactic acid begins to build up rapidly in the athlete's blood.* Another way of saying this is, the speed an athlete can run without a rapid increase in blood lactate levels. The build-up of lactic acid has been identified as one of the limiting factors to endurance performance. If so, it would be important for the athlete to "delay" the accumulation of lactate. Current research has revealed that without increasing VO_2 max, *training* can reduce lactate accumulation at the same pace. Or, perhaps, as the result of one recent investigation with rats on a treadmill, it isn't the "passive" reduction of the lactate production—it is an improved method of lactate removal (Donovan, 1982). What difference does this make?—For practical purposes, probably none.

Initially, practical consideration requires a training target heart rate necessary to bring about a change in the anaerobic threshold. This is calculated by multiplying .85-.90 times the max HR (220 - age = max HR). The difference in the percentages is related to the fitness status of the athlete. Use .85 or 85% for the less fit and 90% for the more highly trained individual.

The target heart rate must be reached and maintained for a least 20-30 minutes during a training session, and must be repeated at least three times per week. More research is necessary to determine the exact effect of interval training on the anaerobic threshold. Perhaps running longer intervals (500's, 600's, 700's) may be even more effective in shifting the threshold further to the right as is observed in continuous running at higher intensities. ("Shifting to the right" is a graphic representation of lactic acid versus VO_2 max, which tells us one can endure a good pace longer, without hurting, than earlier in the training period. See Figure 1.)

The fundamental difference between a

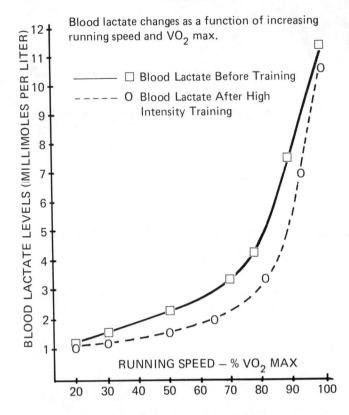

FIGURE 1

Blood lactate changes as a function of increasing running speed and VO$_2$ max.

□ Blood Lactate Before Training

O Blood Lactate After High Intensity Training

BLOOD LACTATE LEVELS (MILLIMOLES PER LITER)

RUNNING SPEED – % VO$_2$ MAX

logically stimulates and simulates the energy requirements of competitive running and may serve to cause a change in the rate of blood lactate accumulation (Sady et al., 1980).

To summarize, one of the limiting factors in distance running may be the accumulation of lactic acid in the blood. The anaerobic threshold is the exercise intensity at which there is a rapid accumulation of lactate in the blood. Research has shown that after training at an intensity above 85% of max HR, the athlete can shift the anaerobic threshold to the right. This allows him to run at a higher percent of his VO$_2$ max before lactic acid levels in the blood rise sharply. This could substantially improve performance by allowing the athlete to run at a faster pace without accumulating acid. □

cardiorespiratory fitness and a distance running training program is one of intensity. If we want to shift the anaerobic threshold by accumulating less lactate or by removing it better, the key may be stress.

Most distance training today is either year long or includes at least a substantial pre-season training period. The cardiorespiratory fitness program is the off-season program in which one might emphasize running long workouts below race pace, at about 70% of max HR. Using the familiar pyramidal system of training during the competitive season, the quantity goes down and quality goes up. Thus, the intensity of the work should go up to the .85-.90 range. This more

REFERENCES

1. Astrand, P.O. and K. Rodahl. *Textbook of Work Physiology.* McGraw Hill, New York, 1977.

2. Davis, J. A., M.H. Frank, B.J. Whipp, and K. Wasserman. Anaerobic threshold alterations caused by training in middle aged men. *Journal of Applied Physiology.* 46:1039, 1979.

3. Donovan, C.M. and G. Brooks. Endurance training effects lactate clearance, not lactate production. Abstract: *Medicine Science in Sports and Exercise.* 14(2) 113, 1982.

4. Costill, D.L., H. Thompson, and E. Roberts. Fractional utilization of the aerobic capacity during distance running. *Medicine Science in Sports.* 5:248, 1973.

5. Fox, E.L. and D.K. Mathews. *The Physiological Basis of Physical Education and Athletics.* Saunders, New York, 1981.

6. Sady, S., V. Katch, P. Freedson, and A. Weltman, Changes in metabolic acidosis; evidence for an intensity threshold. *Journal of Sports Medicine and Physical Fitness.* 20.41, 1980.

VO2 MAX: A MEASURE OF FITNESS

by Arthur Weltman, Ph.D. and Bryant Stamford, Ph.D., U.S.A.

A clear, concise explanation of the methods of determining and interpreting oxygen consumption measurements. From The Physician and Sportsmedicine, *Vol. 10, No. 6.*

A good indicator of cardiovascular fitness is VO_2 which is shorthand for the maximum volume of oxygen that can be consumed per minute during strenuous exercise. Measurement of VO_2 max provides an indirect assessment of energy expenditure because for every liter of oxygen consumed approximately 5 kilocalories will be expended.

VO_2 max is highly stable, and careful measurement should result in an error of 3% or less. Time of day, donation of one pint of blood, prolonged loss of sleep, repeating the test with very little rest between tests, and several other factors have been investigated and found not to influence VO_2 max. But the type of exercise during the test will influence VO_2 max results, because the larger the muscle mass employed, the greater the oxygen consumption. Running uphill on a motorized treadmill is the standard testing format. A stationary bicycle ergometer may also be used but will result in a VO_2 max approximately 10% lower. It may be more appropriate to refer to a *peak* VO_2 when you mean the highest oxygen consumption for a particular type of exercise, because VO_2 max is usually reserved for the highest possible value under any circumstances.

Because body size affects oxygen consumption, VO_2 max is usually expressed in milliliters of oxygen per kilogram of body weight ($ml \cdot kg^{-1} \cdot min^{-1}$) when measured in the laboratory. Resting VO_2 is approximately 3.5 $ml \cdot kg^{-1} \cdot min^{-1}$, and during maximal exercise it may increase by 10 to 20 times depending on your level of fitness.

Consumption of oxygen during exercise depends largely on coordination of several physiological functions that transport oxygen to the muscles. The process begins when oxygen enters the lungs and rapidly diffuses into the bloodstream via the capillaries surrounding the tiny air sacs (alveoli) of the lungs. Blood flow from the heart increases to several times resting rate during maximal exercise due to an increased volume of blood pumped from the heart each beat and also an increased heart rate. At the muscles, the rate at which oxygen is taken up from the blood depends on how quickly and efficiently the muscle cells use oxygen in the energy production process.

Aerobic (oxygen-using) physical training such as jogging, swimming, and cycling can improve VO_2 max by increasing blood volume and the pumping capacity of the heart. This makes more oxygen available to the muscles during exercise and increases their ability to use oxygen. The elite marathoner may consume as much as 80 $ml \cdot kg^{-1} \cdot min^{-1}$ or more of oxygen during maximal exercise compared with approximately 42 $ml \cdot kg^{-1} \cdot min^{-1}$ for the average college-age man. Women typically have a VO_2 max of 10% to 15% less than men. The explanation for this is not entirely known, but contributing factors may be the lower hemoglobin level in women and their additional sex-specific fat. Body fat decreases VO_2 max, but even when oxygen consumption is calculated per kilogram of lean body mass the difference between sexes is not entirely removed.

The average person can expect to make rapid gains in VO_2 max early in training, with changes of 10% to 20% typical for a ten-week training period. As training continues, further increases are difficult and slow in coming as you approach your genetic limit, but even if no gains are made you can still slow the decline in VO_2 max that normally occurs with aging. □

PHYSICAL GROWTH IN THE YOUNG ATHLETE

by Malcolm J. Coomber, Great Britain

The training of young athletes, always a controversial subject, is given very subjective analysis by British Coach Coomber. He offers guidelines for training and outlines the effects that training will have on the growing child.

First we must look at the background of these "bodies" with which we are going to work—the many factors affecting the growth of the young athlete. The age concerning us is probably from 11 or 12 onwards, although the coach must have knowledge of physical development before that age.

At this age the child is changing school and being introduced to a more formal physical education program. It approximates the end of a period of relatively uninhibited movement and discovery, at the latter end of the so called "skill hungry years."

As well as the enlargement of bone and cartilage, growth means increase in number and size of body cells. For the most part, development runs parallel to growth. Development of all the anatomical, physiological and psychological processes takes approximately until age twenty.

Growth has stages of sudden acceleration throughout its process and several tissues develop non-synchronously; and each body part grows at a different rate—between birth and age 20, the head expands to double its original size, while the length of the leg increases by five times during that period.

After the rapid development of the first two years over-all growth is more gradual. While the growth of the upper parts of the body slow down, the growth of the legs is still quite rapid during the pre-school years. By the age of six, the child's proportions closely resemble those of an adult, and growth continues at a relatively slow pace.

Up to the age of ten, there is very little difference in the height and weight of boys and girls, though on average boys may be slightly taller. This position changes just before adolescence, around age 11 or 12 for girls and 13 or 14 for boys, when there is a "growth spurt" (**Figure 1**), and for two or three years until approximately age 15, girls are somewhat taller and heavier than boys. The growth spurt is the last occasion of rapid height and weight gain; after adolescence the growth rate slows considerably. Final height for girls is attained between 16 and 18, and for boys between 17 and 19.

Shortly after this time, final ossification of the skeleton is complete, with the exception of

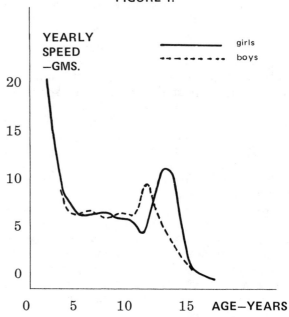

FIGURE 1.

the vertebral column which may take to age 25 to be finished. Ossification is the breakdown of cartilage (from which all bones, with the exception of the skull and collarbones, are formed) and its replacement via the construction of bone tissue. This process is accompanied by the setting down of an increasingly thick layer of bone around the cartilage and from within the cartilage.

Growth of the bone (lengthening) takes place at the junction between the "growing end" and the main shaft, known as *epiphysis*. Although the total process of skeletal growth is hormonally dictated, it is also subject to functional loading. These hormonal effects render the epiphyses relatively vulnerable parts of the body.

Individual organs and organ systems of the body grow at different rates. During the first three or four years, muscles grow continuously and roughly in proportion to the over-all body growth. In the next two years muscle size expands rapidly accounting for approximately 75% of the child's increase in weight during this period.

Mid-childhood finds muscle tissue increases in proportion to general growth. As with most aspects of development, boys tend to be slower than girls in muscular growth. The ultimate development of girls' muscles is not as great as boys', and therefore girls are physically weaker at maturity.

Figure 2 shows the curves of postnatal growth rates of three major types of organs. General body tissue (including bones, muscles, and most of the internal organs) grows rapidly at first and then at a decelerated rate until about two years before adolescence; then the preadolescent spurt brings a second period of speedy growth; finally a slow down occurs until adult size is attained.

Development of the neural system is extremely rapid in the first six years and then slows down sharply. In marked contrast to this the genital system has a period of very slow growth in childhood, and extremely rapid

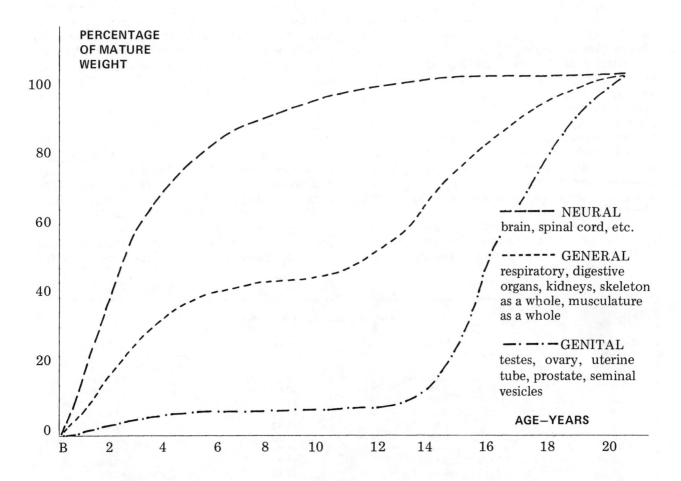

FIG. 2. GROWTH RATES OF THE THREE MAJOR CATEGORIES OF ORGANS (SCAMMON).

development at puberty.

It is not possible to have a complete set of "ground rules" because of the fundamental differences between athletes; therefore training should be designed with due consideration to growth spurts, maturation, puberty, sex and the event. The coach must always be able to adjust and mold the program to the ever changing situation.

At this point it is worth highlighting a situation in many of our clubs which appears contrary to a large part of the foregoing. We have a tendency to place our youngsters with the novice coaches. However we should remember that the work done with young athletes must be well organized and thought out—and this is not the situation for the inexperienced coach.

In the program all aspects must have a long term basis for their maximization. No single factor should be extracted and maximized quickly. To do this would produce the "mini-monster" with which we are all probably familiar—the coach could then have a 14-, 15-, or 16-year-old "failure" on his hands.

Stories of this abuse are legend: an often quoted example concerns a National Coach who was approached by the father of a young middle-distance runner who wanted to know what recovery he should give to his young son between workouts of 12 x 400 flat out. To his eternal credit the coach's reply was, "one week!" Quite frankly, coaches or persons masquerading as coaches who do this sort of thing are at best ignorant and at worst, criminally negligent.

The coach's first serious consideration must be to define competitive or performance success for his young athlete. Always allow the athlete to know why they are doing a particular unit of work and where it fits into their over all program. Too often youngsters work in "ignorance" and will often copy practices they have seen older, more mature athletes performing. And this without their coach's knowledge or agreement. The stages of development are obvious to us but probably not to the athletes involved.

Track and field athletics is just a simple series of tests and measurements, with an overriding principle of "how high?," 'how fast?,' 'how far?' Unfortunately many competitions and techniques are watered down adult versions. Perhaps we should reconsider the way in which these are introduced to young athletes—make changes in the implements, race distances and the rules—". . .if the emphasis was away from that of the adult competitive program the task of learning and of teaching these skills and practices may be easier" (Giles).

Before moving on to the details of training I must issue a word of caution about the approximate ages used. At all times the coach should bear in mind the quite large differences that can occur between chronological age and physical age. Hollman (1968) showed **Figure 3)** that the greatest difference can appear around age 13; and this can be as much as 3.6 years.

A wide area of development, having been described, then poses questions about strength development, endurance, skill acquisition and technique, and the programming of training. Reference to **Figure 4** shows the percentage muscular strength we can expect from young athletes, taking a 25 year old man as 100%.

Figures 5a & 5b show the periods of intense development of the child's physical abilities, giving a guide to the time (age) for

FIG. 3		from BROUNS (after HOLLMAN 1968)	
Chronological age	Retarded	Accelerated	Difference
8 years	7.00 years	9.25 years	+2.25 years
9 years	7.83 years	10.60 years	+2.78 years
10 "	8.85 "	11.00 "	+2.75 "
11 "	9.33 "	12.33 "	+3.00 "
12 "	10.53 "	13.00 "	+2.47 "
13 "	10.89 "	14.25 "	+3.36 "
14 "	12.55 "	15.29 "	+2.74 "
15 "	13.57 "	16.43 "	+2.86 "
16 "	14.86 "	17.40 "	+2.54 "
17 "	16.00 "	18.00 "	+2.00 "
18 "	17.00 "	19.00 "	+2.00 "

emphasis on particular aspects of training.

Excessive loading of the spine should be avoided while the athlete is still growing, and this in any case must be preceded by good development of the trunk musculature—the early emphasis on dorsal and abdominal strength. Before the use of weights and resistance exercises the young athlete must work on a complete range of movement, and initial strengthening must come from mobility and suppling exercises.

Szmodis states that with the favorable hormonal balance present in girls immediately after the adolescent growth spurt, they should be exposed to regular, moderate strength training (around age 13). He also states that in devising the appropriate work for the preadolescent, care should be taken that sufficient amount of stretching exercises be included. There is also a place for those exercises requiring the elongation of the contracted muscle, i.e., eccentric muscle contraction.

Pre-puberty the emphasis should be on steady state aerobic runs, where no oxygen debt occurs and the nervous system is not under stress, as the muscle biochemistry does not favor anaerobic work.

"In repeated high intensity, incomplete recovery training, then, the load placed on the oxygen transport system—and more specifically the heart—may suggest a training effect which is quite different in character to similar training practiced by adults" (Dick).

However the two aspects of endurance cannot be completely separated. It would be impossible to exclude all exercises in which there was an anaerobic part, and also unwise.

In very broad terms, the acquisition of skills and the learning of techniques will come before sweat and the development of strength. This is not to lose sight of the fact that some skills and techniques cannot be established until the body is strong enough. During the "skill-hungry" years—8/11 for girls, 8/13 for boys—the young athlete must be given the opportunity to learn as many techniques as possible.

However, it should be borne in mind that the child is equally capable of learning bad techniques and/or compensatory ones. Therefore the best teaching must be available to them, and at each stage they must have the basic strength, mobility and endurance to perform adequate periods of practice without introducing compensatory movements.

While the initial build up of the technique will be slow to establish the correct pattern of movement, as soon as possible the speed of execution of the correct movement must be included.

With the advent of leagues and age group competitions, the period of adolescence, previously a period of preparation for competition in the post-teenage years, has become a time of high-pressure competition. The problems resulting from excessive bias within the training program have already been dealt with, and so it is to be hoped that the diligent coach will guard against the temptations endemic in these pressures.

The following guide is suggested for training progression:
a) general conditioning: strength, mobility, endurance.
b) basic technical model: preliminary skills, basic drills.
c) special conditioning: speed, speed endurance, elastic strength, maximum strength, strength endurance.
d) advanced technical model.□

REFERENCES

ASTRAND, P-C. & RODAHL, K. *Textbook of Work Physiology*
CRATTY, B.J. *Movement Behaviour and Motor Learning*
KNAPP, B. *Skill in Sport*
MUSSEN, P.H. *The Psychological Development of the Child*
TANNER, J.M. *Growth at Adolescence*
CAIN, G. *Coaching-an Art or Science (Athletics Coach* Vol. 14, No. 3, Sept., 1980)
DICK, F. W. *Training and the Growing Child* (lecture at Midlands Coaching Conference 1977) (paper reproduced *Athletics Coach,* Vol. 12, No. 1, March, 1978)
TRAVERS, P. *Report on Two Visits to the Medical Center at Vincennes (Athletics Coach,* Vol. 5, No. 1, March, 1971)

FIG. 4.

a man of 25 years = 100%

girl of 6	=	+ 20%	boy of 6	=	+20%
girl of 10	=	40%	boy of 10	=	40%
girl of 14	=	50%	boy of 14	=	60%
girl of 18	=	60%	boy of 18	=	90%

from BROUNS (after BAUSENWEIN 1967)

FIG. 5a   Endurance

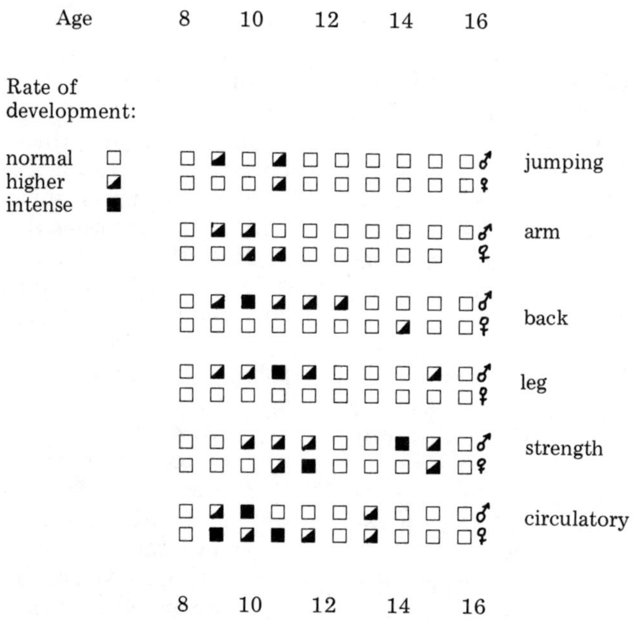

Age   8   10   12   14   16

Rate of
development:

normal ☐
higher ◰
intense ■

♂ jumping / ♀

♂ arm / ♀

♂ back / ♀

♂ leg / ♀

♂ strength / ♀

♂ circulatory / ♀

8   10   12   14   16

FIG. 5b   Speed & Strength

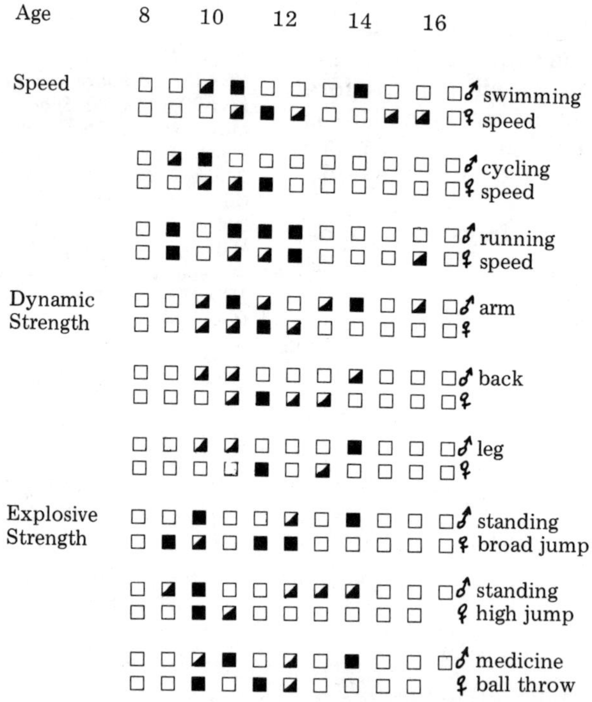

Age   8   10   12   14   16

Speed   ♂ swimming / ♀ speed

♂ cycling / ♀ speed

♂ running / ♀ speed

Dynamic
Strength   ♂ arm / ♀

♂ back / ♀

♂ leg / ♀

Explosive
Strength   ♂ standing / ♀ broad jump

♂ standing / ♀ high jump

♂ medicine / ♀ ball throw

114

STRESS INDICATORS IN MIDDLE & LONG DISTANCE RUNNERS

by Dick Brown, Coach & Physiologist, Athletics West, Eugene, Oregon

Brown's stress indicators are based on a 10-month study conducted in 1978-79 using 15 Athletics West middle- and long-distance runners.

Assumption: World-class athletes are genetically gifted. If they are able to train consistently at the proper level, without loss of training time due to illness or injury, they will compete effectively.

Goal: To provide simple, statistically significant stress indicators enabling the athlete to make appropriate training decisions, which will in turn enable the athlete to train more consistently by reducing training interruptions due to stress related illness or injury.

Stress indicators predicting potential illness or injury problems:
Post PM work-out weight
Evening fluid intake
Time to bed
AM pulse rate
Hours slept

1) .05 is usually accepted as significant. This means the event would occur 50 times in 1000 by chance. .012 means an event would only occur 12 times in 1000 by chance. In other words, for our data, the relationship between the stress indicators and the potential illness or injury is strong and probably not due to chance.

2) Body weight was taken after the PM practice, but if the weight is taken the same time each day (especially AM weight) it should be equally effective.

3) Evening fluid intake was a subjective evaluation of thirst between the evening meal and bedtime. "2" was "normal" and "1" was "more than usual." Thus, when thirst was "more than usual," the score was lower.

4) The AM pulse rate was a one minute count after fully awake and prior to getting out of bed.

How to use the data:
If one or more of the above changes are noted, your potential for illness or injury *is increased.*

This information is a flag to get your attention. Review what you have done the last few days and what is planned for the day the change(s) is noted. Listen to your bodies warning signs and modify the workout. □

Indicator	Mean-healthy	Mean-ill/inj	% Change	Significant	# of Readings
Post PM work-out weight[2]	67.3 Kg	65.3 Kg	3	.026	292
Evening fluid intake[3]	1.77 (near normal)	1.59 (more than normal)	10	.023	721
Time to bed	11:12	11:50	3	.016	946
AM pulse rate[4]	47	52	11	.012	1145
Hours slept	8.0	7.6	5	.009	1004

World Roundup

by Jess Jarver

LONG JUMP MECHANICS

by Dr. E.A. Towbridge

Articles on mechanics of long jumping state that it is usual for athletes to rotate in a clockwise direction after the take-off. The reason for this is attributed to the line of action of the vertical component of impulse force being behind the mass center at the instant of take-off. They surmise that, if such a rotation is unchecked, it would be theoretically possible for the athlete to finish on his head in the sand on the landing pit.

They argue that the only external force acting on the system of particles, constituting the athlete, is the gravitational pull, and therefore the total angular momentum about the mass center of the system must remain constant. This argument is based on the principle that the rate of change with time of the total angular momentum about the mass center is equal to the moment about the mass center of the resultant external force.

They also state that angular momentum is the product of a body's moment of inertia and its angular velocity. Combining these two statements they deduce that the athlete can reduce his speed of forward rotation by increasing his moment of inertia.

Unfortunately, these predictions are based on oversimplified mechanical models. The statement that angular momentum is the product of moment of inertia and angular velocity will apply only to a system of particles that constitute a rigid lamina (or rigid body in uniplanar motion). Even though the arms, legs and the trunk of the athlete may realistically be modeled as rigid rods, their relative movements imply that the system of particles, representing the whole athlete, is not a rigid lamina or body.

The moment of inertia of the athlete, considered as a particle system, will not be constant. It changes with time. Also, more than one angular velocity will be involved in the evaluation of the angular momentum about the mass center. If the athlete is considered as nine rods, two for each arm, two for each leg and one for the trunk and a disc for the head, nine angular speeds will have to be calculated.

In fact, it is more sensible when trying to perform a mechanical analysis of the long jump to consider the nine individual angular momenta, since the mass center of the athlete moves relative to the system as a whole and may even lie outside the system of particles.

Predictions based on statements which consider the athlete as a rigid lamina will necessarily be in error and may lead to the adoption of inefficient long jump techniques. An aspiring long jumper should spend more time acquiring speed and accuracy on the runway and lift at take-off, rather than trying to perfect a nitch kick or hang style that may not give any mechanical advantage.

Athletics Coach (Great Britain)

WHEN ARE ATHLETES IN THEIR PRIME

by Peter Tegen

Athletes and coaches often wonder at what age best performances can be expected and how long an athlete can stay at the top. Answers to these questions do not come too easily but experience and research have provided some information that is useful in designing an individual running career.

Looking at the data concerning the careers of some 305 international-caliber athletes (see Table) shows that sprinters make their biggest improvements between the age of 18 and 20, most reaching their best performances between 19 and 24. On an average, very young champions (16 to 18 years), who were produced in extremely short and intense training programs, have shorter careers and rarely reach the level of those who have been developed gradually on long range training plans.

A similar observation can be made in middle distance running. Most, who start too soon and too hard have shorter running careers. Ninety percent of the top runners who stay up there for a number of years come from long range training programs and it takes them 6.2 years to reach their best.

Long distance runners need the largest preparation but they also stay with it a considerable period. About

TABLE 1.

	Sprint	Middle Distance	Long Distance
First regular training	15-16	17	18
First "prime" performance	17	18	19
Best ever performance	20-28	21-29	22-32
Years of top performances	20%—4 yrs. or less	25%—4 yrs.	12%—7 yrs. or less
	75%—5 yrs.	50%—6 yrs.	63%—7 to 8 yrs.
	5%—5 yrs. +	25%—7 to 10 yrs.	25%—10 to 15 yrs.

half of them, who trained with the pure interval methods, had to cope with many injuries, some so severe that they were forced to stop.

In summary, it can be stated that training at an early age must be carefully planned and only gradually increased in its intensity. It will not pay to hasten to record breaking performances or push young athletes to their maximum levels too soon.

Track and Field Journal (Canada)

MORE ABOUT YIFTER

Short and lean Miruts Yifter of Ethiopia, using his easy but considerably long running stride, dictated the Olympic distance events in no uncertain manner. He ran like a skilled hunter, accelerating and decelerating as he wished, particularly in the 10,000m final where his superiority, assisted by fellow countrymen Kedir and Kotu, ruined all attempts by Lasse Viren to employ a steady pace.

Despite the appearance, Yifter denies that he uses pre-planned tactics in his races. "I never enter a race with any tactical plans," he explains. "As the race begins, I observe what my rivals are doing. My decision to accept the pace offered, or to take over the lead, is usually made after the first five laps, knowing that whatever happens, I can begin my final sprint with 600m to go."

Tactics or no tactics, Yifter's enormous energy reserves have been achieved through training three to four hours a day. According to his coach, Niguse Roba, the Olympic champion trains mainly in forests near his home at 2400m altitude. He places emphasis on running over undulating country, usually covering 20 to 30km in a workout. This often takes place in temperatures close to 40°C. Yifter's track training is made up from a 6 x 800m, 25 x 100m, 20 x 200m and 12 x 400m series. The pace is adjusted according to the demands of a particular period of the year.

Finally, it is interesting to note some views of Yifter and his coach, expressed last year at Ostrava. Yifter explained that he believes it most important for long distance runners to compete early in their careers in 800 and 1500m races, even in the sprints. Roba considers winning far more important than breaking world records. "Some coaches aim for records," he explained. "My aim is to assist athletes to remain among the winners for as long as possible."

Legkaya Atletika (USSR)

PRACTICAL HELP FROM SPORTS MEDICINE

by Paul Schmidt

Athletes and coaches expect considerable assistance from sports medicine to solve complex problems occurring in planning and executing training and competition in running events. Such assistance should not be available only to a small group of internationals but also to lower level performers and particularly to talented young athletes and their coaches.

The performance diagnosis should provide event-specific information that concentrates on data and analysis of parameters relevant to performances. It should also help to solve such problems as providing information on future performance potential, early warning of possible loss of form and precautionary measures to be taken to avoid loss of form.

The following immediate actions are recommended to provide efficient assistance to running athletes from sport medicine:

• Coordination of research through the establishment of a central research unit to avoid unnecessary duplication of similar projects. The central unit should concentrate only on projects that have a practical purpose in consultation with experienced coaches.

• Standardization of existing testing methods and event-specific information to avoid the present confusion with different treadmill gradients and variations in the employed loads and intensities.

• Field research that can be directly used in planning of training and competition. It should include constant monitoring of the actual performance level and the analysis of lactic acid concentration under varying training loads.

• A better understanding of training and racing performances by sports scientists through evaluating training diaries. Sports medicine specialists will have to compare the actual work performed by an athlete with laboratory and field studies to provide an objective and reliable evaluation of the actual performance level.

Leichtathletik (West Germany)

THOUGHTS ON SPRINT TRAINING

by Dr. Kuulo Kutsar

It is important to keep constantly in mind that

muscular contraction energy in the 100 and 200 sprint distances depends on the reserves of creatin phosphate in the muscles. These reserves diminish in the working phase to be replenished during the recovery. However, well-adjusted recoveries cannot only restore creatin phosphate reserves but increase them above the initial level when supercompensation methods are employed.

The athletes should therefore avoid performing numerous repetitions of short (40 to 80m) training distances at 90 to 95% intensity with short recoveries. It will drastically reduce creatin phosphate reserves and affect performances.

The correct approach would be to use series of 4 to 6 repetitions of 40 to 80m with 10 to 12 min. recoveries between the series to create supercompensation. This will lift the creatin phosphate reserves in the muscles above the initial level and improve performances accordingly.

A similar situation occurs in training for the 400 meters. The quarter-milers frequently make the mistake of using in training 300 to 600m repetitions at 80 to 90 percent intensity with short recoveries. Glycogen reserves in the muscles are exhausted and performances suffer. The correct approach would be to create supercompensation by introducing 15 to 20 min. recovery intervals between series of 2 to 3 repetitions.

Modern Athlete and Coach (Australia)

DISTANCE RUNNING TECHNIQUE

by Vladimir Zulin

An analysis of available literature reveals that most authors in middle and long distance running concentrate on the development of aerobic and anaerobic endurance and pay little attention to running technique. While nobody underestimates the importance of maximum oxygen uptake and the tolerance of a high oxygen debt, it is equally wrong to underestimate the value of an economical and efficient running technique.

The lack of information and common terminology has made it difficult to evaluate the efficiency of different technique variations, particularly when individual running styles have to be considered. To overcome this problem the author recommends to base the analysis of a running stride on a three-tiered system as shown in **Fig. 1.**

In the diagram S_o represents the running stride, divided into the non-support (S_1) and the support (S_2) phases. Each of these phases is again sub-divided. $S_{1.1.}$ represents the separation of the feet and $S_{1.2.}$ the closing in of the feet in the non-support phase. $S_{2.1.}$ is the deepest knee bend phase, $S_{2.2.}$ the start of the driving phase and $S_{2.3}$ the end of the driving phase.

A mathematical analysis of these parameters in four runners—Turb (USSR), Sellik (USSR), Yifter (Ethiopia) and Viren (Finland)—reveal how valuable such information can be. The results (full details are included in the article) show that Yifter and Viren employ a far more economical running technique. This is particularly noticeable in the support phase. Turb and Sellik concentrate here on a stressed push-off at the end of the drive to retain velocity. In contrast, Viren and Yifter conserve energy by using an economical rolling action at the start of the support phase.

Spordileht (Estonia)

CHOICE OF POLES

by Herbert Czingon

Pole vaulting is the most expensive event in the track and field program, making the correct choice of poles extremely important. As a general rule, beginners should use poles according to their body weight, grip height and running speed. The first chosen model should allow for the establishment of a bend by the second or third training session. The choice of the next model must be guided by the rules for advanced vaulters, avoiding poles that over-bend close to a 90-degree angle.

One of the most important points in the choice, often overlooked by athletes and coaches, is the correct length of the pole. We regularly find vaulters using poles that they can't grip at the recommended height, around 10 to 30cm from the top end of the pole. They wonder why the pole feels much harder than the kg- or lb-scale indicates and why it breaks without being over-bent.

This is happening because poles are constructed with a vertical bending zone between the optimal recommended grip height and the lower end. **(Fig. 1b).** This zone is reinforced for a uniform bend, created only when the correct grip height is used. When gripped lower than the recommended height, the pole develops a bend

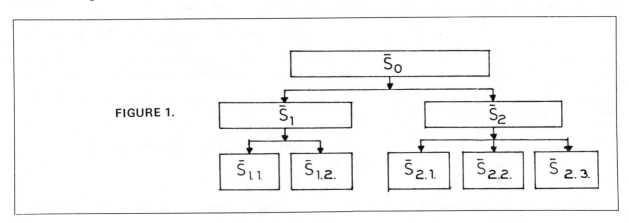

FIGURE 1.

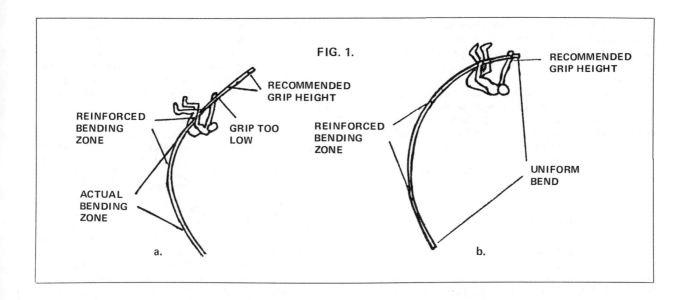

FIG. 1.

RECOMMENDED GRIP HEIGHT

REINFORCED BENDING ZONE

GRIP TOO LOW

ACTUAL BENDING ZONE

a.

RECOMMENDED GRIP HEIGHT

REINFORCED BENDING ZONE

UNIFORM BEND

b.

below the center, which is not reinforced (Fig. 1a). Besides other disadvantages, there is a danger of the pole breaking under the strain.

Leichtathletik (West Germany)

NUTRITION FOR ENDURANCE EVENTS

by M. Saleskij

Athletes training for endurance events can have five or six meals a day. The recommended distribution of caloric intake is 25% for breakfast, 30% for lunch and 25% for the evening meal. The remaining 20% is to be consumed in relatively equal quantities in two or three in-between meals or snacks. The average daily need for female athletes is 4000 to 5000 calories, for male athletes 4500 to 5500 calories.

Most important is to assure that there is a sensible distribution of fats, carbohydrates and protein in the food intake. The optimal distribution for endurance athletes is considered to be 60% carbohydrates, 25% fats and 15% protein, allowing for differences in training. Drastic changes in this distribution take place during recoveries after intensive training to replace muscle glycogen and during the carbohydrate supercompensation prior to major events.

It should be noted that the protein intake during recovery should not be less than 1.5 to 2 grams for one kilogram of bodyweight. The protein-rich meal is recommended to follow about an hour after an intake of a sufficient quantity of fluids and mineral salts. Fats, admittedly in limited quantities, are also needed for recovery. However, it should be noted that fats are filling and could reduce the appetite for carbohydrates and proteins.

An average daily ration for a woman endurance athlete in training should contain 150 to 170g. of protein, 110 to 125g. of fats and 600 to 650g. of carbohydrates. For men, 170 to 200g. of protein, 130 to 150g. of fats and 650 to 800g. of carbohydrates. With a

balanced diet, there should be no problems with minerals but it is advisable to take vitamin supplements, particularly during the periods of large training volumes and when training at high altitude.

Der Leichtathlet (East Germany)

BIOMECHANICS OF THE HIGH JUMP RUN-UP

by J. Lazarev, N. Mihhailou, N. Yakunin

The authors, presenting a biomechanical analysis of the high jump, look in detail into the characteristics of the run-up. They claim that the efficiency of the run-up, usually divided into the acceleration and the preparation for the take-off phases, depends on the rhythm, stride length, speed and execution of the last three strides.

In the straddle, the most common length of the run-up is 7 to 9 strides, with variations between 5 to 13 strides. The average flop run-up is 9 to 11 strides, with variations between 6 to 17 strides. The straddle run-up is straight, approaching the bar at an angle of 30 to 40° (variations between 20 to 60°). The flop run-up begins at an angle of 65 to 90°, before curving to an angle of 25 to 30° to the crossbar. In both cases, the faster the run-up, the sharper is the approach angle.

The transfer from the run-up into the take-off occurs during the last three strides. During this phase the center of gravity of the jumper drops with the bend in the knee joint reaching 86 to 110° in the straddle, but less in the flop, unless a straight lead-leg action is employed. In general, the transfer into the take-off in the flop is less pronounced because the lean towards the center of the curve lowers the center of gravity slightly and there is less backward lean at the start of the take-off.

Good high jumpers reach a stride frequency of 3.70 to 4.50 strides a second in the last of the three final acceleration strides. The speed of straddle jumpers at the end of the last approach stride is 7.0 to 7.5m/sec., compared with 7.5 to 7.8m/sec. in the flop technique. It is reduced by 10 to 20% at the moment of the take-off in the straddle but by only 2 to 5% in the flop. There is also a great difference in the duration of the take-off (0.12 to 0.192 sec. in the flop, 0.174 to 0.265 sec. in the straddle).

The latest trend among leading high jumpers is to lengthen and speed up the run-up, attempting to avoid velocity losses during the last stride by using less pronounced preparatory movements in the straddle and simplifying the transfer phase in the flop.

Legkaya Atletika (USSR)

TECHNICALLY SPEAKING

by Roman Olszewski

The technical program of any sport must take into account the growth patterns of its participants. On the average, girls achieve physical maturity two years before the boys at the age of about 15. The greatest disparity in physical maturity occurs in the 13 to 14 age range at which boys have reached only 89.4% of potential adult height, as opposed to 97.4% for the girls.

In track and field, the Canadian specifications for throwing events have come, through trial and error, or as a result of theoretical considerations, to correlate closely with the growth patterns of teenagers in women's events. In throwing for example, there is no difference in the implements for girls from the age of 13 to 14 years through to senior competition (over 20 years). Girls in the younger age groups seem to adapt well to the situation.

The men's throwing events, however, exhibit a much different pattern. In the javelin event the mass of the implement increases from 600g for the 13 to 14year-olds to 800g—an increase of 25%. The difference in the discus, from 1kg to 2kg is a whopping 100%. Because the development in stature of boys between the ages of 13 and 19 is so rapid as compared to girls, a substantial progression in men's throwing event specification is required if the boys are to attempt to mimic the technique of experienced seniors.

It is obvious that a great deal of scientific study, encompassing all of the factors, growth patterns and sociological and psychological development, is required to establish a basis of age groupings and implement specifications.

Athletics (Canada)

MOSCOW SHOT PUT ANALYSIS

by Wilf Paish

The shot is the only throwing event, for men, where the average age has increased (29 years). The mean height has remained constant at about 191cm where as the average weight (121.72kg) has decreased by about 3kg. From visual impressions this seems obvious as all of the competitors look slimmer, fitter, faster and more athletic.

Most of the throwers wore some kind of wrist strapping. This now seems essential and would suggest a scrapping of the rule requiring medical certificate. The rule regarding finger strapping should also be reviewed as it is unlikely to provide an unfair advantage in this event. Only one thrower seemed to wear a protective waist belt.

During pre-event warm-up very few of the throwers seemed really active. Movement commenced about 45 minutes before the reporting time (30 minutes before the event). Some lifted light weights at speed, some jogged, stretched and did some gentle putting. The Russians all rehearsed the total movement, Baryshnikov, as in training, reducing the circle size by about 30cms. The East Germans seemed to do very little. The three Russians were taken to the medical room about an hour before the report time. This certainly caused some concern with the other throwers.

In discussions with the throwers and coaches at the training track, it would seem as if there is a definite move away from pure strength. The emphasis is placed on power and general athleticism. All emphasized the need to do quality work all of the year round (other than during recovery). There seemed to be little evidence of "periodization" as it has come to be known.

The mean age of female competitors remained at 26 years; the mean height at 175cm while the weight showed a decrease from the last Games of 2kg down to 87kg. Having observed most of them in training one realizes that they are fast, strong and very athletic women.

In the pre-event warm-up very few of the women athletes seemed to do anything very active. Warm-up inside of the stadium consisted of a general mixture of standing puts for the first of their two permitted efforts, followed by a shift for the second.

As far as this event is concerned there are no significant changes in techniques. Indeed, the women offer a tremendous variety of the conventional O'Brien shift with some starting high and other starting very low. On landing from the shift, the putting base varied from the very wide stance of Slupianek to the narrower base used by most others. However, very few really split the circle. Some use a braced front leg delivery while others use a jump and some have a long very late active reverse.

Circle (Great Britain)

HYPNOSIS AND SPORT

by Russell Hawkins

The increasing use of hypnosis in athletics is seen as an example of the recent expansion in scope of psychological contributions to sport. In reviewing the latest literature, it becomes clear that the traditional use of hypnosis, involving attempts to increase power, strength or endurance, fails to succeed. Hypnosis per se does not improve physical performance.

However, motivating instructions given during hypnosis do result in improved performances. What remains unclear is which variables are instrumental in effecting the improvement, since some authors have been able to demonstrate equivalent gains to motivating hypnosis by using motivational instructions without it.

It is suggested that the value of hypnosis in sport lies not in any ability to improve performance through direct suggestion, but in the potential for hypnosis to alter suggestive feelings. Data is available to show that, even while objective indicators of athletic performance remain unaltered, subjective feelings (i.e., perceived exertion) may be substantially modified.

While skill development and the level of fitness components determine physical capabilities, hypnosis offers a means to influence the athlete's state of mind. It has the potential to modify fears, anxieties, confidence levels, arousal levels, motivations, determination and enthusiasm—all factors not to be ignored. From the viewpoint of the coach or the psychologist, it appears that the most appealing quality of hypnosis is that it offers a unique opportunity for efficient message communication.

Sport and the Elite Athlete,
Congress Report (Australia)

LIGHTER JAVELINS FOR YOUNG GIRLS

by Z. Sinitski

Coaches, assigned to study the problems of young female javelin throwers, recommend the use of lighter implements for girls. They believe that the two main problems in the development of potential javelin talent are the start of specialized training at the age of 12 to 14 years and the shoulder injuries that result from the early specialization. The injuries studied were of similar nature and most failed to respond to treatment or improved only slightly.

The reason for the injuries appeared to be in the serious use of too heavy javelins, shots and balls in the training of young girls. It should be noted that the women's discus weighs only half of the men's implement and the women's shot is also virtually half of the men's shot. However, the difference in the weight of the javelin is only 200g (7 oz.). Further, boys use lighter shots and discuses for various age groups, but girls are not enjoying this privilege.

Consequently, the introduction of 300 and 500g javelins, as compared with the present 600g, could well prevent shoulder injuries during the developmental age of young girls, who lack shoulder strength. This, however, would be effective only if the training of talented throwers is not forced and hurried. It is essential that good all-round physical conditioning precedes technical training. Premature technical tasks are not only hard to achieve but are frequently responsible for serious injuries.

Future javelin potential should therefore use many-sided training to lay a foundation for future development for 4 to 6 years. During this period the learning of technique should correspond strictly to the physical development level. After all, Ruth Fuchs made an impact in international competition at the age of 26 and the average age of javelin throwers in Montreal was 26.2 years.

Legkaya Atletika (USSR)

BORN A WINNER

by David L. Costill

The use of muscle biopsies for predictive purposes can only be applied to those individuals having extremely different fiber types. That is to say, only athletes having either very few (30% or less) or very many (70% or more) slow twitch fibers can be considered to have specific potential for a given event. Since the percentage of slow and fast twitch fibers is somewhat fixed from birth, individuals who have a predominance of slow twitch fibers are the ones with the greatest chance of success in events of long duration.

Being born with muscles composed principally of slow twitch fibers does not mean that you will immediately be successful as a marathon runner. It simply means that the latent potential is there for you to develop. Having a high percentage of slow twitch fibers simply means that with proper training and stress, these fibers will develop to provide the aerobic type endurance essential for prolonged effort.

In a number of our studies involving muscle biopsies we have observed untrained, middle aged men, who had over 80% slow twitch fibers in their leg muscles. In most cases these men had never engaged in any sports programs as children. Consequently, their endurance talents were never realized. A few of the men subsequently began running and within a few months were able to out perform better trained and more experienced local runners.

The point of all this discussion about muscle fibers is that we can distinguish elite sprinters from elite endurance athletes, but these groups only represent a small fraction of the population. Over 90% of the subjects we have biopsied have a more even mixture of slow and fast twitch fibers. More importantly, we cannot pick the winner of the Olympic marathon or the 100 meter dash on the basis of their muscle fiber types. I can only say that the 6 or 8 best performers in those two events are certain to have muscle fibers that have enabled them to reach this level of endurance or sprinting success.

Racers' Edge (USA)

SELECTION OF POLE VAULTERS

by Y. Volkov

The selection of potential pole vault talent, according to the father and coach of world recordholder Konstantin Volkov, is a complicated task. It begins with visual observations of boys during physical education periods, taking into consideration height, weight, agility, speed and so on.

The next and the most important step is the organization of the first training session. This begins with a series of tests (see Table 1). While the tests provide some information on performance capacities, their value is often overestimated. Dogmatic conclusions that are based on test results should be avoided. Instead, the coach should carefully observe the youngsters in action and make his own decision. It often happens that

TABLE 1.

Test	Age Indicators				
	10	**11**	**12**	**13**	**14**
30m from flying start (sec)	5.0	4.8	4.6	4.5	4.4
60m from crouch start (sec)	9.4	9.2	9.0	8.6-8.5	7.8-7.6
St. Long Jump (cm)	190	200	215	225	245-260
Long Jump (cm)	320-350	350-375	380-400	410-430	470-500
St. Triple Jump (cm)	580	600	620	700	750
Pull-ups (x)	3	4	5	6	8
Pole vault (cm)	140	160	180	220	240

EVALUATION TESTS

young athletes are relatively slow but have good stride frequency. The coach must understand that stride frequency is inherited but speed can also be improved through training by increasing the stride length.

The same applies to strength. There is no need to hurry and eliminate someone who fails in the pull-up test. Replace it with a push-up test, which is easier to perform and evaluate the result in a ratio of 1:3 (one pull-up = three pushups). Keep constantly in mind that the youngster, whom you have eliminated, could be the one you ask back in two or three years time. It happens regularly.

An important factor, even before the final selection is completed, is the planning of training sessions. They must be made up of drills which lead to the introduction of vaulting and are made up from gymnastics, ball games and other track and field events. The basic exercises in gymnastics are performed on the rope. It is at this stage that the coach can make up his mind about final selection.

Legkaya Atletika (USSR)

AN ANALYSIS OF THE HEPTATHLON

by Y. Primakov

An analysis of over 100 leading heptathlon performances in the world showed a close correlation between the total scores and the results in all single events with the exception of the javelin throw. Obviously high scores require good results in all events. The lack of correlation between the total score and the javelin appears to be in the limited training for this new event and its biomechanical structure that is different from all other heptathlon events.

Looking into the correlation between heptathlon performances and the athlete's age indicated that the age influences the total score and the results in the shot, 800m and 200m. These three events, requiring strength and specific endurance, take longer to develop. At the same time, events like hurdling, long jumping and high jumping can produce reasonably high level results in a much shorter time.

The correlation between the single events of the heptathlon showed that hurdling performances were correlated with all heptathlon events, except the javelin.

The correlation was extremely close between the results of the 200m and the long jump. It was also apparent that the factors responsible for success in the hurdles influence considerably 200m and long jump results, causing the author to conclude that the "key" events of the heptathlon are the hurdles, 200m and the long jump.

The shot put results were closely related to all events and even showed some correlation with the javelin. Apparently the development of strength for the shot is a factor that influences performances in all other events.

In conclusion, the following observations appear to be relevant to the present stage of the heptathlon:
1. The factors responsible for performances are made up of:
   — general training level
   — physical development level
   — strength development level
   — specific endurance level
   — technical preparation level.
2. The time needed to achieve high performance in the shot, 200m and 800m should be taken into consideration in long range training plans.

Teoria i Praktika Fiztsheskoi Kultura (USSR)

SPRINT STRIDES

by E. Andris, G. Arzumanov, M. Godik

A study to establish how closely-isolated components of sprinting technique correlate with the total performance was based on a speedogram record of the reaction time, time and distance over which maximum velocity was reached, duration of maximum velocity and deceleration at the finish.

The study showed that the time to reach maximum velocity was relatively constant and depended little on the athlete's sex, age, or performance level. However, there was considerable difference in the distance, ranging from 32 to 36m for skilled athletes to only 24m for novices.

There were also differences in the maintenance of maximum velocity. While the distance for women athletes remained within 42 to 45m, the better male athletes maintained maximum velocity for 48m, compared with 35m for novices.

The study also revealed that the 100m sprint is, for novices, not so much connected with speed qualities than with speed endurance and that speed endurance has a very high variability (24 to 40%). The last can be explained by the fact that the volume of speedwork in training is about the same for all groups but differs considerably in speed endurance training.

A closer look at the results and their correlations indicated that the competitive performance of novices depends practically on all parameters. The performance of highly ranked athletes, on the other hand, is determined by the development of maximum speed and speed endurance in the finishing stages.

The above fact is closely related to the selection of training methods at different stages of development. It appears inadvisable to employ a restricted number of specific speed exercises in the early stages of training, since they act on a narrow range of motor abilities at a time when the performance needs a wide range of qualities. Early specialization in speed exercises seems therefore unjustified.

Teoria i Praktika Fizicheskoi Kultura (USSR)

DEPTH JUMPING

Depth jumping, like hopping and bouncing, is an explosive exercise designed to improve the strength and recruitment of fast muscle fibers in the quadriceps and gastroncnemius muscles. There are three components of depth jumping that should be considered by all coaches if the exercise is to be given the opportunity to produce its maximum training effect and minimize the incidence of injury.
1.   Establish that the athlete is fit to perform the exercise.
2.   Make sure that the technique used in performing the exercise is correct.
3.   The choice of height from which to jump must be carefully assessed for the individual, guided by the athlete's previous explosive training.

As the fast twitch fibers fatigue rapidly, the number of repetitions in depth jumping should be monitored carefully, especially when starting the exercise. It can be suggested as a guide to begin with three sets of five repetitions, gradually increased to 10 repetitions. Training should take place three times a week in the pre-season phase, reduced to once a week in the first month of competition.

Depending on fitness, depth jumping should start at a height of about 50cm gradually increased to a limit of 10cm. If 50cm appears to be too high for the starting height for a particular athlete, he/she should be given a less demanding explosive exercise program for a build-up. A jump and reach test can be used as an indicator for the starting height.

Finally, coaches should take great care in giving teenagers intensive depth-jump programs. There does not appear to be any significant response to explosive strength training in the adolescent until 9 to 12 months after the onset of puberty. This should be kept in mind to prevent late maturers from being grouped with early

maturers in similar programs.

Sports Coach (Australia)

FLEXIBILITY IN THE THROWING EVENTS

by M. Dodwell, B. Miller, K. Roberts

The biomechanics of throwing events necessitate the rapid generation and application of force by the athlete to an external body. It is the explosive nature of the throwing events and the high degree of load placed on the athlete's body that increases the likelihood of injuries to throwers. Obviously, any training regime that can reduce the incidence of these injuries is to be recommended. Many authors have advocated the use of flexibility exercises as one such pre-event procedure. This text will examine the types of injuries associated with throwers and focus upon a program of flexibility exercises designed to aid injury prevention.

Broadly speaking, there are two types of mobility exercises—active and passive. The former are strongly advocated, but the stretch must be a gradual movement to the optimum point and then held until the muscle fatigues. Alternatively, body weight can be employed to apply force to the joint. However, such actions are not bouncing movements, as this activates a stretch reflex, which causes the muscle to contract long before any training effect can be applied to the ligaments. Passive mobility exercises should only be used by experienced athletes and great care should be taken not to overstretch the muscle concerned. These exercises involve the movement of joints through their maximum range by an external force, often the coach or a partner.

The training effect of a flexibility regime can only be maintained by constant repetition and it is recommended that such exercises are performed on a daily basis. It is also suggested that the exercises should be specific to the movement required by the joint, thus promoting mobility in the desired plain while limiting it in others. A further recommendation concerns the place of a flexibility unit in a given training session. The golden rule is "warm-up to do flexibility exercises, not warm-up by flexibility exercises." In other words, they should be preceded by running, jumping-on-the-spot etc. to pre-warm the body. It should be noted there is one joint where increased mobility is not to be recommended, the knee. The major reason for this is that the functional stability of the knee, while load bearing, depends to a great extent on tight ligamentous attachments and good quadricep strength.

Circle (Great Britain)

ENDURANCE FOR YOUNG SPRINTERS

by W. Olijar and N. Fomin

The authors studied the influence of general endurance training in the development of beginner sprinters in the 10 to 11 and 13 to 14 age groups, using contrasting training programs.

In the first 18 months the experiment study group A used 60% of their training time for pure speed and power development, 25% for general endurance development and the rest for mobility and coordination exercises. Group B employed the opposite approach by spending 25% of their training time on pure speed development and 60% on general endurance development.

The general endurance training was based on warm-up runs, steady pace endurance runs, fartlek type runs, games, swimming and medium intensity cross-country skiing. All endurance training activities were adjusted to a work rate that corresponded to an approximate pulse frequency of 150 to 160 a minute. Speed and power training employed 60m runs at maximum speed and slightly downhill, starts from various positions, jumping exercises, medicine-ball exercises, tumbling and intensive circuit training.

Test results after the first 18 months showed only small differences between the two groups. However, following another 18 months training, during which both groups used 70% of their training time on speed and power development, the advantages of group B (60% endurance training during the first 18 months) became obvious. They produced faster test times in a 30m sprint from a flying start, a 60m sprint from a standing start, a 300m run, as well as better results in relative leg strength tests.

The experiment indicated that a large training volume to develop general endurance is required for beginners in speed and power events in order to benefit fully from the following event specific training program.

Legkaya Atletika (USSR)

DAINIS KULA IN ACTION

by Mart Paama

Moscow Olympics Javelin gold medalist, Dainis Kula, uses a final six-stride pattern, pulling the implement back straight. His trunk remains upright to allow for an acceleration in the following strides.

The third stride in Kula's pattern resembles a modified transition stride. It is performed very actively to establish a slight backward lean while the withdrawal of the javelin in completed. The actual transition stride is Kula's fifth, executed with a strong drive from the left leg, so that the left leg passes the right in the flight phase of the stride.

Although this action brings Kula into an orthodox throwing position, his actual delivery action differs from most javelin throwers. Kula's left side continues to move forward without any hurried forward movement of the hips to create a "bow" position. As the result, the delivery is based on virtually simultaneous linking of the right side of the body into the delivery.

The delivery, that follows the active employment of the right side of the body without the classically stressed extreme "bow" position, applies forces to the javelin without a break forward of a fall away to the left.

DAINIS KULA'S DELIVERY
Trunk upright, implement pulled back straight.

The whole movement is directed forward-upward with both feet in firm contact with the ground.

It is interesting to note that the Soviet national javelin coach, Dimitrussenko, criticizes Kula's early javelin withdrawal, claiming that it creates unnecessary tension in his arm. On the other hand, Dimitrussenko believes that Kula's unorthodox delivery could well be superior to the generally accepted "bow" position in the delivery phase.

Track and Field Supplement to Kehakultuur (Estonia)

CONNOLLY ON THE HAMMER THROW

by Hal Connolly

The first thing you notice about Soviet hammer throwers is that they are not the traditional muscular types. However, the size of their muscles is deceiving. They are very efficient because all their training is geared to a specific event.

As a measure of basic strength they use the squat, power clean and snatch, all dynamic movements. They also use one-legged squats with the bar across the back, alternating the legs, rotational exercises with a 20kg plate and medicine ball throws into a wall with the

124

hammer throw movements always emphasizing the release. As you can see, not much time is devoted to traditional power-lifting and body-building types of exercises.

A lot of throwing is done with varied weight hammers, mixing up the heavier and lighter implements. They also throw hammers of varying length.

The Russians say that, in general, an athlete should continue to improve until he is about 30-years-old. If he hits a plateau, then it's not him but his training program which is faulty.

An athlete who trains one day at high intensity must cut back 50% the next day. The third day should be cut back to 20% and the fourth day should be an active rest. Athletes who train at 80 to 90% intensity for three or four consecutive days are doomed to injuries, plateaus and staleness.

Physiological tests and coaches' observations have discovered that world-class athletes can exert maximum effort only a certain number of times in a training session. Some throwers can take up to 30 throws in a workout, while others can manage only five all-out throws. The rest of the deliveries have to be at 80% or less effort to develop neuro-muscular patterns for technique.

Circle (Great Britain)

POWER EXERCISES FOR YOUNG ATHLETES

by Dr. Gunter Fritcshe

The development of leg power is important not only for athletes competing in jumping events but also closely related to performances in throwing events and sprints. Jumping exercises, carefully adjusted to the biological development of young athletes, should therefore find an important part in every training program.

The adjustments in the load and choice of exercises is particularly important in the 10 to 13 age range when most of the structural changes in muscular development take place. There are favorable neurophysiological advantages for power development in this age range but anatomical disadvantages in overcoming large outside loads, such as using the barbell. The skeletal system, including the spine, is still not completely ossificated and unable to tolerate high pushing and pulling stresses. Similarly, the ankle, knee and hip joints should be protected from injuries by careful progression to higher training loads.

In general the choice of exercises includes:
- Double leg take-offs, both vertical and horizontal.
- Single leg take-offs, left and right, vertical and horizontal.
- Partner and competition games.
- Multi-jumps to develop rhythm.
- Springboard take-offs to develop coordination.

In the performance of exercises that include some components of competitive jumps the technical development should not be overlooked. Emphasis should be on the ability to take off from varied length approaches with a flat (long jump) or vertical (high jump) flight curve, active foot placement at the take-off and full extension of the take-off leg.

Finally, the exercises developing jumping power from single- or double-leg take-offs, both horizontal and vertical, should be performed by using only the athlete's own body weight for resistance. No jumping exercises are to be performed by additional resistance in the form of weighted jackets, sandbags, or weights in the 10 to 14 years age range.

Der Leichtathlet (East Germany)

RACE WALKING TECHNIQUES

by Boris Klubov

Most coaches prefer to develop the orthodox technique with a straight lead-leg placement. However a minority is convinced that better results can be achieved by placing the lead leg to the ground with a slight bend in the knee joint. Although the leg is bent when it contacts the ground, it will straighten before passing the vertical axis and the action remains within the international rules.

There have been studies conducted to discover which of the two walking techniques produces more efficient performances. One of such studies included several top-class race walkers, who had virtually equal ability in both techniques. The analysis of the results indicated convincingly that the bent knee technique was by far the most effective. It was more economical and required less energy.

Legkaya Atletika (USSR)

TEACHING DECATHLON EVENTS
by Y. Primakov and G. Popov

A study was conducted to find the most efficient method and sequence of teaching the techniques of single events to potential decathlon talent during their basic training phase at 12 to 13 years of age. The study revealed that the total score depends largely on the results in the hurdles, the pole vault and the javelin throw. It also established the following sequence of teaching single events in a three-phase training plan as the most efficient:

Phase 1: 1. Teaching of preliminary and specific exercises that assist in the development of pole vault, hurdles, javelin, high jump and discus events.

2. Teaching of pole vault, hurdles and javelin techniques.

Phase 2: 1. Teaching of high jump and discus techniques.

2. Development of pole vault, hurdles and javelin techniques.

3. Teaching of preliminary and specific exercises that assist in the development of long jump and shot events.

Phase 3: 1. Teaching of long jump and shot techniques.

2. Development of all the previously established event techniques.

Teoria i Praktika Fiztsheskoi Kultura (USSR)

LATENT AND REACTION TIMES

by Toni Nett

It appears that most coaches and athletes are unaware of the difference between latent and reaction times in the sprint start.

Latent means hidden, not visible. It can be described as the time span that the central nervous system needs to acknowledge the starters gun until responses are spread over the entire nervous system and put into muscular movement. It happens without conscious awareness and without visible reaction. Practice can hardly ever change latent time.

Zaciorski of the U.S.S.R. divides latent time into five components:

1. Appearnace of the stimulus at the receptor (sensual stimuli for the receptive organs and sensory neurons leading to the central nervous system).

2. Dispersement of the stimulus throughout the whole nervous system.

3. Transfer of the stimulus in the cerebrum from sensory neurons to the motor neurons (formation of the order to the effectors).

4. Entry of the nervous system signal into the muscle.

5. Stimulation of the effector and the beginning of mechanical response in the muscle.

Reaction time begins when latent time comes to an end. It is visible and conscious in direct opposition to latent time. The movements commence after the recognition of the command by the athlete.

Reaction time, longer than latent time, is the time span between will and ability to produce locomotion. According to Zaciorski the visual-motor reaction in non-athletes varies from 0.20 to 0.35sec. In trained athletes it is 0.15 to 0.20sec., sometimes even as low as 0.10sec.

Leichtathletik (West Germany)

HURDLE RHYTHM

by Brent McFarlane

Speed is the product of stride length and stride frequency—the number one prerequisite for the sprint hurdle events. Or is it? Many Eastern European countries have placed rhythm ahead of sheer speed.

What is rhythm and how does stride frequency relate to it? We know that stride frequency can only be improved by approximately 17% and only for a short period of time. Add 10 hurdles with three strides between each and frequency becomes even more restricted. To differentiate between rhythm and frequency would be very difficult. Why is it that most hurdlers take eight strides to the first hurdle, three strides between hurdles and six strides to the tape vary in times from 13.0 to 20.0 seconds? They all took the same number of strides in the race.

For an answer consider the following statements:
- "Rhythm is the type of speed which allows hurdlers to use their technique to the maximum."
- "Rhythm work increases the speed of the run."
- "I place the hurdles low so I can practice without tiring and make sure my technique is smooth. I can stay in rhythm and not lose pace between the hurdles."

For simplicity, rhythm is the running part between hurdles. If the hurdles are lowered, hurdling technique becomes of secondary importance, turning hurdling into a faultless sprint. Assuming, of course, that few technical errors exist for those doing the quality work of rhythm.

In high level sprint hurdles races the hurdles "come up" closer as the race progresses. Rhythm work can therefore also involve the hurdles closer together to rehearse this "feeling", while maintaining the elements of good technique, speed and speed endurance.

Many questions revolving rhythm work have yet to be considered and answered. Is there any value in a 7-stride rhythm? How about combination runs of 3-5-7 strides rhythm? Could rhythm work over 15 hurdles serve a purpose? Could hurdle frequency be improved through downhill drills, etc.?

Track and Field Journal (Canada)

MARATHON CONSIDERATION

by John Humphreys

Because low lactates have been observed in marathon runners at the end of fast uniformly run races, it has been assumed that anaerobic work is of no importance in marathoning. However, claims that all marathon training needs to be aerobic do not take into consideration pace changes, such as a fast start, hills and a fast finish, that occur in high-class marathons.

To be able to step up the pace when a group of elite marathoners are locked together requires to train the LA/O_2 energy systems. It is therefore the opinion of this writer that top marathoners must be highly trained at 5000 to 10,000m distances, as well as being capable of a fast 1500m in order to dictate the race.

Marathoners, concerned too much with L.S.D. should not overlook that, in order to tax the aerobic system 100%, some LA/O_2 interval work and fast aerobic training is necessary. Fair emphasis should also be given to intensity to get accustomed to glycogen storage, dehydration, etc. It may well be that L.S.D. training is not as efficient as fast continuous aerobic running to improve the percentage a marathoner can utilize of his VO_2 max while racing.

It is extremely difficult to set a training load that gets a maximal physiological training response without a breakdown, as adaptation levels selected by an athlete may be below the thresholds required for optimal improvement. Is is the authors opinion that progressive overload has to be applied with regards to training intensity, duration and frequency, bearing in mind that a fully trained race horse can afford and benefit from periodic sustained rests.

Athletics Coach (Great Britain)